AQUARIUM
❧ DESIGNS ❧
INSPIRED BY NATURE

AQUARIUM

DESIGNS

INSPIRED BY NATURE

Peter Hiscock

BARRON'S

First edition for the United States and
Canada published in 2003 by
Barron's Educational Series, Inc.
First published in 2003 by Interpet
Publishing
Original edition © 2003 by Interpet
Publishing

All inquiries should be addressed to:
Barron's Educational Series, Inc.
250 Wireless Boulevard
Hauppauge, NY 11788
http://www.barronseduc.com

International Standard Book No.
0-7641-5549-0
Library of Congress Catalog Card No.
2001099147

Credits
Created and designed: Ideas into Print,
Box Cottage, Claydon, Suffolk IP6 0AB,
England.

Author

Peter Hiscock began keeping fish and aquariums as
a child, inspired by his parents, both accomplished
marine biologists. He was appointed manager of a
retail aquatic outlet at just 17 years of age and went
on to complete aquatic studies at Sparsholt College
in Hampshire, UK. He entered publishing with
contributions to the aquatic press and has since
written several books. His main interests include
fish behavior and the interaction of fish with their
environment, as well as aquascaping and the
natural habitats of aquarium species.

Aquarium photography: Geoffrey Rogers
© Interpet Publishing
Computer graphics: Stuart Watkinson
© Interpet Publishing
Production management: Consortium,
Poslingford, Suffolk CO10 8RA, England.

Printed in China
9 8 7 6 5 4 3 2 1

Left: *These two
elegant angelfish
(Pterophyllum
spp.) are content in
a densely planted
aquarium that
simulates their
Amazon River
home.*

Contents

PART ONE

Practical section

In the first part of this book we take a look at the ingredients required to create an aquarium based on the needs of the fishes and their environment. All fishes behave in a certain manner that reflects years of evolutionary refinement, enabling them to survive in their natural environment. Their behavior and body shape provide clues to their needs, which can be incorporated into the planning stages of the aquarium. For example, by observing a particular catfish, we may be able to tell simply from its shape, size, and color that it requires a dark, rounded substrate, hiding spots under wood or rock, and that it may be sensitive to sudden light changes. Fish movement provides further clues; many tetras shoal tightly together, often swimming around or through plants. This tells us that they need to be kept in groups in an aquarium with plenty of dense vegetation.

Providing the right environment involves a great deal of planning and preparation. Aquarium size, location, lighting, substrates and decor, water quality, and plant care are all important factors. In the following sections all of these are discussed in detail and with reference to the fishes' needs. Once such choices have been carefully made, there is the task of constructing the display and fitting items of decor together to create a natural and impressive design. In the substrates and decor and aquascaping sections, a wide range of materials and methods of construction are discussed. This part of the book opens with a look at the path of a typical river and the environments through which it flows; mountain streams, winding rivers, pools, swamps, and flooded forests are all described.

The topics discussed in these sections will provide you with a basis for planning and creating a stunning aquarium that takes its form and inspiration from nature, because it is always nature that makes the best aquariums.

River story

A river collects its water from an area called the river basin. If water falls onto this mass of land, it will end up in one particular river, although it may travel through many other streams and rivers to reach its destination. Eventually, the water collected in the river basin will end up in a wide stretch of river and head out to the ocean.

Each river system is unique and complex in "design." Often, it is the geological and ecological surroundings that determine a river's speed, size, path, and even its water quality. However, most larger river systems have many common elements and these can be divided into distinct habitats. This opening section explores these zones and the fish life they support. But first, we consider where the water comes from in the first place.

THE NATURAL WATER CYCLE

Water is continually moved around the world in a vast natural water cycle. Without this cycle there would be no weather, rivers, or vegetation. A convenient point to join the cycle is the stage when water evaporates or transpires into the atmosphere. Most evaporation occurs from the surface of the ocean, while transpiration is the process of water loss from the leaves of terrestrial plants. As the water vapor rises, it cools and forms clouds, and when air pressure becomes low enough or when the clouds become too dense, the water vapor combines to form droplets that fall as rain, snow, or ice (hail). Air pressure is often low around higher areas of land, so the vast majority of rainfall or snow occurs in mountainous regions. Heavily vegetated areas absorb heat instead of reflecting it, so water droplets also form more readily above large areas of vegetation such as forests – hence the term "rain forests."

As the rains fall, the water flows over and through the ground and topsoil into waterways, streams, and, eventually, rivers. Some of the rainfall will travel down to reach the underlying rock layers and emerge later as underground springs. As water travels through the rock, it picks up minerals, and when these springs occur in riverbeds or waterways, dense patches of aquatic plants often thrive on these outflows of mineral nutrients.

When rain or snow is first formed high in the atmosphere, it is pure and contains no contaminants. As it falls, it becomes slightly acidic from the absorption of atmospheric carbon dioxide, but remains relatively unchanged. It is only when water travels through or over soil and rock that its properties begin to change. Rainfall or meltwater from snowfall in high regions causes the formation of small, clear, and highly oxygenated mountain streams that are often the start of larger river systems.

MOUNTAIN STREAMS

The water in mountain streams has traveled a relatively short distance from its atmospheric origins and flows across terrain that is often rocky, steep,

THE NATURAL WATER CYCLE

Carbon dioxide and nitrogen oxides make rain and snow mildly acidic. At this stage, the water is devoid of minerals and salts.

As the warm, moist air rises, it condenses to form droplets in which the greenhouse gas (carbon dioxide) and airborne pollutants, such as nitrogen oxides from motor vehicles, dissolve.

Water percolates through the ground and sediments, picking up minerals and salts.

Water runoff – notably in areas of granite, which is impermeable to water – collects humic acids.

Groundwater runs into streams and rivers, and these flow into lakes or the sea.

Evaporation from rivers, lakes, and seas, plus transpiration from trees and other plants. This is pure water without any minerals, salts, or contaminants.

Above: *This mountain stream contains few organic or mineral compounds. This is only the start of the water's journey and it will change dramatically before it reaches the sea.*

LOWLAND STREAMS

River systems that begin in lowland hilly areas start out in an environment that is very different to the mountains; instead of rocky ground, the streams flow through a deeper soil substrate. Because water from rainfall is almost pure, it contains no mineral elements or natural hardness to act as a "buffer" against changes in its acidity. As it flows through the lowland areas, the water picks up a small amount of organic matter from the soil, causing it to become soft and acidic.

The fishes found in these streams do not have to cope with fast-flowing waters, although they often feed on the same types of food. Loaches scavenge along the streambed for small aquatic creatures, and small shoaling fishes hide among the aquatic vegetation. In many places, the natural waterways have been replaced by developed farmland and take the form of ditches and irrigation canals, but most of the aquatic life still remains.

TRIBUTARIES

As streams, ditches, and small waterways combine, they form larger streams and small rivers that head toward the main river system. These tributaries may have different water conditions and fish species to the main

and covered with only a thin layer of soil. The water has had little time to pick up organic matter, although it may contain some mineral elements from the surrounding rock. It is highly oxygenated and slightly hard and alkaline.

As streams combine, they form waterways large enough to remain permanent throughout the year and to support small fish that feed primarily on insects or algae. These insect-feeders are midwater swimmers and often have streamlined bodies and short fins. This body shape allows them to dart quickly from place to place, avoiding the strongest areas of flow. Using their highly adapted mouths and fins, the algae-eaters are able to secure themselves to rocks and graze the algae coating against the strong water flow.

Apart from algae, there is little aquatic vegetation in these streams. High-oxygen conditions, fast-flowing water, and a lack of organic nutrients mean that only the hardiest of aquatic plants are able to survive.

ENDEMIC OR WIDESPREAD?

A river basin may contain a number of pools, lakes, swamps, and waterways that never connect to the river and are geographically isolated. Many fish can be found even in these areas. In larger isolated lakes, such as many in East Africa and North America, species of fish can be found that exist nowhere else in the world. These are known as endemic species. In Lake Malawi, for example, one of the Rift Valley Lakes in East Africa, there are over 600 endemic fish species, making this an important habitat worthy of preservation in its natural state.

While certain species of fish are endemic to particular river basins, others can be found in river systems across the world. These widespread species are often hardy and adaptable fish that feed off a number of food sources. Many thousands — or even millions — of years ago, these fish would have "traveled" to different river systems while landmasses were still joined together. Today, these river systems have moved with the continents and may be separated by vast distances, although the widespread fish species remain, often unchanged.

Above: The middle and lower sections of a river often contain the calmest waters. Vegetation provides shade where many fish will retreat, while the undulating landscape ensures that the river's path rarely changes.

river. In the massive Amazon River Basin there are many tributaries, some of which are larger than most smaller river systems around the world. Each one of these tributaries has been formed from the collection of water in a particular area, and different rock and soil types (as well as the surrounding vegetation) will have created unique water conditions. Some of the fishes in the tributaries can also be found in the main river and in other connecting tributaries. Other species may be found in only one tributary, "unwilling" to move into the main river, where conditions may not be suitable. In the Amazon region, there are many species of small corydoras catfish, differing only slightly in size and coloration,

each of which is found only in particular Amazonian tributaries.

The tributaries are shallower and narrower than the main river and often more likely to have dense patches of aquatic vegetation. Aquatic plants thrive in shallow, slowly moving water, where they can capture a greater intensity of light and absorb the rich supply of nutrients that have dissolved from the surrounding soil.

THE MAIN RIVER

Once a few tributaries have joined the main river, it becomes a wide expanse of water that can support a population of larger fishes and animals. Depending on the location, the center of the river may be home to barbs, cichlids, catfish, and carp species that can grow to over 1m (39in) in length. These are often predatory species feeding off smaller fishes. At the river margins, some vegetation, dense reed beds, or small marginal plants provide hiding and breeding spots for smaller fish species.

The water quality in the main river rarely fluctuates, although it may change throughout the year as dry and rainy seasons affect water levels. When two large rivers join, they may have entirely different water conditions and it will be a considerable distance before the two are fully mixed together. The main river may flow through a number of different landscapes, each of which creates a different underwater habitat. In tropical regions, the river may pass through dense rain forest regions that provide a wealth of food sources, ranging from forest fruits and seeds to waste from plants and animals. Further down river, the rain forests may give way to open savannahs or dusty desert.

In more temperate regions, the river winds through flat grasslands, cutting a path of erosion that alters over a number of years. As the faster-flowing water on the outside of a bend cuts through the riverbank, silt and sediment are deposited on the calmer sandbanks on the inner side. Over long periods of time, this causes the river to "'snake" across the landscape.

FLOODED FORESTS

The volume and velocity of small streams and tributaries alter every year depending on the dry and rainy seasons. But these smaller waterways have a limited collection area, so they rarely flood or burst their banks. However, there will be a much greater annual fluctuation in the main river. When the rainy season arrives, the water from all the feeder streams and tributaries increases at the same time, creating a massive influx of water.

Unable to cope, the river bursts its banks, flooding the surrounding land. In major tropical river systems, substantial floods are an annual event and often cover many thousands of square kilometers. The flooding opens up a new and vast habitat for the fishes, and many breed during this period. Flooded vegetation may live through the deluge or it may die, along with many small land animals, creating an influx of biological material that is fed upon either directly by fish or by

CHANGING TO SURVIVE

Fish species may alter and adapt in a relatively short time in response to changing environmental conditions, although this still takes tens of thousands of years. When this happens, fish become specialized and undergo physical changes that allow them to survive in certain environments.

For example, fishes from the dim and muddy swamps of Southeast Asia may have reduced eyesight and rely instead on heightened senses of touch and smell to locate their food. In fast-flowing mountain streams, most fish have torpedo-shaped bodies that minimize drag – hence the term "streamlined." Some fishes have even developed methods of leaving the water and traveling across land if their habitat dries up.

From the mountains to the sea

Many rivers start in the mountains. As rain falls, tiny streams form and join together.

Here the vegetation is heavy. In tropical environments, rain forests form and life in the river changes. Fruits and seeds, plus animal and plant waste offer plentiful food for the fish.

The joining of two rivers causes a great disturbance this far downstream. Often, the quality of the water in one river is very different from the other and it may be some distance before the two are truly mixed into one.

The main body of the river is formed as the streams join. In this area the river is still a rocky and barren environment, interspersed with waterfalls and rapids.

Finally the river meets the ocean. Spreading out over a wide expanse, the river is now heavily laden with sediment. Salt water moves up and down the final run of the river, creating an ever-changing estuarine habitat.

Emerging from the forest, the river takes with it organic matter that alters the water chemistry. Now it is soft, slightly acidic, and may be muddy or brown.

Now the river is a great mass of water. The soil here is easily carved by the river as it winds back and forth across the land. As it turns, the water moving on the outside of the bend is faster and carves away at the land. On the inside bend, sediment is deposited, creating sandy banks.

small aquatic animals and fish fry that in turn become food for fish and larger river creatures. Tall trees and large bushes often drop their fruits and seeds into the floodwaters and these are carried to new locations, where they may root and grow.

As the waters recede, many small pools remain, along with isolated populations of fish. Most of the pools eventually dry out and the fishes perish, but others persist until the following year's floods, together with their communities of fish.

LOWLAND SWAMPS

Swamps in lowland tropical habitats also fluctuate in size with the floods and the dry seasons, although they remain throughout the year. In these low, flat areas, the soil is saturated and rarely dries out. The shallow water of the swamp is crammed full of aquatic vegetation and home to many fish

Below: As a river continues its winding path through flat lowland areas, there are no hills or valleys to contain the annual influx of water. In tropical regions, such as here in Brazil, lowland floods can last for several months.

species. In this environment, oxygen levels become very low at night as the plants and animals use up the scant supplies for respiration. And in the almost stagnant conditions, there is little exchange of gases at the water surface. Many fishes that live here are well adapted to the dark, murky, low-oxygen waters. Some are able to take gulps of atmospheric air at the surface from which they can absorb oxygen. Many bottom-dwelling catfish and loaches have poor eyesight, but rely instead on touch and smell to locate prey lurking in the muddy substrate. In many tropical areas, temperatures in the swamps can reach over 30°C (86°F) as the shallow water quickly absorbs and retains heat.

BRACKISH WATERS

As the river eventually reaches its destination, the ocean, it begins to mix with salt water from the sea, creating brackish habitats. Brackish waters occur not only close to the sea but can extend for many kilometers inland as the waters move up and down stream with the tides. Although a few of the river fishes live in these waters, the majority are brackish species found only in this habitat. Brackish fish are adapted to

cope with changing concentrations of salt in the water and to feed upon the food sources found in the sandy substrate. The nutrient-rich substrate contains a number of small animals and crustaceans that feed on the organic debris deposited by the river.

In many tropical areas, mangrove swamps flourish around the brackish waters. These adaptable plants provide cover, food sources in the form of fruits, insects, and other terrestrial animals that live among them, and stabilize the substrate, creating a clear water environment.

In time, the river will spread out to cover a wide expanse of land before mixing out into the ocean. Evaporation from the ocean will then form atmospheric water vapor, eventually forming clouds and rainfall, and the cycle will begin again.

Below: Mangrove swamps can be found in tropical regions where the river meets the ocean. These habitats are rich in organic load and support a complex web of life, including many unusual fish and other creatures.

Central America

The Central American region, including the United States and Mexico, encompasses a number of river and stream systems. The larger rivers of Mexico and Central America are home to many of the imposing, predatory cichlids, while the streams and waterways contain smaller fish. Of particular interest to aquarists are the small livebearers, such as mollies, swordtails, and platies.

South America

The vast majority of aquarium fish originate from South America, which is home to the vast Amazon River system and its tributaries. The most popular and best-known aquarium fish, such as angelfish, tetras, and discus, come from the Amazon Basin, as do many catfish. Within the mountains, rain forest, and lowland areas of South America are many different habitats, each with their own individual fish species. Acid pools, mountain streams, open rivers, mangroves, flooded forests, and tributaries are all present in South America, and provide a rich source of habitats and aquascapes for the hobbyist to recreate.

China

The larger river systems of China have been ecologically damaged by human activities, although barbs and carp species can be found here. However, most fish of interest in this region live in the numerous mountain streams that contribute to larger river systems. These include many small loaches, both scavengers and algae-eaters, along with a few small catfish. Fish such as the White Cloud Mountain minnow and Chinese hillstream loach are often seen in the aquarium trade.

Europe

The climate of Europe can be considered temperate, and many fish from this region are highly adaptable to cooler conditions. Small fish suited to these environments include minnows, sticklebacks, bitterlings, sunfish, and larger species of rudd and carp, which are often sold for ponds. Some loaches and algae-eaters are also found in European regions, although catfish species are limited.

Southeast Asia and Indonesia

Due to the relatively small size of the Indonesian islands, there are few large river systems. However, there is plenty of rainfall and many fish thrive in the lowland swamps, streams, and brooks. Common aquarium fish found in this region include a large majority of gouramis, smaller barbs such as the tiger barb, rasboras, and many loaches, including the clown loach, kuhli loach, and red-tailed black shark.

Mangroves

Mangrove regions occur throughout the tropics and are home to the majority of fish suited to brackish aquariums. Mangroves are highly fertile, containing many organics and minerals picked up by the flow of the rivers. At first glance, the underwater habitats appear muddy and barren, but many organisms live in the fertile mud and provide a valuable food source for fish. Brackish aquarium fish, such as scats, monos, mudskippers, and archerfish, can be found in these habitats, along with species of tropical crabs.

Africa

Africa is home to some of the world's largest river systems, including the Congo (Zaire) and Zambezi, and also houses the three large Rift Valley Lakes – Tanganyika, Victoria, and Malawi. The diversity of fishes in Africa is immense, and the number of African species commonly found in aquariums is rivaled only by those from South American regions. The Congo is a fast-flowing river in many places, where catfish such as Synodontis spp., and large African cichlids can be found. In contrast, areas surrounded by rain forest vegetation and numerous pools and tributaries are home to many smaller fishes. The Rift Valley Lakes offer thousands of cichlid species, of which many common varieties are readily available for the aquarium.

Australia and New Guinea

The landscape and ecology of Australia are incredibly diverse, ranging from temperate scrublands to tropical rain forest. In central regions, desertlands contain many small waterholes, brooks, streams, and seasonal rivers with many isolated and diverse fish populations. Although there are many interesting Australian fish species, only a few are offered in the aquarium trade. This stems largely from strict controls on imports and exports of animals. However, fish from the beautiful rainbowfish families are readily available for the aquarium, as are a number of individual catfish.

How fishes live

Along with cats and dogs, fishes are among the most popular and widely kept animals in the home. At first glance they appear to offer little as companion animals, being unable to return affection or communicate with their owners. Their popularity among experienced fishkeepers often stems from the observation of behavioral traits that are unique to each species. With many hundreds of species available to the aquarist, there is a wealth of colors, sizes and behaviors to be observed. Unique feeding, breeding, and territorial activities ensure that a well-stocked aquarium always provides a fascinating view of the natural world.

Trying to make sense of such observations is a fundamental human desire and the first step in our journey of understanding is to look at the way a fish's body works and how it lives in the watery environment. It is also important to understand how they have evolved and come to live in such diverse habitats.

THE EVOLUTION OF FISHES

Fishes first developed in the oceans and it is likely that complex land animals, including reptiles, mammals, and birds, evolved from the early fishes. On current figures, there are over 20,000 known species of fish, although it is likely that there are thousands more undiscovered or unclassified species. Of the known fish, over 40% are found in freshwater environments, yet the world's freshwater habitats contain a minuscule proportion of water in comparison to the oceans. This "imbalance" is due to localized environmental conditions. In the oceans, water quality may vary slightly in certain coastal areas, but in general it is relatively stable and consistent across the world. Although many marine fish confine themselves to a particular area for safety and the availability of food,

Left: The shape of the marbled hatchetfish (Carnegiella strigata) is due to an enlarged muscle connecting to the pectoral fins. The fish uses this extra muscle power to launch itself above the water to escape danger.

the oceans represent one vast environment with few natural "barriers." By contrast, the water conditions in freshwater environments may vary dramatically in a relatively small area, and natural land barriers create many isolated habitats. Whereas a marine fish may have a whole reef system, or even the entire ocean in which to roam, a freshwater fish may be confined to just a portion of a river or a lake.

Over the course of millions of years, marine fishes moved into freshwater areas, where they became isolated in specific habitats and changed independently to form new species.

Below: All fishes are evolved to survive in a particular habitat. These highly vegetated, clear Brazilian waters are home to many plant eaters, predators, and scavengers.

Different combinations of water conditions, food sources, predators, and environmental factors in freshwater habitats have created a vast number of ecological niches. Fish have spread into these niches, evolving into separate species ideally suited to the conditions in these natural habitats.

One of the most dramatic and geographically small-scale examples of this can be found in the Rift Valley

HOW EVOLUTION WORKS

The process of evolution occurs when a slight genetic change in a single animal either helps or hinders its survival. If it is a help, then the genes that include this change are passed on to some of its young, which themselves have a greater chance of survival and of passing on the genes to their young. If the change is a hindrance, the fish may have a lower chance of survival, thus reducing the likelihood that it will breed and pass on its genes to the next generation. Although these genetic changes are tiny, over time they may completely alter an animal's size, color, appearance, or behavior, and even affect its internal biology.

Lakes of Africa, most notably in Lake Malawi. Due to their territorial and rock-dwelling behavior, the Lake Malawi cichlids – a group closely related to marine fishes – tend to remain in particular rocky outcrops. This causes individual groups of fish to become isolated and to evolve independently into separate species, developing physiological changes that help them to survive in their particular rocky outcrop. The end result is that over millions of years, the first few fish species developed into over 600 species.

THE SENSES

Fishes have the same senses of touch, taste, smell, sight, and hearing that humans and other higher animals possess. They also have another sense, the lateral line system, which detects pressure changes, and some fish can

Below: The highly branched barbels on the underside of this Synodontis robertsi *allow the fish to identify items of food in the substrate without relying on sight.*

Below: The rock-dwelling cichlids found in the African Rift Valley Lakes are highly specialized feeders. The mouth of numerous species contains many small "teeth" used to graze algae.

use an additional sensory system based on electrical fields. The acuity of any one of these senses depends on its usefulness in a fish's environment. For example, catfish that live in debris-ridden substrate at the bottom of muddy rivers would find sight a relatively useless sense. No matter how good their eyesight, they would be unlikely to see much of any value, so they rely on other senses instead. On the other hand, large predatory fish in clear, open waters rely heavily on good eyesight to catch their prey, as do smaller fish that feed on insects at the water surface. So,

although all fishes share the same basic sensory organs, how the senses develop is dictated by a fish's evolutionary path and there are wide variations between species.

FEELING IN THE DARK

Most catfish have long whiskerlike appendages that sense the surrounding physical environment, helping the fish to move about and locate food. These barbels are not only sensitive to touch, but also contain taste receptors that can pick up chemical signals and even identify water quality parameters, such as temperature, oxygen levels, and salinity. Fishes with smaller barbels, such as members of the carp family (including goldfish), smaller catfish such as *Corydoras* species, and loaches, use their barbels to find items of food in the top layer of the substrate. This enables the fish to search constantly for food while still being able to see what is happening around them.

The barbels on some of the larger predatory catfish may be even longer than their bodies. They are used for locating prey before attacking them and to feel around the immediate environment. The effect of the barbels can be seen when these larger catfish are fed in the aquarium. Almost as soon as a suitable food source enters the water, the barbels begin to move, signaling that the catfish can sense the smell or chemical signals coming from the food source. As soon as one of the barbels touches the food source, the fish knows exactly where it is and whether it is suitable to eat, at which point the fish will swiftly swallow it.

The anabantoids have similar appendages, which are extensions of the ventral fins, and are also covered with taste and chemical sensors. In the

19

low-visibility environment of the swamps in which the fish live, these "feelers" are able to sense areas of higher oxygen content and to "test" objects. In the aquarium, these fish can often be observed touching other fishes or food sources in order to obtain more information.

UNDER PRESSURE

Fish detect changes in water pressure using the lateral line system. Along the flanks of most fishes it is possible to see a line of small pits, or pores, that extends from the head to the tail. These allow water to pass into a tiny canal running the length of the fish beneath the skin. Pressure changes near the fish cause the water in the canal to move, disturbing tiny hairs connected to nerve cells lining the canal and these send impulses to the brain.

The ability to sense changes in water pressure allows fishes to detect objects and the movement of nearby fishes. Pressure changes can be compared to the wake produced by a boat. As a fish or other object moves by, it produces a small wake that other fish pick up as

pressure changes through their lateral line systems. Using the same system, fish can sense the change in pressure and the movement of water as they approach an object.

The ability to sense pressure changes enables a fish to move around its environment and to negotiate objects quickly if it is chased by a predator. It also allows shoaling fish to sense each other's movements and thus keep close together without constantly colliding with each other. In the aquarium, pressure waves can be created by external vibrations, such as loud noise or people tapping on the glass. When this happens, the pressure waves generated "sound" to the fishes like a gun being fired next to our ears. Clearly, this is very stressful for them. Shoaling fish have an enhanced sensitivity to pressure waves and they immediately change direction and flee in response to such stimuli.

AN EYE FOR ALL OCCASIONS

Fishes' eyes are quite similar to our own and those of other higher animals. However, they do have a few

adaptations, and some fishes have better eyesight than others. Water tends to bend light to a higher degree than air and rapidly reduces its brightness. Thus, estimating distances is more difficult for eyes developed for terrestrial use, and the deeper you go, the less light becomes available. In fact, many fish cannot sense distance to any noticeable degree. This is because the eyes are placed on either side of the head and the visual fields do not overlap. However, the advantage is that they have an almost 360° view around them, which may be far more useful when it comes to avoiding predators than the ability to judge distances.

Generally speaking, sight in fish falls into one of two categories: color perception or light sensitivity. Color perception is useful for fishes that live in clear, sunlit waters and is used to identify mates or dangerous fishes. Reef fishes depend heavily on color perception, which is why so many of them are brightly colored. However, fishes that depend on other senses for their survival and that live in dark waters or are nocturnal by nature may

THE LATERAL LINE SYSTEM

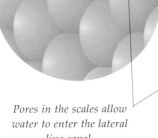

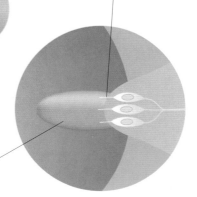

Outer layer of scales

Sensitive hairs embedded in the gelatinous cap trigger nerve impulses when they move. Some respond in one direction more than another.

Pores in the scales allow water to enter the lateral line canal.

Cavity of lateral line canal

Nerve fiber carrying impulses to the spinal cord and then to the brain.

Gelatinous cap responds to the movement of water in the canal.

ALL-ROUND VISION

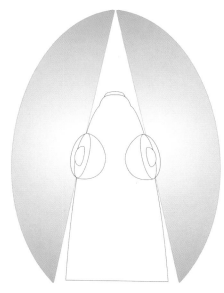

Above: The visual fields of these laterally placed eyes cover a wide area but do not overlap to provide a stereoscopic view, making judging distances difficult.

find that an increased sensitivity to light is more useful. In many catfish, for example, eyesight is geared toward light perception and as a consequence, these fishes are rarely brightly colored.

BODY SHAPE AND MOVEMENT

By observing the body shape and features of a fish you can pick up clues about its natural environment. Mouth shape is a good indicator of how and where a fish feeds. An upturned mouth – common in livebearers and anabantoids – indicates that the fish feeds at the water surface, possibly on insects or floating seeds. On the other hand, downturned mouths, as seen in loaches, indicate bottom feeders. Centered, or terminal, mouths are found in midwater swimmers that feed both from the surface and in open waters.

Body shape also indicates how the fish behaves in nature. Fishes with tall, laterally compressed bodies, such as angelfish and gouramis, would not do well in fast-flowing water, where their bodies would produce a large amount

of drag. Instead, these fish live among the vegetation in calmer waters, where their body shape allows them to maneuver gracefully between the stems. Some catfish and loaches have a flat body shape that is far wider than it is tall. This helps the fish to remain unnoticed and also allows them to hide in gaps under rocks, wood, or other objects. Most fishes have a torpedo-shaped body that minimizes drag and allows the fish to move through open water with minimal effort. All fishes that constantly swim in open water have similar torpedolike body shapes.

In some groups of fishes, the body has developed into an unusual shape or size. In most cases, this is "designed" to aid the fishes' survival. For example, hatchetfish are flat on top, with a semicircular profile to the lower part of the body. The flat top and upturned mouth are clear indications that these fish are surface dwellers. The semicircular profile houses strong muscles that enable the fish to jump suddenly from the water to avoid

MOUTH POSITION

A longer lower jaw gives the mouth a distinctive shape and shows how the fish feeds by approaching food from beneath.

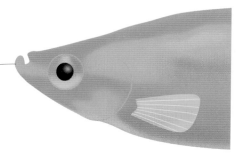

Terminal mouths are typical of midwater fish and allow the fish to approach their food head-on.

Extended upper jaws are seen on fish that approach food from above, such as bottom-dwellers feeding on the substrate.

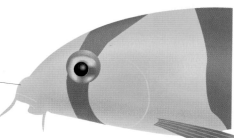

predators. Another species with an unusual body shape caused by muscle extensions is the archerfish that fires jets of water at insects on overhanging branches (see page 195).

Other fishes use body shape and color for camouflage. Catfish from the *Farlowella* and *Sturisoma* group have very long, thin bodies that imitate twigs on the substrate floor. The leaf fish (*Monocirrhus* spp.) is aptly named for its leaflike body shape and color and it often swims in a "drifting" manner, like a fallen leaf. A few catfish have even more bizarre camouflage techniques; they develop skin extensions that make them look like pieces of debris on the riverbed, thus avoiding the attentions of predators.

SHOALING OR SCHOOLING

Many fish exhibit unusual behaviors in the aquarium and these almost always stem from their natural environment, where such behavior aids their survival. Shoaling or schooling are the most familiar behaviors and normally seen in small or medium-sized fishes. A shoal is a group of fish that stay close together and often follow each other's movements, whereas in a school, the fish remain at a set distance from each other and move almost as one object, with each fish copying the movements of the fishes around it. In the oceans, schooling fish use this behavior to appear as a much larger object and thus deter predators. If a predator should arrive, it becomes confused when the school splits into smaller schools and heads off in different directions. Without being able to focus on one fish, it becomes much harder for the predator to make a catch. Shoals work in a similar fashion, and for many fishes, including most tetras, staying in shoals increases their chances of finding food and decreases their chances of being eaten.

TERRITORY AND MATING

Territorial behavior is common in some aquarium fish and is seen in almost all cichlids. The cause of territorial behavior normally stems from the need to protect young or to attract a suitable mate. In nature, fishes rarely come into conflict and a series of "threat" displays normally allows two individuals to identify the dominant fish, which remains while the other simply swims away. In the aquarium, however, swimming away is not an option and this is why conflicts are far more common and "bullying" can occur.

Displays can also be used to attract a mate and often consist of shimmying and displays of finnage and color. Males are often more colorful than females, and when conditions are good for breeding, their colors become even more intense. A female of the species will often pick the most colorful male, as an indicator of a healthy male ready to breed.

THE AQUARIUM ENVIRONMENT

As we have seen, evolution has "molded" the size, color, and behavior of fishes, and these visual clues will help you to identify the type of environment each species requires. In practical terms, providing a suitable environment depends on a number of factors, including seemingly insignificant choices such as the type of plants, color of substrate, and flow of water. To keep most fish correctly, it is important to be familiar with their natural environment and way of life. Tetras must be kept in groups, many catfish need hiding spots, anabantoids need heavy vegetation, dull-colored fish may not appreciate bright lighting, cichlids should be chosen to avoid territorial "bullies" – the list is endless. Providing a sympathetic aquarium that recreates the elements found in the natural environment or habitat will improve the fishes' health, color, and resistance to disease, as well as encouraging natural behaviors such as breeding. An aquarium "in tune" with nature is much healthier for the fish and a more interesting environment for the fishkeeper to observe.

Right: The Odessa barb (Puntius ticto) *is a shoaling species and will stay in groups. This increases the chances of finding food and decreases the chances of being eaten.*

A HOME AWAY FROM HOME

In unsuitable surroundings, fish become stressed and unhealthy. Although water conditions in the aquarium may be ideal, a fish that has developed to survive in one particular environment will still suffer if it placed in a completely different one. For instance, a fish accustomed to a densely planted environment with plenty of hiding spots will feel highly vulnerable in a relatively bare tank. The fish does not "know" that it is free from predators and, without the safety of hiding spots, will be continually stressed. Eventually, it succumbs to disease and may even die.

Substrates and decor

The "hard landscaping" in the aquarium – the substrate, wood, rocks, and pebbles – together make up the decor, and how you combine these items creates the individual appearance and style of the display. However, decor does not just have an esthetic value; it also plays an important role in creating an environment that suits the aquarium's inhabitants. For example, choosing the right combination of substrates will provide a good rooting medium for plants, supplying nutrients for their continued growth and overall health. Decor can also be used for practical purposes, such as hiding bulky filters or pipework in the aquarium, or to encourage breeding in some fish species.

CHOOSING SUBSTRATES

Many styles and types of substrate are available, but in general only choose those designed for aquariums. Although gravel and other substrates can often be obtained in bulk at low cost from sources other than aquatic retailers, many mixed substrates contain calcareous compounds that may alter the water quality. In some cases, metal-based contaminants may be present. However, in the majority of cases, single-type substrates such as broken shale (slate) or granite chippings are relatively safe.

The right substrate is vital in any aquarium with live plants. Plants obtain a large amount of their nutrients from the substrate, and although a standard substrate may provide suitable anchorage for plants to grow in, it is generally devoid of nutrients and therefore of little benefit to the plants. A mixture of substrates, including specially designed nutrient-rich and inert, or lime-free, substrates, contain large amounts of available nutrients and are more beneficial. Mixing substrates in this way helps to recreate in the aquarium the conditions that plants experience in nature. You can take this approach one step further by placing heating cables in the base of the tank before adding any substrate. The cables gently heat the substrate and move the nutrients around, making them easily available to the plant roots (see page 28).

Fish also have substrate preferences, based on the type of substrate they would encounter in the wild. Fish that

Above: A typical riverbed is a mixture of muddy, silt-laden substrate and pebbles or rocks. In fast-flowing waters, the silt is removed, leaving exposed rock, while in calm waters it settles out on the bottom.

Below: In this calm and slow-flowing waterway, sediment is deposited and builds up on top of a rocky bed. Toward the edges, the sediment is deep and provides an ideal substrate for plants to root.

Below: *Many large algae-eaters, such as this stunning* Panaque nigrolineatus, *use sandy or muddy substrates to carve out hiding spots and venture into rocky areas to graze algae.*

originate from small streams and river tributaries may be accustomed to small, light, rounded gravel substrates, equivalent to aquarium pea gravel. Corydoras catfish, for example, happily spend their time searching this type of substrate for small animals and other sources of food. On the other hand, small shoaling fish, such as tetras, hide in plants around riverbanks and prefer plenty of hiding spots and cover. In the wild, they inhabit areas where the substrate is often dark and soil-like. The fish take advantage of these shadowy conditions in their camouflage, because from above they blend in with the substrate, while from below they appear pale against the brighter, sunlit surface. Some loaches, particularly those from areas of Indonesia, are found in slow-moving, swamplike environments and prefer a muddy, soil-like substrate in which to burrow for food and hide from predators. Although this type of substrate is tricky to recreate in the aquarium, certain small-grade substrates are close enough to suit the fishes' needs.

Without additional decor, an inappropriate substrate can have an adverse effect on the health of some fishes. Timid species kept in an aquarium with an unfamiliar substrate (for example, shy tetras kept with a

very bright or pale substrate) can become stressed, suffering a drop in their immune system and increased susceptibility to disease. Choosing the right substrate is, therefore, more important than may appear at first glance and requires some thought. Try to balance the needs of both the plants and the fish. In most cases, the fish are only concerned with the visible top layer, whereas the plants' requirements lie in the middle and lower layers.

TYPES OF SUBSTRATE
While some substrates serve a practical purpose, normally relating to plant growth, others have decorative qualities that are useful when setting up a specific type of environment. Substrates need not be used singly; indeed, mixing different ones together can produce some interesting results. Most aquarium substrates are inert and therefore do not alter water quality, although you should always check this before making a purchase. Some substrates, such as coral sand or coral gravel, are designed for marine aquariums and are high in calcium. If you add these to a freshwater aquarium, the pH and hardness levels would rapidly rise. Keep only hardwater species, such as some African Rift Valley Lake cichlids, with these types of substrate.

For plants, use only inert substrates or those that do not raise water hardness, and small-grade is preferable to a large particle size. Water passes easily through a large-grade substrate, removing nutrients and preventing a nutrient buildup in the substrate. If you wish to use a large-grade substrate with live plants, a good compromise is to cover a small-grade, main substrate with a thin (1-2cm/0.4-0.8in) layer of larger substrate.

Pea gravel is so-called because of its small, rounded, pealike appearance. It is very similar to the kind of substrate you would find in a stream or mountain river and is the most commonly used aquarium substrate. In most cases it is inert, although sometimes there are a few rock types within the gravel that may raise pH levels slightly (i.e., make the water more alkaline). A number of grades are available, ranging in diameter from 1-2mm (0.04-0.08in) to over 10mm (0.4in). For aquatic plants, the smallest grade will make the best rooting medium, although lime-free quartz gravel is often a better alternative. For a realistic "riverbed" display, use a mixture of all the grades and combine them with some small, rounded cobbles or pebbles. Pea gravel can also be used as a top layer over a finer substrate, which may be a better planting medium. Pea gravel is usually quite pale in color, although it could be made darker by mixing it with a contrasting black quartz or black gravel. These mixtures can look very effective, especially in pool or flooded forest aquariums.

Quartz gravel is often labeled as a "lime-free" substrate and is completely inert, making it an ideal substrate for plants and softwater aquariums. Quartz gravel is normally a pale golden-brown color, useful for recreating an authentic downstream river, but it is also available in black and bright white. Black quartz is ideal for aquariums with timid, shoaling fish such as tetras, and has a striking but not unnatural appearance that enhances the color of both fishes and plants. The small grade size (1-2mm / 0.04-0.08in) makes quartz an ideal main rooting substrate for aquatic plants. In an aquarium with many plants, use quartz gravel as a main substrate, but add a nutrient-rich layer as well.

Sand can be found in a number of forms – and even particle sizes – although grains of sand are generally less than 1mm (0.04in) in diameter. You can use any type of sand in an aquarium, but only "silver sand" is completely inert and is the type normally sold by aquatic retailers. Being very fine – almost dusty – silver sand will compact in the aquarium and virtually stop any water flow, resulting in a lack of oxygen, and stagnant anaerobic conditions in the substrate. When this occurs, the affected areas may turn black and begin to release toxic substances such as hydrogen sulphide, which can be dangerous to fish. This foul-smelling gas will also rot plant roots and may encourage algae.

To prevent compaction and allow oxygen into the substrate, gently disturb the sand with your fingers. A shallow sand substrate is less likely to compact than a deep one.

Due to its tendency to compact, sand is not ideal as a rooting medium for plants, although some will happily grow in a shallow (3cm / 1.2in) layer. *Vallisneria, Sagittaria,* and *Eleocharis* species should cope with a sandy substrate reasonably well if other aquarium conditions are good. Silver sand has a unique appearance in an aquarium and is particularly useful for recreating brackish or estuarine habitats, or Australian waterways and riverbanks.

Colored gravels in various shapes and sizes are available for aquariums. Although they are inert, they occasionally color the water slightly, but this normally stops after a few months. A thorough wash before use

A SELECTION OF SUBSTRATES

Silver sand (also inert) needs care to avoid compaction. Excellent decorative and supporting medium.

Black quartz can be used to darken the overall substrate.

Lime-free gravel is inert and will not affect water conditions. An ideal planting medium.

A finer grade of pea gravel allows less water movement and creates a better planting medium.

Pea gravel is the most common form of aquarium gravel and has a number of uses in the aquarium.

can prevent any discoloration. The artificial colors are created by covering the gravel with a colored plastic coating, which gives it a very smooth appearance

Your choice of color is a matter of personal preference, but it is true to say that orange, purple, bright green, pink, fluorescent shades, and color mixtures do not lend themselves to a natural-looking aquarium! However, darker (and more subtle) colors, such as black, dark red, and brown, can be very effective in the right situation.

The large grade of colored gravel (with a particle size of 4mm/0.16in or more) does not make a good plant rooting medium, but you could use it as a top layer over a finer substrate. Colored gravels can be useful in small amounts, mixed in with other substrates to add a little variation and/or color, or as a single substrate if you want to create a darker base.

Soil is not often used in the aquarium because it is hard to manage in a small area and will often dirty the water or release nutrients that may encourage algae. However, many natural environments have a muddy or soil-like substrate and the fish in the aquarium do not mind muddy water. In fact, for many species this is closer to their natural environment. Nevertheless, it is not normally esthetically pleasing and can cause problems with tank filters. However, in certain circumstances, soil can be used with care without muddying the water too much.

The nutrients released by soil are ideal for plant growth and if there are many plants in the aquarium, with enough light and carbon dioxide to grow healthily, they should take up the nutrients fast enough to prevent algal blooms. Plant roots will also "hold" the soil together enough to reduce any dirtying of the water.

If you use a soil substrate, either cover it with a top layer of another substrate to prevent muddying, or put the soil and plants in place at least a month before switching on the filter or introducing any fish. During this period the soil will "settle," plants will grow roots, and the water should clear. Allowing the soil to settle is important, because as soon as the fish are introduced, many of them will disturb the substrate and an "unsettled" soil layer will quickly muddy the water. Although you should never introduce large, bottom-dwelling fish into a tank with a soil substrate, smaller catfish, such as *Corydoras* species, should cause no problems.

Not every type of soil is suitable for the aquarium; many contain harmful substances, especially those with added fertilizers and, sometimes, pesticides or herbicides. Potting soil is normally safe, but always check the label for any

Subtle-colored gravels are ideal for aquascaping.

Brightly colored gravels are available (including white), but few look natural.

Aquarium soils can be used beneath a top layer of gravel to provide a natural planting medium that stores large amounts of nutrients.

Nutrient-rich planting substrates such as this laterite clay-based medium are high in iron and other vital plant nutrients. This substrate can be mixed or layered with other mediums.

Coral gravel is designed for marine aquariums but can be used to good effect in brackish aquariums.

Calcium-based gravel will raise water hardness and pH so should be used only with hardwater or brackish aquarium fish.

artificial additives. Never use soil from the garden or other outside source. Even if no harmful chemicals are present, it will undoubtedly harbor many creatures that will decompose and pollute the water.

A soil substrate will add a very "real" look to a downstream river, flooded forest, pool, or swamp-style aquarium. However, it should be used only by aquarists with the experience or confidence to manage it.

Nutrient-rich substrates are used solely for the benefit of plants. Although nutrients can be added to the aquarium by other means, normally in the form of liquid additives, a nutrient-rich substrate is a long-term source of vital plant nutrients that are continually available to all the plants. The most common nutrient-rich substrates are designed to be used in small quantities, "sandwiched" between two layers of another substrate, such as lime-free quartz or fine-grade pea gravel. If they are used as a top layer, they may float or muddy the water, and will also be

largely inaccessible to plant roots. In some cases, the nutrient-rich substrate can be mixed in with the lower half of the main substrate.

Some substrates, often laterite- or clay-based ones, are designed to be used as a main substrate, while also slowly releasing nutrients. Nutrient-rich substrates will benefit plants even more if they are used in conjunction with a substrate heating cable.

Substrate additives, much like nutrient-rich substrates, are designed to release nutrients slowly over a long period of time. Additives are usually supplied in the form of pellets (5-10mm/0.2-0.4in or more in size), placed directly beneath an area of roots, where individual plants can benefit from them. Additives can have an advantage over nutrient-rich substrates in situations where only a few plants are used, or where only certain areas of the aquarium contain plants. For example, in an aquarium containing a few large *Echinodorus* species, which require high amounts of iron, placing

pellets beneath the plants means that they will obtain nutrients but the rest of the aquarium will not be overfertilized, which could cause algal blooms.

OTHER SUBSTRATES

When creating a particular style of aquarium, it is important to choose the substrate that best represents that style, but, of course, a "style" does not have to be a representation of a particular habitat in nature. For example, a quarry bed, pebble shoreline, or "rocky" style may not represent any particular habitat, but may still suit a certain group of fishes. For such aquariums, you can draw on some unusual materials such as coal, or even broken driftwood chippings, to create a unique setting. Rock chippings, such as granite, quartz, sandstone, slate, or basalt, can represent a wide variety of styles and colors. In many cases, chippings can be combined to good effect with larger rocks of the same kind. Pebbles and/or cobble, mixed with large-grade pea gravel will create an interesting aquarium for larger fish, such as some

INSTALLING A HEATING CABLE

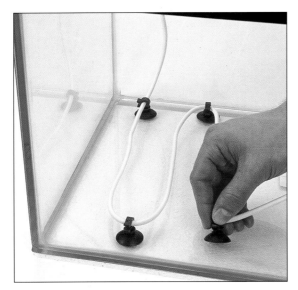

1 A heating cable helps to distribute nutrients and must be installed with a 5-10cm (2-4in) space between the loops to work effectively. The ideal spacing depends on the cable wattage.

2 Sand is very fine and distributes heat evenly from the cable while holding it securely in position. Cover the cable with about 2cm (0.8in) of sand, creating an overall depth of around 5cm (2in).

3 Place a thin layer of nutrient-rich substrate on top of the sand. Then add a top layer of small-grade lime-free gravel, which is a good inert plant-rooting medium. This should make up at least two-thirds of the overall depth.

Above: *A gravel cleaner is an essential maintenance tool for any aquarium. Water is sucked up the wide tube by siphonic action and whisks away debris from the gravel. Avoid disturbing nutrient layers.*

cichlids, or for African Rift Lake fishes. For hardwater or brackish aquariums, coral sand and/or coral gravel can be mixed with a few shells to create a brackish or marinelike beach effect.

Used in small amounts, many of these alternative substrates can add a welcome realism or texture to an existing substrate. An aquarium with only one visible, uniform substrate across its base often looks quite artificial and too unnatural to represent a habitat. Many of these alternative substrates are used in the "world tour" sections featured later in this book for particular habitat designs.

SUBSTRATE HEATING CABLES
In aquariums with a large number of plants and a relatively fine substrate, such as a quartz gravel or fine pea gravel, combined with a nutrient-rich layer, heating cables can be used to distribute nutrients around the substrate and prevent some stagnation. A heating cable works by gently raising the temperature of the lower portion of the substrate. This creates convection currents that cause the warmer water to rise and cooler water from the aquarium to be drawn down through the substrate. The gentle water flow also moves nutrients around the substrate, rather than leaving them concentrated in the nutrient layer. Nutrients that move around the substrate are more likely to come into contact with plant roots and then be taken up by them.

A heating cable must be surrounded by a very fine substrate that can quickly distribute and diffuse the warmth, so that the whole of the lower portion of substrate is heated. Silver sand is ideal for this purpose, but you need use it only around the heating cable; a deeper sand layer may compact and stagnate.

Heating cables are not essential in an aquarium with plants, but a heavily planted aquarium with a nutrient-rich material in the substrate, strong lighting, and carbon dioxide fertilization will benefit greatly from the addition of a heating cable.

PREPARING SUBSTRATE
Most substrates, especially lime-free quartz, contain a lot of dust and debris that will cloud the water unless they are thoroughly rinsed out. Even substrates labeled "pre-cleaned" should be rinsed before use. The only substrates that do not need rinsing are silver sand, nutrient-rich substrates, and soils. To clean substrates, simply run small amounts under a tap or hose until the water runs clear. This may take some time, but it is better than a murky aquarium. Even with the best cleaning, once the substrate is in place and the aquarium filled, the water will cloud slightly, although this should clear within a few days.

MAINTAINING THE SUBSTRATE
Over time, the substrate will compact and accumulate large amounts of debris. This can cause algal blooms or encourage a proliferation of harmful bacteria that could infect bottom-feeding species such as many catfish.

To prevent this, gently disturb the substrate at least twice a week. Simply "rake" the gravel by pushing your fingers firmly down to the base of the substrate layer.

If there is only a single type of substrate, regularly remove the waste by suction using a siphon-action gravel cleaner. You can do this at the same time as carrying out a water change. For aquariums with layers of different substrate, just clean the top layer with a gravel cleaner, as this is the area where most debris will collect.

ROCKS AND WOOD
As with substrates, there are many types of rock and wood available for the aquarium. Your choice should reflect the style of aquarium being created. For example, large, jagged pieces of slate may look odd in a swamp or downstream Amazon River, but are ideal for a mountain stream or a rocky lake aquarium.

THE FIZZ TEST

To test if a rock is likely to alter water quality, simply pour on some acidic substance such as vinegar. If the rock contains any calcareous substances, it will begin to fizz gently. If there is no fizzing, the rock should be safe to use in the aquarium.

Below: *A sharp eye is needed to check for bubbles, or "fizz," that occurs when an acid is added to an alkaline rock.*

TYPES OF ROCK

As well as the "standard" types of rock, unusual rocks with interesting patterns and markings caused by geological and volcanic activity are readily available for aquariums. Some of these are ideal for creating a distinctive display, while others, such as some dyed or "glass" rocks, look distinctly unnatural.

Not all rocks are suitable for all displays; some release calcareous compounds that alter the pH value of the water and raise hardness levels. Common calcareous rocks include chalk, limestone, marble, and tufa. You may come across rocks with names used only in the aquarium trade, such as ocean rock and spaghetti rock, and these are also calcareous. Rocks with several holes or a "Swiss cheese" appearance are often calcareous. The holes are usually created by the erosion of brittle calcareous substances within the rock. Calcareous rocks are safe in hardwater or brackish aquariums, and may even be beneficial in maintaining high pH and hardness levels.

Inert rocks that are safe to use in any aquarium include coal, basalt, flint, granite, sandstone, quartz, slate, and lava rock.

On their own, rocks can appear static and uninteresting, but if you position them carefully in the aquarium, you can create some dramatic effects. Rockfalls or a scattered appearance can be achieved with a few large rocks surrounded by smaller pieces and chippings of the same type of rock. For a bolder display, choose one or two very large rocks, plus a few smaller pieces. Use rocks to break up areas of the display, such as planted or barren areas, or to create caves for fish to hide or even breed in.

FIXING ROCKWORK

If the aquarium has only a few individual large rocks or an arrangement of small ones, simply place them on the substrate or, for greater security, sink them into the substrate. A safely built, moderate stack of light or porous rocks, such as lava rock, should not need additional fixing. However, a substantial collection of rocks, possibly stacked on top of each other, must be firmly fixed in position. Heavier rocks or taller rockscapes should be siliconed in place before the aquarium is filled with water to prevent a collapse that may crack the aquarium glass. Build up a tall rockscape in stages to prevent collapse during construction. The best method is to use the rocks in order of size, with the largest toward the bottom. You can

ROCKS AND WOOD

This Westmorland rock has an attractive reddish color and striking markings.

Granite has an unusual sparkling texture and will appear more natural with time.

Slate is a heavy, angular rock available in a range of shapes and sizes. Position it carefully.

Rounded boulders have great impact in aquarium displays and make good grazing spots for algae-eaters.

Chippings are available for many rock types. These slate chippings mix well with larger pieces of slate.

Broken pieces of lava rock can be used with larger pieces or to create an unusual substrate.

Washed coal is a good choice for creating a darker display.

Small rounded pebbles are ideal for creating a riverbed.

30

build and silicone together the first section of rocks up to about 30cm (12in) high without much risk of collapse. Allow this section to dry before adding the next layer of rock and securing it. Continue like this each day until you reach the required height.

To create overhanging rocks, build up the initial rockscape and then carefully lay the aquarium on its back or at an angle. Construct the overhang vertically and when the silicone sealant is dry, restore the aquarium to an upright position. Be sure to silicone the rock wall to the back panel of the tank.

TYPES OF WOOD

The standard type of wood commonly used in aquariums is bogwood or driftwood, so called because it is taken from bog areas such as peat marshes, where it will have been naturally soaked and preserved for many years. This process creates wood that will not quickly rot or cause fungal or bacterial blooms when submerged. Driftwood is available in a few styles and often called "jati wood" or "mopani." Mopani has been cleaned by a sandblasting process that creates a two-toned wood. One side is dark and the other is smooth, with a paler, sandy color. Mopani wood is particularly effective in displays with a sandy substrate, such as a brackish or sandy riverbank aquarium. Another type of wood, simply called "twisted root," can represent the roots of trees that sometimes grow into a riverbank. Twisted roots suit almost any aquarium, but look particularly at home in riverbank, swamp, mangrove, or flooded forest-style displays.

Other types of wood, such as bamboo, brushwood, or cork bark, can also be used in aquariums, although some of these may need preparing first. Bamboo is highly effective among dense plants, creating a swamplike style. Brushwood (dried branches) creates the impression of tree roots or overhanging vegetation and is particularly good for imitating the roots of mangroves. Cork bark is sometimes sold by aquarium retailers; use it to hide equipment such as filters, to create an attractive background or as hiding places for bottom-dwelling fish species.

Over time, many types of wood, but particularly driftwood, release tannic acids that may turn the aquarium water a brown, tealike color. Tannic acids are not harmful to fish, although they may lower the pH and/or hardness of the water. In many cases, slightly discolored water can give an aquarium a more realistic appearance, but many fishkeepers do not like it.

Mopani driftwood is precleaned and has a rough dark side and a smooth paler side.

Driftwood is ideal for providing hiding spots, breaking up planted areas, and representing fallen or dead vegetation.

Twisted roots can be used to represent overhanging branches and tree roots.

Cork bark is buoyant and will need to be weighted down or fixed in place. An ideal material for hiding tank equipment.

A chemical filter medium such as activated carbon will remove any discoloration as the water passes through the filter. Alternatively, you can soak driftwood before use to remove the majority of the tannins, but this may take a few weeks.

Apart from the woods described here, or any sold specifically for aquariums, you should avoid placing any other types of wood into the aquarium. If wood is not totally dead or has not been soaked for a long period, it may contain organic elements that will quickly cause bacterial or fungal blooms. These are not only dangerous to fish, but may also severely cloud the aquarium water. Only if the wood is relatively thin, has been dead and dried or soaked for some time, and then prepared for the aquarium, is it likely to be safe.

PREPARING WOOD

Driftwood is safe to place straight into the aquarium, but bamboo must first be dried and varnished to prevent bacterial and/or fungal blooms. The inside of bamboo often has a protective layer, or "skin," which should be removed before varnishing. Then cover

Below: Large bamboo pieces will soon rot unless they are properly varnished inside and out. Make sure the wood is thoroughly dry and use a suitable varnish.

BUILDING A LAVA ROCK CAVE

1 Once you have selected a few rocks, use the largest pieces for the base and apply sealant to the highest points or those that will touch the next segment.

2 Firmly press the "roof" of the cave onto the siliconed areas. Depending on the shape of the cave, you may need to position the structure at an angle to dry.

3 Fill gaps with silicone and smooth the join with a wet finger. These areas should be hidden in the finished cave, although you can cut excess sealant away.

4 Leave the finished cave to dry for a few days and trim off any excess silicone sealant to improve the appearance. The cave is then ready for use in the aquarium.

all visible areas with a clear polyurethane varnish and leave it to dry. Do not use other types or colors of varnish, as they may contain chemicals harmful to aquatic life.

Brushwood does not need to be varnished, but it is a good idea to break or cut it at the widest point to check that all the wood is dead. If there are any green areas or the wood is pliable rather than brittle, do not use it. Normally, if the branches are less than

1cm (0.4in) in diameter and break easily, the wood is safe to use. Brushwood may float, but can normally be wedged into position.

Both bamboo and cork bark are very buoyant and must be weighted down or fixed into position. Wood can be secured by siliconing it to a heavy object, such as a large rock, or onto a flat piece of slate or glass. When this is placed beneath the substrate, the wood appears to be resting on the substrate.

To create a cork bark background, silicone the wood to the back panel of the aquarium several days before filling the tank.

ARTIFICIAL DECOR

For aquascaping purposes, artificial decor can be placed into one of two categories: natural and unnatural. The latter includes novelty items such as skulls and fluorescent bridges, and although these have their appeal, they play no part in creating a natural aquarium, or an aquarium based on the needs of the fish. However, natural-looking artificial decor can be very useful and makes a good alternative to rocks and wood. It can take the form of synthetic roots, stones, caves, or wood. Often, artificial decor begins to look natural only when it has been established in an aquarium for a few months. By this time, a small amount of algae will have grown and the decor appears a little "weathered." The advantage of artificial decor is that many pieces provide welcome hiding

A variety of plain or "natural scene" backgrounds are available for aquariums – here tree trunks and rocks.

places for fish and useful shapes for creating different levels of substrate or planting areas. Some items are designed to fit around filters and/or pipework, and are an easy way of hiding aquarium equipment. Manufactured "stone" walls or caves are also available and eliminate the risk of heavy rocks collapsing. Using such items also means that you do not have to make them yourself.

BACKGROUNDS

A background can make a big difference to the overall appearance of the aquarium. Without one, pipes, cables, or the wallpaper behind the tank are clearly visible unless a large number of plants or other decor covers the entire back panel of the aquarium. Often, a simple black background is enough to hide the hardware. Black backgrounds also help to show up the colors of fish and plants effectively without detracting from the display. Alternatively, there are backgrounds with designs such as rockscapes or dense planting. Although these may not appear completely natural, they

These plastic sheet backgrounds have length markers along the base. Remember to allow a little extra for trimming.

This plastic background (about 1cm/0.4in thick) has a textured surface and is easy to cut to size. Use it inside the tank.

can add an element of depth to the display, particularly if the background matches the rest of the decor.

Structured preformed backgrounds have a natural-looking texture, creating more of a three-dimensional feel. Some are designed to represent a rockface or large tree root. These backgrounds are generally made of a tough polystyrene or a hard foam material and are usually very buoyant. For this reason they must be permanently fixed to the rear panel of the aquarium with small quantities of silicone sealant. Fix the background in position and allow it to dry for at least two days before filling the aquarium with water. While you wait for the silicone sealant to dry, you can place substrates and other rockwork into the tank. Structured backgrounds make a good medium on which to grow certain nonsubstrate-rooting plants, such as Java fern, Java moss, or *Anubias* species.

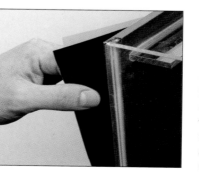

Left: *A variety of methods can be used to attach backgrounds although a few well-placed pieces of sticky tape usually works. You can trim the background to fit, so careful positioning is not always vital.*

33

Using plants in the aquarium

Although some aquarium displays are intended to be rocky or appear barren, in many cases it is the plants that, along with the fish, bring vibrancy and life to the display. As with other items of decor, plants – the "soft landscaping" – should represent the style of display being created. From a practical point of view, the plants' nutritional and other needs must be catered for and they should be compatible with the fish species in the aquarium.

The subject of proper plant care is a complex one, but there are some universal requirements to consider when introducing plants to the aquarium. They are light, nutrients, substrate, and water quality.

LIGHT

Plants obtain their energy and food by converting carbon dioxide and water into glucose. This process – called photosynthesis – harnesses the power of sunlight to break down and rebuild the chemical bonds between the carbon, oxygen, and hydrogen atoms. In the aquarium, you cannot rely on natural sunlight as a source of illumination because it is unpredictable and may cause algal blooms. The alternative is to set up some means of artificial lighting.

Although a single fluorescent tube will illuminate a display aquarium, most plants need far more light than this. Aquariums featuring a moderate number of plants normally need three or four fluorescent tubes, complete with reflectors to bounce the maximum amount of light into the tank. However, it is important to choose fluorescent tubes with the correct spectral output.

White light is made up of many different colors in a "spectrum" of wavelengths. The spectral output of a light source depends on the quantity of each wavelength it produces. Sunlight has peaks in the blue and red/yellow areas of the spectrum, and fluorescent tubes are available that have an

ZONES OF LIGHT AND PLANT GROWTH

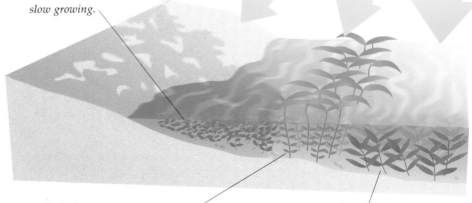

At the water's edge, light is shaded by overhanging vegetation. Plants are small and slow growing.

In deeper water, thick-stemmed plants obtain bright light from the surface.

Plants at the center receive bright light, but the flow is faster and they must bend with water movement.

equivalent spectral output. This type of tube may give the aquarium a slightly odd pinkish purple hue. To offset this, use a single full-spectrum light tube as well. A typical lighting setup could include two or three tubes designed for plant growth and a single full-spectrum tube to balance the visible light and create a more pleasing color.

Powerful lamps, such as mercury vapour or metal-halide lamps, are ideal for heavily planted and/or deep aquariums. Not only do they provide suitable light for the plants, they also improve the appearance of the whole aquarium.

NUTRIENTS AND SUBSTRATES

Plants require a constant supply of about 17 different nutrients in varying amounts to carry out their biological functions. Although a few of these nutrients occur in sufficient quantities in most water sources, aquarists introduce the others artificially to satisfy the needs of plants in the aquarium. Nutrient-rich substrates,

substrate additives, and liquid fertilizers are all methods of adding nutrients that plants can then assimilate through their leaves and/or, more often, through their roots.

Liquid fertilizers are a quick and easy way of introducing nutrients to the aquarium. Most liquid fertilizers must be added at least every two weeks, because oxygen, minerals, and organics in the water will often bind with liquid nutrients, rendering them unusable by plants.

Two important nutrients often lacking in the aquarium are iron and carbon dioxide (CO_2). Iron can be introduced by the methods described above, but carbon dioxide is taken up by plants as a dissolved gas. However, being a gas, CO_2 is lost from the aquarium and into the atmosphere at the water surface and if the surface is highly agitated or the aquarium receives additional aeration, CO_2 is lost even more quickly.

Carbon dioxide is largely used during photosynthesis, which only occurs in light conditions. In many cases, additional fertilizers or extra lighting will not benefit plants unless there is a sufficient quantity of dissolved carbon dioxide in the water. Carbon dioxide must therefore be added continually to the aquarium using a proprietary carbon dioxide fertilizer system. These systems ensure that the water retains a high dissolved CO_2 content by introducing the gas and keeping it in contact with the water for a sufficiently long time for some of it to be absorbed by the plants. In larger aquariums, external CO_2 cylinders can be used together with a control regulator and a bubble counter. Depending on the design, the bubble counter allows bubbles of gas slowly released from the cylinder to travel upwards in a "zigzag" or circular fashion before collecting near the surface and finally being released into the atmosphere. While the bubbles are in contact with the water, the gas is absorbed, increasing the aquarium's dissolved CO_2 content. More complex systems incorporate functions such as switches that prevent CO_2 from being released at night, when the plants do not need it.

There are compact units suitable for smaller aquariums. These are not

INTRODUCING CO_2 FROM A CYLINDER

This carbon dioxide (CO_2) system uses a pressurized cylinder and is ideal for larger aquariums.

A timer connected to a valve cuts off the supply of CO_2 when the lights are off.

Compressed CO_2 gas is held in a cylinder and released at a controlled rate through a regulator.

Aquarium lighting provides the energy for photosynthesis.

A "bubble counter" inside the aquarium maximizes the contact time between water and CO_2.

controlled, but still release a steady supply of CO_2 gas. They normally consist of two sections: a canister into which you place either a tablet, some powder, or liquid and powder, and a collection cup where the CO_2 gas is held. A chemical reaction in the canister slowly releases the CO_2, normally over a period of a month, and it is absorbed into the water from the collection cup. Again, the CO_2 must be released

continually during daylight hours to maintain a sufficient level of dissolved gas in the water. Providing an aquarium has suitable lighting and a relatively fine substrate, adding liquid fertilizers and a supply of CO_2 gas will be enough to supply adequate levels of plant nutrients.

For aquariums with a greater number of plants, substrate fertilization offers a much longer-term and more

DIFFERENT LIGHTING STRATEGIES

Above: *The pink-purple hue created by this fluorescent tube helps plants to grow and shows up fish colors. On its own, the effect can look a little strange, but when mixed with other tubes, the hue disappears.*

Above: *White, or full-spectrum, tubes create a realistic and balanced lighting effect, which is good for both plants and fish color. A full-spectrum tube is often brighter than purpose-specific tubes.*

Above: *Spotlights provide a high-intensity light, ideal for plants and reasonably good for fish colors. Spotlights also pick out details more dramatically and can be used to highlight plants or aquarium features.*

Above: A mixture of substrates provides a more useful planting medium than a single material. Each substrate has a different function vital to optimum plant health.

useful method of creating a constant supply of nutrients for all the plants. Substrates are discussed in detail on pages 24-33, but in short, a good substrate should be relatively fine grade (1-2mm/0.04-0.08in), contain nutrient-rich compounds, and be at least 5cm (2in) deep. A nutrient-rich additive in the substrate allows all the aquarium plants to access nutrients via their roots, and because of the low-oxygen conditions of most substrates, the nutrients are always in a usable form.

WATER QUALITY

Depending on their natural origins, many plants have a preference for hard or soft water and may not do well if placed in an aquarium with the opposite water characteristics. This is because in the wild, the nutrients used by plants occur in different quantities in hard and soft water. A plant from a hardwater area will easily assimilate the nutrients found in hard water, while a softwater plant will be accustomed to the nutrients in soft water. You can compensate for this by adding to the aquarium water the correct quantities of those nutrients required by each group of plants. This will allow you to introduce hard- or softwater plants into aquariums with "unsuitable" types of water.

Another potential difficulty is that the surrounding environment, such as the salty water of a brackish aquarium, will not suit certain plants. Nor do some plants appreciate the fast-flowing waters of a mountain stream aquarium. Such waters are high in oxygen, which binds to nutrients, rendering them useless to plants. The high surface agitation in such an aquarium also removes beneficial carbon dioxide as quickly as it can be introduced.

Water problems such as these cannot normally be resolved by adding nutrients. In these situations, the only way to ensure successful growth is by making a careful selection of plants. Many hardy or slow-growing plants are suitable for such environments; good examples are Java fern *(Microsorium pteropus)*, *Anubias*, *Vallisneria*, *Sagittaria*, and some *Hygrophila* species. In many cases, you may need to choose suitable plants on a "trial-and-error" basis.

Many other environmental conditions also affect plants. In common with fish, plants come from areas of differing water temperature, and it is vital to match this in the aquarium. The temperature of the water will govern a plant's metabolic rate – the rate at which its cellular systems function and how fast it uses up food and grows. In warmer water, a plant will typically grow more quickly, but it will also require more light, nutrients, and carbon dioxide to sustain this increased growth rate.

Pollutants in the water can affect plants in much the same way as they do fish. Water containing a high level of metal contaminants and/or biological pollutants will cause a decline in plant health, a reduction in growth rate, or even the death of the plant. However, small amounts of some pollutants, such as ammonia and nitrates, are beneficial to plants and used as a source of nitrogen, an important plant nutrient. This does not mean that ammonia and nitrates should be added to the aquarium. Although filters and good aquarium maintenance will remove such pollutants, small amounts are continually released by the activities of fish and bacteria. Plants will assimilate these pollutants, often more quickly than a filter can remove them. In effect, the plants act as a filter, removing harmful substances from the water.

SELECTING PLANTS

There is a wealth of plants available for the aquarium, and choices for almost any position in any type of display. A look at the habitats discussed in part two of this book will reveal some suitable plants for specific purposes. Plants for biotope, or habitat, aquariums can be chosen either on the basis of their origin or simply to represent the types of plant found in that location. In a typical aquarium, the plants can be grouped into background, midground, and foreground species, based on their eventual heights, with the tallest in the background. To complement these, add floating plants and rock- or wood-rooting plants in various locations.

The appearance of plants can also reflect the display being created. For example, plants with long, thin leaves, such as *Vallisneria* species, would suit a streamlike or fast-flowing aquarium. They will "bend" with the water flow and enhance the effect of the moving

Foreground plants can be used in a variety of ways. Sagittaria platyphylla *can be planted alone, in a group or among other plants.*

A variety of leaf shapes is important in a well-planted aquarium. Many cultivated species, such as this Hygrophila guianensis, *have interesting leaf colors or shapes.*

also welcomed by many fish. They can provide shade from bright light, hiding places and even breeding sites for some species. As with other abovewater plants, good ventilation is important to stop the leaves from overheating under the aquarium lights. Most floating plants are very adaptable and hardy, and may grow so quickly that they need regular thinning. Floating plants are particularly effective in swamp, lake, or pool-style aquariums.

A number of tropical lilies are available for aquariums, although they will not attain the same leaf size or spread as temperate species sold for garden ponds. However, given good lighting and nutrient availability, a tropical lily in a heated aquarium will quickly reach the surface and produce a number of leaves, so give it plenty of growing room.

TERRESTRIAL AND BOG PLANTS

In many situations, plants that are not "true" aquatics can be used in aquariums to create some interesting displays. In tanks with an abovewater element, terrestrial, moisture-loving plants, such as mosses, ferns, and alpine plants, can be attached to rocks and wood above the water. Some of these plants require only a little substrate and can be planted in small amounts of potting soil in gaps, dips, and crevices

in rockwork. Many marginal bog plants, such as those sold for ponds, can be planted either completely underwater or in shallow water, so that the majority of the plant is above the surface. When plants are used above the water in this way, it is important to keep the air above the aquarium well ventilated and to ensure that the aquarium lighting does not produce too much heat, otherwise the leaves will dry and burn. In some cases, spraying a fine mist of water to create a humid atmosphere above the aquarium will be beneficial.

A few plants sold for aquariums are in fact terrestrial plants that naturally grow in areas that periodically flood. These "nonaquatic" plants will survive for many months underwater before they need replacing and some have quite striking leaf patterns or shapes. By contrast, some true aquatic plants can be used above water in wet conditions; many foreground plants experience terrestrial growth when the water level drops in their natural habitat. Java fern, *Anubias* and *Eleocharis* species and some *Echinodorus* species can all be grown above water if their roots remain very damp and the surrounding air is humid.

The thick, bold leaves of Echinodorus osiris *will make a statement in the aquarium and may grow above the surface.*

water. For swamplike designs, choose smaller, bushy plants with a messy appearance, such as stargrass (*Heteranthera zosterifolia*) or Japanese cress (*Cardamine lyrata*), together with floating plants that produce long, trailing roots. In a swamplike aquarium, the plants should not be obviously grouped but should blend into each other, with individual species dotted around the aquarium. The shallow areas of a downstream river may feature beds of plants such as cryptocorynes, or taller, emerging plants, such as *Echinodorus* species.

Selecting a suitable group of plants for your aquarium should be based on aesthetic considerations – a mixture of sizes, leaf shapes, and colors – and plants that best represent the style you are trying to create. Do not forget the practical aspects, such as water quality and temperature, growth rates, and compatibility with fish in the aquarium.

PLANTS FOR THE SURFACE

Floating plants are not only very decorative in natural displays, but are

PLANTING TECHNIQUES

Plants will need some preparation before being placed in the aquarium to ensure that they establish quickly. First remove any dead or dying leaves and, in the case of good-sized plants such as some *Echinodorus* species, any leaves that are significantly larger than the rest, even though they are healthy. This reduces the plant's nutrient requirement when it is first placed in the aquarium. Once it becomes fully established in the aquarium, it will produce new leaves that may grow bigger than the previous ones.

Next, trim the roots of the plant to 2-3cm (0.8-1.2in). Long roots are easily damaged when the plant is placed in the substrate. Again, this encourages new growth as the plant establishes. Plant aquatic species much as you would terrestrial plants. Make a dip in the substrate, set the plant into it, and cover the roots with substrate. Arrange stem plants in groups, leaving at least 2-3cm (0.8-1.2in) between them, depending on the size of the leaves. Larger-leaved plants can be placed further apart.

PLANTING ON ROCKS AND WOOD

A number of plants have adapted to root above the substrate on solid objects such as rocks and wood. *Microsorium, Anubias, Vesicularia,* and *Bolbitis* species all prefer to be grown this way, rather than in the substrate. The advantage of this in the aquarium is that plants can be grown vertically on a piece of wood, rather than horizontally along the substrate. This method of planting can help to introduce some interesting visual effects into the aquarium. Alternatively, plants can be secured to a large rockscape, a tank background, or even to rocks above the water.

To grow plants in this way, trim the long, thin roots to about 2-3cm (0.8-1.2in) and attach the thick root, or rhizome, to the wood, rock, or other object with fishing line or black cotton. Once the plant is secured, position it in the display. As it grows, the new roots attach to the surface and, if conditions

are good, begin to spread. For the best effect, combine a few different plants on the same piece of rock or wood. A particularly good strategy is to feature a couple of larger plants together with a smaller moss, such as Java moss (*Vesicularia dubyana*), around the roots and base of the plants.

PLANTING AN ECHINODORUS

1 The base of the plant, normally embedded in a rockwool planting medium, should be gently eased from the pot. Trimming away excess roots first may help.

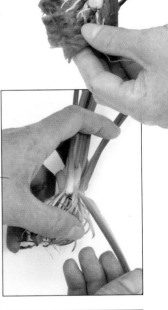

Carefully remove the planting medium surrounding the roots.

2 Trimming the long roots reduces any damage caused by planting. Once in the substrate, the plant will respond by quickly producing new and healthier roots.

Remove any leaves that show signs of damage. The leaf "stem" can be gently pulled away from the base.

3 Putting the plant in place is much like terrestrial planting. Hold the plant in one hand and create a dip in the substrate with the fingers of the same hand.

4 Place the roots in the hollowed-out area and surround the base of the plant with substrate. Be sure to cover the white area at the base of the plant.

ATTACHING A PLANT TO WOOD

Black cotton is hard to see and will eventually break down in the aquarium.

2 *Remove as much excess root as possible from the plant, but be careful not to cut or damage the main root (rhizome). Old or damaged leaves can also be removed.*

1 *Many of the plants that root on objects such as wood have a tangled mass of roots in the pot. Gently disengage the rockwool planting medium from these roots.*

3 *Wrap a length of cotton several times around the rhizome to ensure that the plant is firmly fixed. The plant will produce new roots that will attach to the wood.*

MIXING PLANTS AND FISH

Although most fish in the wild live in environments where plants are present, this does not mean that all fish and plants will coexist happily in the confines of an aquarium. For most fish, plants are welcome in the aquarium as a place to hide in and breed, or just because they provide familiar surroundings. Most fish occasionally nibble at plants to supplement their diet, although they rarely cause lasting damage; often, they eat the decaying parts of the plant. However, for some fish, plants are a major element of their natural diet and they do not lose this instinct in the aquarium, despite the regular availability of alternative foods. Common herbivorous fish, or plant eaters, include species such as silver dollars (*Metynnis* spp.), headstanders (*Abramites* spp.), scats (*Scatophagus* spp.), *Distichodus* species, and some cichlids. Many of these fish can quickly decimate a planted aquarium and will certainly consume most plants more quickly than the plants can produce new leaves.

A similar problem can arise with boisterous fish, such as large barbs, catfish, or cichlids, which damage plants not by eating them, but by sheer clumsiness. Some cichlids, such as oscars, attempt to move objects around the aquarium to establish territories and this includes plants. In many cases, large fish such as these will rip leaves apart, simply because the plant is there!

On the other hand, some fish can actually benefit plants. In any aquarium, you will find some algae growth, often on the leaves of plants. This can undermine plant growth and health. Small algae-eating catfish, such as *Otocinclus* or *Peckoltia* species, are perfectly adapted to feeding off such algae without damaging the plants. Some livebearers and loaches also remove algae from plant leaves.

As well as algae, debris from fish, plant waste, and decomposed material in the aquarium can collect in the foliage of finer-leaved plants, particularly low-growing foreground ones. A buildup of debris between the leaves will block out light and hinder photosynthesis. To prevent this buildup, introduce small scavenging fish into the aquarium. In their constant search for food items, they disturb the leaves of plants, dislodging any collected debris. *Corydoras* species and kuhli loaches (*Pangio kuhlii*) are ideal for this purpose.

Below: *Peaceful* Otocinclus *catfish provide a welcome "cleaning service" for plants.*

Creating the right water conditions

It is easy for the aquarist to alter and care for the visible "hard" and "soft" landscaping in the aquarium, but for fishes and other living inhabitants, it is often the invisible water conditions that make it a home away from home. Even in apparently ideal surroundings, some fish will never be completely healthy or display their full colors and behavioral traits unless the water around them has all the correct properties. A good aquarist should be a "water keeper" as much as a fishkeeper.

Right: Dissolved salts and minerals, collectively termed "hardness," are not visible to the naked eye. The fishes of Lake Malawi require hard water and would be prone to disease without the presence of these dissolved compounds.

THE INVISIBLE ENVIRONMENT

It is rare to find crystal-clear waters in nature all year-round and in many places where aquarium fish are found, the waters are often murky and full of suspended debris. Fish, therefore, are not overly concerned with the color or appearance of the aquarium water. A lack of silt and debris in an aquarium, combined with constant mechanical

Below: The clear water in this vegetated river gives the impression of a healthy environment, but the elements that create unhealthy water are also invisible.

filtration, ensures that the water is clear, while chemical media can be used to remove any discoloration. A good filter, proper feeding, and regular maintenance will remove any invisible pollutants such as ammonia and nitrites, which are dangerous to fish. The resulting environment is free of pollutants and crystal clear, which would at first appear to satisfy all the fishes' requirements. However, the water in which fish live in the wild (and in the aquarium) is not pure; it contains a number of chemicals,

organics, and minerals, and it is the balance, or quantity, of these that makes up its composition.

A fish's physiology is adjusted to the typical water values found in the area from which it originates. Water values vary in different habitats because of the surrounding landscape and the properties acquired by the water from the moment it falls as rain until it reaches a particular habitat. For example, around the African Rift Lakes the landscape is rocky and relatively barren. The rainfall around this area travels through various rocks, many volcanic in origin, and picks up large quantities of minerals. Some of these minerals bind with other elements, creating carbonates. It is the mineral content of water that is responsible for the water hardness; more minerals create harder water. The water in the African Rift Lakes is relatively hard and the fish (mostly cichlids) from these lakes will not do well in an aquarium with soft water. By contrast, the tetras and some cichlids, such as angelfish and discus, found in tributaries of the Amazon River prefer softer water. The water in these rivers and tributaries has passed through masses of soil, which is full of organics that remove minerals and introduce acids. This has the effect of lowering the water's hardness and pH. In areas such as this, pH and

THE pH SCALE

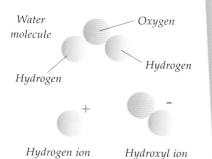

Water
molecule

Oxygen

Hydrogen

Hydrogen

+ −

Hydrogen ion   Hydroxyl ion

Water (H$_2$0) is made up of positively charged ions (H$^+$) and negatively charged ions (OH$^-$). The pH level is a measure of the ratio of these two ions in a body of water. Acidic water has more hydrogen ions; alkaline water more hydroxyl ions. Neutral water has an equal number of both.

The pH scale is logarithmic, meaning that each unit change in pH, say from 7 to 8, is a ten times change; from 7 to 9 is a hundred times change, and from 7 to 10 reflects a thousand times change. This is why sudden changes are stressful to fish.

pH 9

pH 8

pH 7

Above: *Liquid test kits involve adding a specified number of drops of one or more reagents to a water sample. Hold the bottle vertically. Compare the final color change to a printed chart.*

Above: *This broad range pH test shows a value of 8.5, reflecting alkaline water conditions. More specific high-range and low-range pH tests are available for tanks with critical tolerances.*

hardness levels can fall so low that hardwater species, such as the Rift Valley Lake cichlids, would not survive.

The fish described above are examples of alkalophiles (alkaline-loving) and acidophiles (acid-loving) fish, but many species are suited to a happy medium. Some are highly adaptable and will live in water that does not always have to conform exactly to certain conditions. However, to keep your fish in the best of health, you should make an effort to recreate conditions that are close to those they would experience in nature. There are various ways of altering the properties of water before adding it to the aquarium, but you should first understand the factors that influence the pH scale and what makes water hard or soft.

THE pH SCALE

The degree of acidity or alkalinity is measured on the pH scale, which ranges from 1 to 14. The scale represents a difference in the ratio of positively charged hydrogen ions (H$^+$) and negatively charged hydroxyl ions (OH$^-$). Pure water (H$_2$O) with a neutral pH of 7 has an equal ratio of ions. If a body of water has more hydrogen ions, it can be considered acidic (pH below 7); if it has more hydroxyl ions, it is alkaline (pH above 7). The pH scale is logarithmic, meaning that a change of 1pH (say from pH 7 to pH 8) is a change by a factor of 10, a change of 2pH (pH 7 to 9) is a change by a factor of 100, and a change of 3pH reflects a factor of 1,000, and so on. Because of the logarithmic nature of the scale, a sudden change in pH by more than 1pH can be quite a shock to fish, whereas a change by more than 2pH may be enough to kill some delicate species. If the change occurs slowly over a period of time, fish can adjust to it within their own physiological limits. In nature, aquarium fish are normally found in water that ranges from pH 5 to pH 9, depending on geographical location, but for the majority, a pH level around 6.5-7.5 is suitable.

Some fish from Amazon tributaries and similar locations have been found surviving and breeding at levels as low as pH 3, although this is extreme and need not be recreated in the aquarium.

FACTORS THAT AFFECT pH

The pH value of water is very closely linked to the amount of dissolved carbon dioxide (CO$_2$) it contains. Carbon dioxide releases carbonic acid into the water, which causes the pH level to drop (becoming more acidic). Other natural acids, such as humic or tannic acids, are produced in the aquarium and these also lower the pH level over long periods of time. Driftwood, waste from plants and fish and from some bacteria all produce pH-lowering acids. Therefore, in most aquariums, the pH level will tend to drop over time.

Certain materials have the opposite effect: they raise pH levels. Some rocks and substrates contain calcareous elements such as calcium that bind with acids produced in the aquarium

NIGHT AND DAY IN THE AQUARIUM

DAY

Carbon dioxide is used up by plants during the day, while oxygen binds with organic matter. This reduces the production of acidic compounds and pH rises.

How the pH level changes in a 24-hour period

NIGHT

Carbon dioxide is produced by plants and other organisms, while oxygen is used up. The release of acidic compounds lowers the pH level.

FISH

All living organisms – including fish and bacteria – respire, using up oxygen and releasing carbon dioxide.

FISH

Bacteria and plants continue to respire at normal rates, while most fish respire at a slower rate.

PLANTS

In sunlight hours, plants photosynthesize, using up carbon dioxide and producing oxygen.

PLANTS

Plants cannot photosynthesize without light, so they neither use up carbon dioxide nor release oxygen.

and prevent drops in pH. If enough calcareous elements are present, the acidic hydrogen ions will also be removed, leaving a larger ratio of hydroxyl ions, thereby raising the pH level and creating more alkaline conditions.

THE DIURNAL CYCLE

As we have seen, pH levels are closely linked to dissolved carbon dioxide levels in the water. Carbon dioxide is continually produced in and removed from the aquarium by living organisms. In general, it is constantly produced by all organisms during the process of respiration – oxygen is used up and carbon dioxide is released. The greatest producers of carbon dioxide through respiration in the aquarium are bacteria. However, carbon dioxide does not normally build up to dangerous levels in the aquarium because it is constantly removed through an air/water exchange at the water surface, and oxygen is replenished at the same time. As a result of respiration and the

air/water exchange, oxygen and carbon dioxide levels are kept relatively constant throughout a 24-hour period, so there is little effect on the pH level. However, another process occurs in the aquarium and it can dramatically alter this balance and introduce a diurnal (daily) cycle. This is the process of photosynthesis by plants and, to some degree, algae.

During photosynthesis, plants use up carbon dioxide and produce oxygen. This reduces the normal carbon dioxide levels so that carbonic acid is no longer released, causing the pH level either to stop falling or to rise (depending on the other factors already described). Because plants do not photosynthesize in the dark (at night) but do continue to respire, oxygen levels drop and carbon dioxide levels increase at night, resulting in the production of carbonic acids and a fall in pH.

The fluctuations in the diurnal cycle are increased in aquariums containing many plants and/or constant carbon dioxide fertilization. Most fish are used

to this cycle in the wild and should not be adversely affected. However, in the aquarium, the effect is often more pronounced than in nature, and should be monitored in a heavily planted tank. If the diurnal pH change is about 1pH or more, use additional aeration at night to increase the air/water exchange and prevent an excess build-up of carbon dioxide. Aeration should be used only at night, because during the day plants need carbon dioxide to photosynthesize.

WATER HARDNESS

Water is often described as hard or soft, and water hardness is closely linked to pH levels. In nature, acidic waters are usually soft and alkaline water is usually hard. Water hardness is a measure of the dissolved salts and minerals in the water; a high concentration of salts and minerals creates hard water, while a low concentration creates soft water. Hard water, which contains many minerals and salts, often creates alkaline (high pH) conditions because any acidics and organics that would normally lower the pH are quickly removed through binding with the minerals. In contrast, soft water contains few minerals, so any acids released are free to lower the pH level.

In tapwater supplies, a combination of hard water with a low pH is possible. This can occur when minerals or salts that do not bind with organic or acidic substances are added to the water. The same happens when acidic substances added to water (such as carbon dioxide fertilization) "outweigh" the minerals and salts in hard water.

A GOOD SOURCE OF WATER?

Depending on where you live, your water supply may have pH and hardness values that match those required by the fish you intend to keep. However, more often than not, you need to alter the water or find another source that suits your fish. Although tapwater is a convenient source of water, there are other factors to consider and an alternative supply may be preferable.

TAPWATER

In most cases, tapwater will always require some level of treatment before it is safe to use in the aquarium. The three main concerns (other than pH and hardness) are chlorine/chloramine content, nitrate content, and heavy metals. Chlorine and chloramine are added to tapwater to kill bacteria that may be harmful to humans, but they also kill useful bacteria in the aquarium and can damage the gills of fishes. Although good aeration for a 24-hour period will virtually remove all chlorine through the air/water exchange (chlorine is introduced as a gas), the chloramine (which releases chlorine over an extended period of time) cannot be removed by aeration. To remove both chlorine and

chloramine, you must use a suitable dechlorinator to treat the water before introducing it into your aquarium. Dechlorinating additives are available from aquatic dealers and remove chlorine and chloramines almost instantly. Some also remove the heavy metals that are sometimes present in sufficient quantities to damage certain delicate fish, such as discus or clown loaches. If your aquarium is densely planted, heavy metals are of less concern, because plants are very efficient at removing such pollutants.

Finally, some tapwater supplies may be high in nitrates, although again, the levels are normally dangerous only to

very sensitive fish species. Nitrates can be removed by prefiltering the water through activated carbon or a similar chemical filter medium. Alternatively, use nitrate-removing media as part of the aquarium filtration.

RAINWATER

Many aquarists use rainwater for their aquariums and it can be a good source of water with virtually no hardness, which is particularly good for acidophiles, such as most tetras and Amazonian cichlids. However, rainwater should always be prefiltered with a chemical medium, as it often picks up atmospheric pollutants on its

HOW HARDNESS AFFECTS pH VALUES

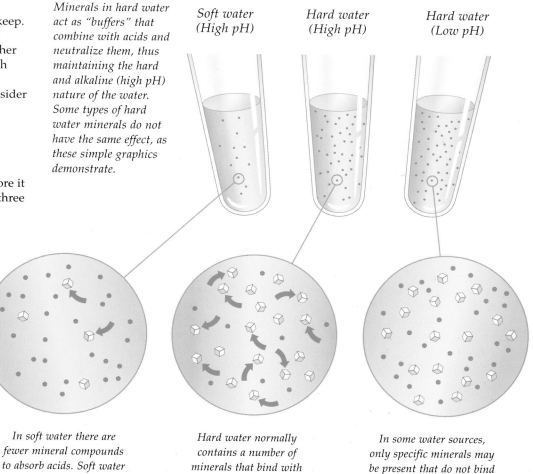

Minerals in hard water act as "buffers" that combine with acids and neutralize them, thus maintaining the hard and alkaline (high pH) nature of the water. Some types of hard water minerals do not have the same effect, as these simple graphics demonstrate.

Soft water (High pH)

Hard water (High pH)

Hard water (Low pH)

In soft water there are fewer mineral compounds to absorb acids. Soft water is therefore normally acidic and may fluctuate.

Hard water normally contains a number of minerals that bind with acids, maintaining a high pH without fluctuations.

In some water sources, only specific minerals may be present that do not bind with acids. This produces hard water with a low pH.

Above: Rainwater is a good source of almost pure water with no hardness and slight acidity. The water should be filtered through a chemical medium before use to remove any harmful contaminants.

way down to the ground. Apart from these pollutants, rainwater is virtually pure and has a zero hardness and a pH of 6.5-7. (The pH value of rainwater in the U.S. can often be lower than this.) Once any contaminants have been removed, you should mix rainwater with some tapwater or add a proprietary treatment to introduce "trace elements." These include substances that add a little hardness and help to reduce any dramatic pH changes once the water is introduced into the aquarium.

REVERSE OSMOSIS WATER

To obtain virtually pure water, all the additional elements must be removed, and this can be achieved in a reverse osmosis unit. Reverse osmosis (R.O.) is the process of forcing water through a very fine membrane that allows only water molecules to pass through; any

larger molecules are discarded as waste. The resulting water is pure and very similar to rainwater, with a zero hardness and low or neutral pH.

The advantage of reverse osmosis water over rainwater is that the possibility of contamination is much lower. However, as with rainwater, R.O. water is too pure to be used directly in the aquarium and must be mixed with tapwater or have trace elements added to it before it is suitable for tank use.

MAKING SOFT WATER HARD

Creating conditions suitable for hardwater fish, such as African Rift Lake cichlids or Mexican livebearers, is relatively easy as it involves adding substances to the water. Proprietary trace element treatments are available specifically for this purpose. Alternatively, you can add calcareous rocks and/or substrates to the aquarium to introduce minerals that will raise the water hardness level and, consequently, lift pH levels above neutral and prevent pH drops. Such rocks and substrates should be used

REVERSE OSMOSIS

Water has a natural ability to even out the compounds within it and spread dissolved salts and minerals. Reverse osmosis is a form of mechanical filtration and is the forced opposite of "natural" osmosis shown here.

R.O. units contain mechanical and chemical prefilters that reduce the load on the main unit.

Above: A commercial R.O. unit produces water with a pH of 6.5-7 and no hardness. Buffers, trace elements, and nutrients must be added to it before it is able to sustain plant and fish life in the aquarium.

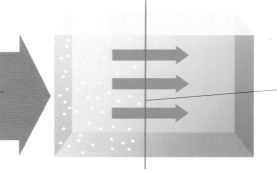

In 'natural' osmosis, water in a dilute solution flows into a concentrated solution through a partially permeable membrane.

In reverse osmosis, water is forced through a very fine membrane, leaving dissolved salts and minerals behind.

The membrane is so fine that only water molecules can pass through, thus producing pure water.

BUFFERING CAPACITY

All natural water sources have a hardness level and a closely related buffering capacity that helps to prevent severe changes in pH. Some fishes require water conditions that are tied to different buffering capacities.

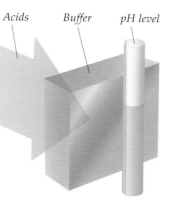
Acids   Buffer   pH level

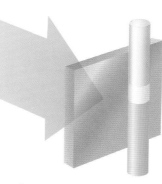

A large buffering capacity removes or binds acidic compounds as they are released, preventing pH change.

Over time, or often in softer water, buffering capacity is reduced. Some compounds are not bound and cause pH fluctuations.

If buffering capacity diminishes completely or in water with no hardness, severe pH changes are caused by acidic compounds.

Calcium is a highly effective buffer, but use it only with hardwater species. Calcium-based gravels prevent pH fluctuations.

Fish and plants from hardwater areas will thrive in well-buffered aquarium conditions.

Fish from softwater areas and most plants are used to minor fluctuations.

Sudden changes in pH are harmful and can kill both fish and plants.

only in tanks housing alkalophiles, as hardness can rise dramatically and pH levels may reach about 8.5. For fish that require only a slight rise in hardness levels, trace element additives are normally the preferred method.

MAKING HARD WATER SOFT

Because reducing water hardness involves the removal of elements, it is a little more difficult to do than increasing hardness. First, you can change the source of your aquarium water and use R.O. water or rainwater to soften it. Alternatively, you could add acid-releasing materials, such as bogwood, to the tank and/or use carbon dioxide fertilization to remove hardness-causing salts and minerals from the water. However, the success of this last method depends on the actual

salts and minerals present in the water; some may remain unaffected by acidic substances, resulting in water that has a low pH level but is still relatively hard. Proprietary chemicals are available for lowering hardness and pH, but these should be used only in water that already has a pH of about 7-8 or lower. At higher pH levels, carbonates are made insoluble by some treatments, resulting in cloudy water (caused by previously dissolved minerals), which can clog filters.

BUFFERING CAPACITY

Buffering capacity describes the ability of a body of water to maintain a stable pH level, or more accurately, to withstand drops in pH levels. Water contains buffers, often in the form of carbonates, that reduce fluctuations in

hydrogen ions, thereby reducing any severe drops in pH. Buffering capacity is closely linked to water hardness, and the same substances apply for both parameters. Hard water is generally better buffered and has a higher alkalinity (pH) than soft water. The buffering capacity of water can be kept stable by regular water changes. It is vital that carbonate hardness is regularly measured in planted aquariums, as the use of CO_2 can reduce the aquarium's buffering capacity and/or hardness. If all the available carbonates are used up, a severe drop in pH can occur that will be harmful to fish in the aquarium.

Plants are also affected by changes in pH, but not as drastically as fishes. Most aquarium plants are happy in water with a pH value of 6.0 to 7.5.

Planning an aquarium

To create a stunning display aquarium, particularly one based on a specific habitat, requires a good deal of planning and preparation. As well as selecting a favorable location for the aquarium – one where it can be viewed to the best advantage and where conditions are suitable for its inhabitants – the equipment and decor must be carefully designed to suit the desired display. The aquarium hobby has advanced significantly in recent decades, and obtaining a wide selection of tanks, equipment, and decor is now relatively easy.

CHOOSING A SUITABLE LOCATION

In any home, there are good and bad locations for an aquarium, although some of the poor sites may not seem obvious at first. However, once the aquarium is installed, it will be very difficult to relocate should any problems arise. There are three main considerations to bear in mind when choosing a site: the best spot for viewing the tank; the most practical place for setting up equipment and carrying out maintenance; and the surrounding environment from the point of view of the fish. A suitable location for viewing is largely a matter of personal preference, but there are several factors to consider with regard to the aquarium equipment, maintenance, and the surrounding environment.

EQUIPMENT AND MAINTENANCE

In most cases, the aquarium will be supported on a cabinet or stand and most of the ancillary equipment, including any external filtration, can be stored underneath. There should be space around the back and sides of the aquarium for wires and/or pipework – 7.5cm (3in) or more should be sufficient. An electrical socket nearby is essential. To prevent water from traveling down wires to an electrical socket, make sure the wires drop below the socket before rising up toward the plug. There should also be plenty of space above and around the front of the aquarium for carrying out water changes or cleaning filters. A source of water close by is not vital, as you can transport water to and from the aquarium in containers.

THE SURROUNDING ENVIRONMENT

The sounds, vibrations, movement, heat, and light around the aquarium all have a direct effect on the health of the fish inside. Many external environmental factors can stress fish and undermine their well-being. Choosing a good location based on the surrounding environment will therefore help to keep the fish healthy, confident, and full of color. Vibrations from household equipment, such as washing machines, television, or stereos, or from any loud noises will travel through the aquarium and directly affect the occupants. Fish are very sensitive to vibrations and use them to detect other fish and objects in the aquarium. If there are too many vibrations from external sources, the fish can experience a "sensory overload," which may lower their immune system, causing health problems and sometimes death. Sudden vibrations caused by doors closing, people moving past the aquarium, or tapping on the aquarium glass will have the same effect. Ideally, choose a quiet spot against a wall and opposite the door, where the fish will be able to see people walking into the room from a long distance away.

Also consider the ambient light around the aquarium. While the aquarium is illuminated, the lighting in the room should not have any influence

Left: An aquarium is a piece of furniture in its own right and should be carefully chosen and positioned to fit in with the room decor and surroundings. Once in place, an aquarium is not easy to move, so any practical considerations should be considered before setting it up.

POSITIONING THE AQUARIUM

Space around and behind the aquarium is essential for maintenance and cables or pipework. Space beneath the aquarium can be used for storage of food or equipment.

If possible, fit a dimmer switch to the main room light. This will eliminate any sudden light changes that will shock the fish.

Heat from sunlight and radiators can affect the aquarium. In this room, direct sunlight will reach the tank for only a small part of the day.

Electrical sockets should be nearby but not directly underneath. Make sure any cables fall below the wall socket to prevent water from reaching the plug.

Vibrations from audio equipment such as TVs or stereos can disturb fish. Make sure any such equipment is not too close to the aquarium.

Doors opening and closing suddenly can stress fishes. The aquarium in this room is positioned where the fish can see the door at a safe distance.

on it. Sudden changes in the room from bright light to complete darkness can have the same detrimental effect on fish as vibrations. In most cases, this situation can be avoided by setting the aquarium lights to come on after dawn, when the room is in partial daylight, and to switch them off at least 20 minutes before turning off the room lights. Finally, do not site the aquarium in front of a window where direct sunlight can reach it, as this may cause the aquarium to overheat in summer and can encourage algae blooms that turn the water green. Avoid heat sources such as radiators, to prevent the aquarium from overheating.

SELECTING A SUITABLE AQUARIUM

There are endless options for shapes and sizes of aquarium, and choosing the right one depends largely on your budget and space restrictions. In general, it is best to choose the largest aquarium that will fit the available space. A good-sized aquarium is often easier to maintain than a smaller one, because it is easier to stabilize a substantial volume of water. (Any pollutants or excess waste in the aquarium will have less effect in a larger volume of water because the pollutants will be more diluted.) Also, you will have more freedom to create an interesting aquascape, although this does not mean that a small aquarium cannot be a basis for a stunning display.

Next, consider the style of the aquarium. Some are supplied complete with hoods and cabinets, or you can buy these components separately. Although it may be cheaper to buy a system complete with filters, lighting, and heating, remember that it may be difficult to make any alterations to it, as the filtration or lighting units are often fixed in place. Bow or angle-fronted aquariums are also available, and if the tank is to fit a particular space, many aquatic dealers will be able to order a specially made aquarium in almost any size and shape.

SITING THE AQUARIUM

An aquarium filled with water is very heavy and will place a great deal of pressure on the floor. If it is to stand on a wooden floor (particularly upstairs), it is worth establishing where the joists are and placing the cabinet or stand feet over them. The weight of water also puts pressure on the tank's glass base, which must be properly supported. If the water pressure is concentrated on one area of the base, the aquarium may crack. To avoid this risk, many modern tanks have a rim around the base that lifts them up from the cabinet or stand beneath. If the aquarium does not have a supporting rim, place a sheet of polystyrene or a plastic foam mat between the aquarium and the cabinet or stand. This layer will absorb any imperfections in either the cabinet or the aquarium and distribute pressure evenly over the base.

CHOOSING A BIOTOPE "STYLE"
The style of aquarium you wish to create will have an influence on the equipment you use. For example, an aquarium representing a mountain stream may require additional pumps, while a Lake Malawi aquarium may require a larger filter to cope with an increased amount of waste from a heavily stocked aquarium. A biotope with a large number of plants may require bulky CO_2 fertilizer systems or a specific substrate. It is important,

therefore, to know what type of biotope aquarium you want to create before buying or installing any equipment. Of course, your choice is largely a matter of personal taste, but do take maintenance into consideration. A heavily planted and stocked aquarium with specific water requirements will require far more care, expertise, and time spent on it than a relatively barren aquarium with no specific water conditions.

CREATING AN AQUASCAPE
With the exception of prefixing rockwork and backgrounds, building up an aquascape is best done in a single session. This way, the aquarium will turn from an empty box into a worthy display, and items can be positioned and rearranged in one "artistic" sweep.

Once you have established the style of aquascape you want to create, the next stage is to decide where to place the decor and plants and the quantities of each that you will need. To help you, it is a good idea to prepare simple

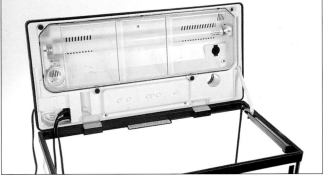

Left: This specially designed tank hood has a built-in light compartment and cable tidy, allowing one electrical socket to power the lights, heater, and filter.

Right: A "bare" tank can be used to create a customized setup incorporating items of equipment for specific purposes. This 90x30x45cm (36x12x18in) tank is used for the aquarium displays shown in this book.

THE BASIC EQUIPMENT

All aquariums will require certain basic items of equipment, including heaters, filters and lights.

Aquarium heaters
Heater/thermostats (heaterstats) are all very similar in function and appearance, but some have added features, such as strengthened glass, which may be useful in tanks with large amounts of rockwork or boisterous fish. Certain filters contain built-in heaterstats or compartments in which heaterstats can be placed. Whatever the design, the most important factor is the wattage of the heater unit; the larger the aquarium, the higher the wattage of heater required. Bear in mind that heater wattages are based on use at room temperature or slightly below. If the aquarium is situated in a location where the surrounding air is a great deal cooler, a higher-than-normal wattage heater will be required.

Below: Heater guards protect the heaterstat from physical damage (from solid objects or fish) and safeguard fish against overheating if they should stay too close to the heating element.

Aquarium filters
The main considerations when choosing a filter for a particular aquarium style are the flow rate, the volume and the location of the filter in relation to the tank. Larger filters tend to have higher flow rates, but fast-flowing water is undesirable in an aquarium with a large number of plants or one that represents a slow-flowing swamp or pool-like environment. As well as hindering plant growth, fast-flowing

Above: An external canister filter provides more efficient filtration and frees up space inside the aquarium for aquascaping. You can use different filter media to control the water conditions more closely.

water also reduces the impression of a quiet, undisturbed habitat. However, a fast flow rate is vital in a mountain stream or fast-flowing river aquarium, and a fast-flowing filter may even need to be supplemented by additional pumps. For aquariums such as these it may be worth installing a venturi or narrow outlet on the filter, to accentuate the appearance of flowing, well-oxygenated water.

The volume of a filter is directly related to its biological performance in removing organic pollutants, such as ammonia, nitrites, and sometimes nitrates. Internal filters (placed inside the aquarium) have a small volume, for practical and aesthetic purposes. An external filter generally has a far greater volume. It can be as large as the space available in a cabinet or other location. The extra volume can be used for additional mechanical filtration (sponges),

biological filtration (sponges and specific media) and chemical filtration (activated carbon and other media). This extra capacity is particularly useful in tanks with a high stocking density (e.g., Rift Valley Lake aquarium), large fish (e.g., South American cichlids), or fish with high demands on water quality, such as discus.

In well-planted aquariums, a relatively small internal filter can be easily hidden behind dense planting or items of decor, but in a rocky Rift Lake aquarium or an open brackish tank, an internal filter may not be so easy to hide. In these cases, an external filter will reduce the appearance of bulky equipment in the aquarium.

Aquarium lighting

In general, aquarium lighting is provided by specially designed fluorescent tubes, although in some cases, you can use overhanging spotlights or high-intensity lamps. Fluorescent tubes are powered by a suitable ballast, which must be the same wattage as the tube, although for some tubes, a variation of a few watts is acceptable. The ballast must be situated outside the aquarium and although it will resist a few splashes, it should not be allowed to get wet. Ideally, place it in the cabinet beneath the aquarium. The ballast will be supplied complete with cables and caps that attach to each end of the fluorescent tube.

Fluorescent tubes do not get very hot and are not overly damaged by water splashes. However, if condensation is continually formed on the tube over a long period, the lifespan of the tube may be reduced. To prevent

this from happening, place a condensation tray or glass cover between the fluorescent tube and the water surface.

Spotlamps, such as metal-halide or mercury vapor lamps, are ideal for highlighting certain areas of the aquarium and for improving plant growth. These bright lamps are more expensive than fluorescent tubes, but they produce far more light and make a significant difference to large displays, particularly tanks that are more than 45cm (18in) deep. Spotlamps should be suspended from the ceiling or a suitably strong support and the main unit containing the bulbs should be at least 45cm (18in) above the water surface. Because spotlamps are suspended over an open aquarium, there may be a significant amount of evaporation, so regular water changes will be required to maintain the correct water level.

Below: Fluorescent tubes are the most popular form of aquarium lighting. Different tubes are available for specific purposes, such as plant growth or enhancing colors. A combination of fluorescent tubes creates the best effect.

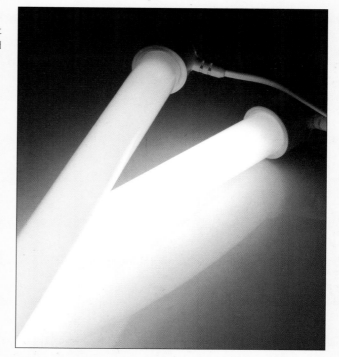

overhead and front-view sketches of the proposed display. Spending a little time working out the details often inspires the ideas and small touches that result in a stunning effect. Consider the needs of the fish at this planning stage; would they appreciate the odd cave, a dense planting area, floating plants, or hiding places? If you are feeling ambitious, you might want to try to breed fish in the aquarium, so think about materials that will create suitable breeding sites. Anabantoids will require a number of small floating plants, fine-leaved species such as *Cabomba,* and a calm surface on which to create a bubblenest. Dwarf cichlids, such as *Kribensis* or *Apistogramma* species, appreciate caves or small flat rocks and well-defined territorial areas. Making a list of all the "ingredients" in the display is also a good way of making sure that all the items you will need are ready and waiting when you come to start work.

SETTING UP THE AQUARIUM
Once the aquarium is in place, make sure that it is level and that the edges are aligned with the cabinet or stand. Also check that there is enough space around the back of the aquarium for wires and pipes, and to thread electric wires and plugs through.

FIXING THE BACKGROUND
Always make the background the first item you install. Once

Above: It is good idea to make a sketch of your aquarium display before you start. Remember to consider the fishes' needs as well as the overall design and appearance.

other equipment and decor are set up in the aquarium, fixing or moving a background becomes much more difficult. Simple, colored plastic sheet backgrounds can be cut to size and secured in or outside the aquarium. If the tank is likely to house a large amount of decor and the background is used simply to hide pipework, cables, and wallpaper from view, secure it to the outside with sticky tape. However, if the furnishing is relatively sparse, placing the background inside the

aquarium will avoid the typical bubble-like patches that occur when condensation is trapped between the aquarium and the background. In this case, secure the background inside the tank with sticky pads available from your aquatic dealer.

ADDING THE SUBSTRATE
Depending on the aquascape, the substrate may be a simple layer of pea gravel or a complex arrangement of different substrates to suit a heavily planted environment. Whichever it is, you must wash it thoroughly before placing it in the aquarium (see page 29). After rinsing them, you can place "single" substrates directly into the aquarium and spread them out as desired. For more complex planting substrates, the layers must be added in a particular order. If you are using a heating cable, now is the time to put it in place (see pages 28-29).

Below: You can create raised planting beds by using larger decor pieces and filling in behind them with a suitable substrate. This major feature is part of the aquarium display shown on pages 142-143.

Right: This stunning aquarium design, dominated by driftwood, is based on the division of areas and has been created by careful planning and preparation.

The substrate can be laid flat or banked toward the back of the aquarium to create a sense of depth. The substrate is often the most unnatural element in a display; remember that in nature the substrate is rarely completely uniform and flat but is more likely to be undulating and littered with bits of stone, wood, and organic debris. In the aquarium, adding some alternative materials, such as rock chippings, pebbles, and broken wood scattered over the main substrate, looks much more natural. To enhance the effect, try piling up substrate over rocks and wood. This works particularly well if you are creating the appearance of water movement, such as in a stream or fast-flowing river. In this case, the "banking" should always be in the same direction and preferably in line with the water flow.

INSTALLING THE EQUIPMENT

The filter, lights, and heater must be installed before the aquarium is running. Installing the heaterstat is relatively easy; place it in an area of water flow at an angle of 45°, with the thermostat at the top, facing the flow of water. This maintains an even temperature distribution and ensures that the heat rising from the heating element does not immediately affect the thermostat. Never switch on the heaterstat when it is out of water, as the glass casing will crack, rendering the unit unusable. Place the heater about halfway down the aquarium glass, so that it is completely covered by water and away from any large rocks that might damage it if they fell down. Plastic guards are available to protect the heaterstat from any disturbance caused by falling rockwork or the attentions of large boisterous fish.

Position internal filters so that the outlet is about 5cm (2in) below the water surface. The flow of water does not need to be strong; if a little water movement is visible at the surface, the aquarium should be suitably oxygenated. You can hide internal filters behind decor or plants, but make sure you can remove them easily for regular maintenance.

External filters should be situated below the aquarium. Although it is possible to site them at the side – or even above – the tank, they must be below the tank when they are first switched on or after maintenance, so that you can prime them properly. Make sure there is enough pipework to reach down to the filter and back to the aquarium, and that the filter can be easily accessed for maintenance. The inlet and outlet pipes should be situated at either end of the tank to produce a flow of water across the whole aquarium. The inlet should be just above the aquarium floor, where it will pick up the most debris, and the outlet just below the surface, so that the water is well oxygenated. If the flow of either an internal or external filter is too strong, it can be distributed by a spraybar, which will spread the outflow over a wider area.

PLACING DECOR

The positioning of plants, wood, rocks, and other decor is largely artistic, but there are a few useful rules worth following. To create a varied environment for the fishes, make sure there are plenty of hiding places and areas of cover, but also sufficient open areas for swimming. Decor and/or dense planting around the edges and rear of the display aquarium not only provide hiding spots but also conceal equipment, while leaving a central open area for swimming.

With the exception of the plants, the decor should all be of a similar style. Use the same type of driftwood throughout the aquarium. The same applies to rocks; choose just one or two types of rock, preferably those that match the composition of the substrate. Limiting the decor in this way will create a more distinctive style of aquarium and looks far more natural. Creating a natural rather than an artificial-looking aquarium is not always easy; success often hinges on several small elements in the display, rather than on the big items of decor.

And finally, remember that your first attempt at aquascaping need not be the final version. Over time, items can be moved around or changed until you are happy with the results.

FILLING THE AQUARIUM

Now you can fill the aquarium with water. To avoid disturbing the substrate too much, carefully pour the water onto an object such as a plate or bucket inside the aquarium. This will distribute the flow of water evenly and keep disruptions to a minimum. Tapwater is safe, but if you are using a hosepipe, first allow the water to run for a few minutes to get rid of any old water that is in the pipe. Once the aquarium is filled, add a dechlorinator to remove any chlorine or chloramines. Finally, switch on and check the filter, heater, and lighting to make sure they are all working properly. Leave the aquarium to heat up and settle for at least three or four days before introducing any fish. During this period you can add the plants and make finishing touches to the aquascape.

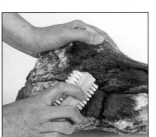

BUILDING UP AN AQUARIUM DISPLAY

These photo segments track the key stages of creating an aquarium display. Take your time to complete each stage carefully.

Fine-grade pea gravel is a good planting medium.

Medium-grade pea gravel, a good mixer.

Large-grade pea gravel can be scattered over sand for streambeds.

The background is the first item to put in place. Use pieces of adhesive tape to fix it to the outside of the back glass.

Stage 1

Wash the substrate thoroughly before placing it evenly across the base of the aquarium. Use a small container and add the substrate gently. If you pour in large quantities from a height, pieces of gravel may bounce and scratch or chip the glass. Keep back some of the substrate for creating raised areas later on.

Stage 2

Place the larger items of decor in the aquarium first. Make sure that any heavy items such as large rocks are firmly in place and unlikely to topple against the glass. Equipment such as filters, heaters, or pipework can also be put in position at this stage. Do not switch on any equipment until the tank is filled with water.

Stage 3

Tapwater is safe to use, although if you are using a hosepipe, let it run for a minute or two first to remove any stale water. Run the water slowly over a large rock or saucer placed in the aquarium to minimize disturbance. The plants and decor still to be added will displace some water, so do not fill the tank to the top. Once filled, add a suitable dechlorinator and switch on any equipment.

Stage 4

Now add the plants. Try to group a number of plants of the same species together but remember to leave room for growth. Check the equipment at this stage to make sure heaters or filters are operating properly. External filters may take a few minutes to work efficiently as any trapped air bubbles gradually work their way through the pipework.

Stage 5

At this point you can add the finishing touches to the substrate. Adding sprinklings of larger substrate or pieces of rock, wood, or pebbles can have a significant effect, making the whole display appear more natural. Use rock types and wood chippings that match the substrate and any larger wood pieces.

Stage 6

Once all the plants and decor are in place, fill the aquarium to the top. The aquarium will need time to heat up and settle down before any fish are introduced. It is best to leave the aquarium for several days and introduce fish slowly over the next few months. During this maturation time, establish a suitable maintenance and plant feeding regime that you can carry out for the whole life of the display aquarium.

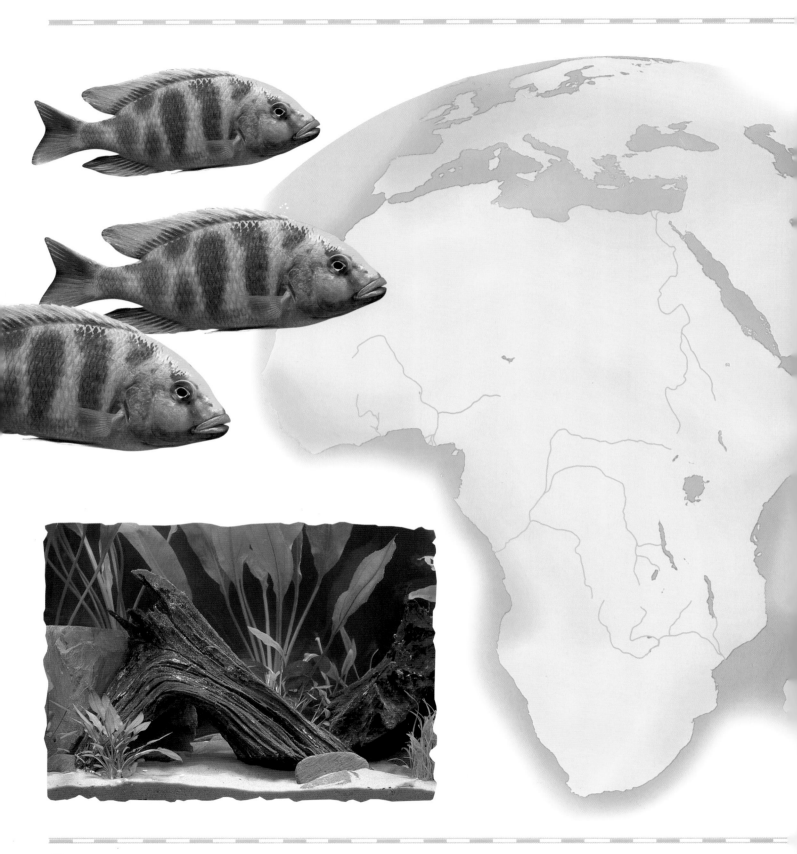

PART TWO

Aquarium displays

Many elements combine to form the basis of successful fishkeeping, and even though an aquarium may be perfectly healthy, established, and well cared for, if it does not look authentic, one aspect of the hard work is somehow lost. To bridge the gap between a healthy display and a stunning one, the fishkeeper must learn from nature. A vast array of natural habitats and environments exists, each housing different groups of fish, all with their own unique habits and needs. A great deal can be learned from the physical properties of an environment, such as its rainfall, water quality, surrounding vegetation, and substrate, as well as from the behavior and physiology of the plants and animals within it. For example, a quick glance at the natural environment of the White Cloud Mountain minnow reveals a clear, oxygen-rich, fast-flowing habitat with little vegetation. From this we can tell that the fish are accustomed to a fast flow rate and room to swim, so we provide them with a powerful filter and open space. But this does not make a stunning aquarium. Take a wider look at the natural environment and you will see waterfalls, scattered rocks, alpine plants, and fallen branches or shrubs; all these natural elements can be incorporated into the aquarium display.

This approach can be applied to any environment or group of fish. Tetras can be associated with dense tree roots embedded in a riverbank and debris-ridden substrate, while gouramis can be found in swamps filled with vegetation, both above and below the surface, and interspersed with tall bamboo canes. Some environments are incredibly simple, such as that of the Lake Malawi cichlids. It consists of boulders and a sandy substrate. However, take this into the display and you can build up a stunning aquarium.

In this section we look closely at a number of natural environments and habitats, at the surrounding geology and landscape and the water quality and vegetation. Each environment is recreated incorporating decor and elements found in nature. And the result is a healthy vibrant display suited to both the fishes and the aquarist.

Chinese mountain stream

In most cases, a river starts with numerous small streams that collect together and form larger tributaries or small rivers before joining the main river. In sizable expanses of flat land, these streams start from bogs or swamps at the lowest point where water collects, or from underground springs near the main river. However, in the majority of cases, the stream begins far higher up, in mountainous or hilly regions. Rainfall is far greater at high altitude than in the surrounding lowland regions. Condensation from clouds – often on a daily basis – leaves the thin soil waterlogged, sometimes even throughout the summer months.

Some of the rainfall travels through the underlying rock and emerges lower down as underground springwater, but most of it does not travel far and quickly arrives at the surface to form small waterways. These increase in volume as a result of surface runoff and water that travels through the thin topsoil. As these small streams combine, they soon create a waterway large enough to house a number of species, forming a complex food chain that includes many small fish species.

Mountain streams can be present at any time of year, but their volume at any particular location varies with the seasons. During the rains, the streams that are large enough to harbor fish extend to the highest points. In dry seasons, these higher-altitude streams become little more than a trickle of water at the center of a dried streambed. However, at lower altitudes the largest streams still exist during the dry season and this is where many of the stream fish can be found. At this time, low-altitude streams are relatively calm, but as soon as the rains begin to fall they quickly become overfull and turn into raging, fast-flowing water bodies bubbling with foam.

MANY TREES, MANY FISH

The plant and animal life that inhabits the mountain streams also varies, largely depending on the surrounding geology. In hilly but low-altitude areas, the soil may be deep enough for trees and larger vegetation to take root and these in turn support many larger animals, other plants, and numerous small mammals and insects. Together, this wide biodiversity provides food sources for aquatic life, including fish. Fruits, seeds, insects, vegetation, and many tiny organisms that feed on the forest "wastes" are all sources of nourishment for small fish, which themselves become food for larger species. The roots of trees and other vegetation also retain substantial amounts of water in the underlying soil. This "reservoir" protects the larger streams from major seasonal variations in water volume, allowing fish to remain in some streams all year long.

Mountain streams

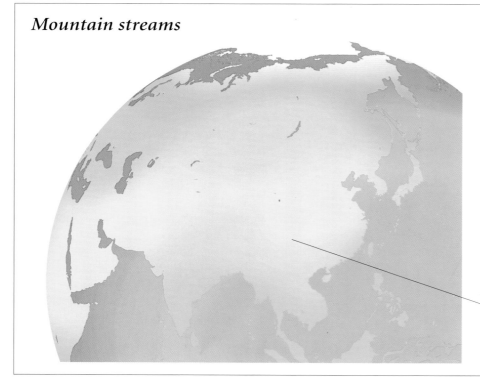

At the source of a river there are many small streams that vary in appearance from season to season. The water here is clear, well oxygenated, and low in organic load. The number of species in these habitats is limited, but those that do live here survive against the odds and manage to find abundant food despite the harsh environment.

Mountain streams can be found throughout the world, although many aquarium species originate in the Chinese mountains.

Above: A stream in the Woolong Reserve in Sichuan Province, China flows through mixed forest that is home to the giant panda. The waters of the stream abound with fish.

In high, steep regions, however, the topsoil is thin and there are no trees or large plants, which need a deep soil in which to root. The vegetation in these regions consists of ferns, mosses, small shrubs, and grasses. Some insects and fruits still provide food for a limited population of fish, but for most of the time, the fish must find food elsewhere.

THE CLOSER YOU LOOK, THE MORE YOU FIND

The mountain stream is not a good habitat for plants; the water in these streams has picked up little organic matter and is low in nutrients. The nutrients that are present are often unusable by aquatic plants, having been oxidated or bonded with minerals in the fast-flowing, highly oxygenated water. There are virtually no taller plants, as the soil is not deep enough to support substantial root structures, and the yearly variation in water volume gives plants little opportunity to become truly established. However, the lack of vegetation in the surrounding landscape does allow plenty of light to reach the shallow streams, and this is used for photosynthesis by algae, small marginal or bog plants, and mosses that often grow beneath the water.

In many cases, the streambed consists largely of open rocks with no soil except at the edges or in small pools near the main stream. Only algae are found in these rocky areas, although such sparse vegetation still provides the basis for a food chain. Many tiny animals and infusoria live among the algae and underwater vegetation. Some small fish will feed on these, but they provide a more complete source of food for many filter-feeders, insect larvae, amphipods, and other invertebrates and crustaceans. It is these organisms that provide the food to support small fish.

Fishes from mountain streams often have barbels, or whiskers, that "feel" for food along the streambed, while smaller catfish and loaches have adapted to feed solely on the algae growing on open rocks.

AVOIDING A SUDDEN ATTACK

Although the small size of many mountain streams and the comparatively limited food chain prohibit many larger, predatory fish from occupying this environment, the smaller fish species are not completely safe from predators. In most areas, a number of birds and other land-based animals readily fish in the mountain streams for a meal. There are few places to hide from such predators and sensing an oncoming attack is virtually impossible. The best defense is a quick reaction, and the fish found in mountain streams are ideally equipped for quick bursts of speed to escape a dangerous situation. Their highly streamlined, often torpedo-shaped bodies are designed to minimize drag in the fast-flowing waters.

To complement this body shape, many fish have short, rounded fins that enable them to cover short distances very quickly, with rapid acceleration and deceleration. This darting motion is used both to avoid a sudden attack and to transfer between suitable resting or feeding sites.

Above: Pseudogastromyzon fasciatus *has the shape of a fish that lives in fast-flowing currents. The streamlined body deflects the flow of water, allowing the fish to graze algae from the rocks with ease.*

As well as the ability to swim very fast, fish from this habitat can also adopt a hovering action, remaining in the same location with a jerky up-and-down motion caused by quick, sharp movements of the pectoral fins. This is seen when they are hiding or resting in calmer waters, perhaps behind a rock or in deeper water. Even in these situations, the current may be flowing unpredictably, and slight adjustments of the fins help to keep the fish upright and in the same location.

Stream fish and other substrate-feeding fishes have a certain way of feeding. Midwater swimmers hover above the substrate and appear to be "picking" at individual stones or items of debris on the substrate. In most cases, they are taking organisms from the substrate that are so tiny that they are often invisible to the naked eye, and searching for larger creatures among the stones.

OTHER NATURAL ADAPTATIONS

Instead of a torpedo-shaped body, some fish from the mountain stream environment have a completely different shape. Algae-eating loaches and catfish are all relatively small, but more importantly, have a very horizontally compressed body. A typical example is the Chinese hillstream loach *(Pseudogastromyzon cheni)*. It grows to about 10cm (4in), but when viewed from the side, it is no more than 1cm (0.4in) in height. This dynamic, compressed body allows the loach to attach itself with a specially designed mouth to rocks and stones in fast-flowing areas, and graze from abundant sources of algae. The body shape acts in much the same way as the wing (or aerofoil) of a plane, reducing most of the drag from an oncoming flow of water. Fish with this type of body shape typically spend most

Smoothed rocks are created by the weathering action of flowing water and are often found in mountain streams.

WATER CONDITIONS

The water found in mountain streams is rarely acidic and nutrient-rich because it has had little time to pick up organic matter, which would soften it. Mostly, the water quality is neutral to slightly alkaline and medium-hard due to the minerals picked up from the surrounding rocks. The water in many mountain streams, even those in tropical regions, is normally relatively cool, and the temperature is certainly lower than that found in downstream rivers and waterways. The fish that inhabit these regions may not appreciate high temperatures and it follows that most of the aquarium fish for this type of display prefer water between 20 and 22°C (68-72°F) and certainly no higher than 24°C (75°F).

*Angled rocks
are used to create
the waterfall in the
display. The flat surfaces
direct the flow of water.*

of their time on the streambed and so
have little need of a highly developed
swimbladder. Instead, when they move
from place to place, they use their
underside against the water to create a
"lift" effect before gliding back down to
the substrate.

A MOUNTAIN STREAM AQUARIUM
A good way to create the impression of
a shallow stream with fast-flowing
water is to "enclose" the open water
space with large rocks and introduce an
above-water element, where flowing
water can be seen entering the
aquarium. To do this, the aquarium
should be only a half to three-quarters
full, with a waterfall at one end. In
larger aquariums, it may be
possible to construct
two waterfalls –
one small and
one large –
for added
interest.
However, a waterfall is not essential to
introduce the impression of moving
water. Additional powerheads or filters
with venturis and airpumps will also
convey the impression of a turbulent
water environment.

Plant life beneath the surface should
be minimal, since, as we have seen,
many plants would not appreciate this
kind of environment. To add a little
vegetation, plants can be used above
the water among rocks and even
outside the tank, allowing leaves and
branches to trail into the aquarium
view. Because few, if any, aquatic
plants grow beneath the surface, the
substrate can be kept relatively simple.
Ideally, choose a large-grade substrate
such as pea gravel for the base, with a
number of small pebbles or cobbles on
top. These should be the same type of
rock, or similar in appearance to the
rocks used in the waterfall and/or
around the sides of the aquarium. The
substrate used in the featured aquarium
is silver sand, covered with a sprinkling
of pea gravel and rounded slate
pebbles. In this aquarium, the silver
sand provides a good base on which to
construct rockwork, although it does
not accurately represent the types of
substrate found in most mountain
streams around the world.

CONSTRUCTING A WATERFALL
In this aquarium, slate is used to create
the rocky waterfall. These rocks are
large, heavy, and angular and thus
present a significant risk if they
are not
secured
properly.

*Use sticklike pieces
of driftwood
sparingly to
imitate fallen
branches that have
become trapped
against rocks in a
stream.*

As with most rockscapes (see page 30),
place larger rocks at the bottom, with
progressively smaller or lighter pieces
further up.

A major consideration in this type of
display is where to locate a suitable
pump. In this aquarium, it is housed
within the waterfall, where it is hidden
from view. In larger tanks, the pump
could be situated elsewhere in the
aquarium or even outside it in a
separate "sump" tank.

Wherever the pump is positioned,
it must be easily accessible for
maintenance. Here, the waterfall is
constructed in two sections. Behind the
rocks that make up the lower section
there is plenty of space for the pump
and pipework, while the top section
forms a "lid" to hide any equipment.
Both sections should be built with care
and each rock securely siliconed to any
adjacent pieces. The "lid" section
should also be fixed together, but
should be easy to remove from the
aquarium to gain access to the pump.

The pump itself should be powerful
enough to recreate the strong flow of a
mountain stream. The actual flow rate,
is a decision for you and depends on
the desired display. You may wish
to recreate a raging stream or
simply a trickle from a small
waterway or spring. In this
aquascape, the flow rate is quite
strong and represents a turnover rate of
20 times the volume of the aquarium
per hour. To maintain such a strong
flow, a small pond pump may be
preferable to a large aquarium
powerhead or filter. Make sure that any
pumps have a suitable prefilter or
sponge attached to the inlet to prevent
fish from being sucked into the unit.

OVERGROUND VEGETATION
Without a little greenery, this type of
display may appear somewhat barren,
especially as a significant proportion of
the aquarium does not contain water.
The rocks that make up the waterfall
and the rockscape have plenty of dips,
cracks, and gaps into which you can
place some hardy terrestrial plants. The

These alpine plants, Sedum rupestre *(left) and* Arenaria caespitosa *"Aurea" (right), will thrive in gaps in the rockwork.*

small rooting area will limit the number of suitable plants, but the same happens in nature, so this should not be a significant problem. Three types of terrestrial plants are ideal for this display: mosses, alpines, and some ferns. All the mosses and many alpines and ferns are well equipped to grow in damp areas with little substrate and should do well in the aquarium environment. Mosses and alpines should spread across the rockwork and soon dominate the above-water element of the display.

Certain aquarium plants are suitable for this type of environment, including varieties such as Java moss (*Vesicularia dubyana*), Java fern (*Microsorium pteropus*), *Anubias* and *Bolbitis* species, and many marginal pond plants. For added interest, place pot plants behind or above the aquarium and allow them to drape naturally into the display.

SUITABLE FISH

Many aquarium fish are well suited to this type of display, although only a few are found in similar habitats in nature. Others simply come from river systems that may be fast flowing, or from lowland streams. Fish that do come from a mountain stream

environment include many species from China, such as the Chinese hillstream loach (*Pseudogastromyzon cheni*), the sucking loach (also called the Chinese or Indian algae-eater, *Gyrinocheilus aymonieri*), and the White Cloud Mountain minnow (*Tanichthys albonubes*). Small algae-eating catfish are particularly suited to this fast-flowing environment, although larger species, such as the popular plecostomus (*Hypostomus* spp.), which are South American in origin, may become large enough to risk knocking over rocks.

For the midwater area, many small-medium barbs and danios are a good choice of fish for an active aquarium. The danios (*Brachydanio* spp.) are very active fish that enjoy a strong water

flow. A group of the smaller zebra danios (*Brachydanio rerio*), accompanied by a few giant danios (*Brachydanio aequipinnatus*), can produce a worthy display almost on their own.

Small barbs, such as the golden barb (*Puntius sachsi*) or Odessa barb (*Puntius ticto*), are also suitable, although some larger species (up to about 10cm/4in), such as the striped barb (*Puntius eugrammus*), arulius barb (*Puntius arulius*), and rosy barb (*Puntius conchonius*), may look more striking.

Below: *The White Cloud Mountain minnow (*Tanichthys albonubes*) – named after the mountain in China where it lives in the wild – is a popular and reliable aquarium fish and ideal for this display.*

Left: Gyrinocheilus aymonieri *is an efficient algae-eater often found in Chinese and Asian waters. Although it is a useful aquarium fish, it is territorial and often fights with others of its own species.*

Below: *The zebra danio (Brachydanio rerio) is a constantly active fish that appears to enjoy swimming against a strong flow of water. Any of the danio group of fishes would be highly suitable for this aquarium.*

61

Chinese mountain stream aquarium

Although there is almost no vegetation beneath the surface, the fast flow of water and the "raw" appearance make this display visually exciting.

You can position moisture-loving houseplants above or behind the aquarium and allow the leaves to hang over and into the water.

This piece of driftwood softens the impact of the rockwork and imitates a fallen branch or root.

Slate rocks are useful in background areas. Although this rock looks large, it only takes up a small part of the substrate.

Smaller rounded pieces of slate scattered across the substrate continue the rocky theme.

A fast flow generated by a concealed pump creates this vigorous "whitewater" area.

The flow of water must be carefully directed over rocks to create a lively impact without too much splashing.

Alpine plants will root in gaps and should spread over the rockwork in time.

A sprinkling of pea gravel completes the streambed effect.

Sand may be moved over time by water movement so placing a gravel tidy (plastic mesh) underneath can help to stabilize the substrate.

These rocks are heavy and should be placed with extreme care.

Central American stream

Unlike the rivers and waterways of the nearby Amazon region, where the water is soft and acidic, conditions in the streams of Central America are hard and alkaline. In many areas, the soil and substrates contain calcareous elements, often resting on a limestone base. In these areas the pH level rarely drops below 7, and is often as high as 8-8.5. The hard water makes it difficult for plants to obtain nutrients and many areas have sparse vegetation. Where aquatic plants do occur, they often grow in dense patches in calmer water, usually around underground springs, where an influx of nutrients is always available. The vegetation around the streams also varies depending on their location. Some streams are surrounded by dense forest, while others flow through lowland vegetation and exposed rocks. A typical Central American stream often alternates between calm stretches of water that gently flow over a shallow, muddy or sandy substrate and fast-flowing patches over rocks and pebbles.

It is not only the streams that house fishes and aquatic life; throughout Central America; there are many swamps, lagoons, pools, and small rivers, and all these environments share similar fish populations. In most places, the streams are clear and well oxygenated and many fish rely on sight to locate their prey.

SMALL FISH, SMALL PREY

Apart from the substrate-dwelling catfish, most of the fish found in these streams are surface-feeders that prey almost solely on insects and insect larvae. Insects, and mosquitoes in particular, are abundant around the streams, especially in areas surrounded by dense vegetation. The mosquitofish (*Gambusia affinis*) is so called because of its almost exclusive diet of mosquitoes and their larvae. This tiny fish is so effective at consuming mosquito larvae that it has been artificially introduced into many areas for the sole purpose of

Central American streams

Many of the small Central American livebearers are also found throughout Mexico and the southern United States.

Many streams occur in the central mountain ridges and flow into pools and waterways before connecting to the larger rivers.

The fishes that inhabit the streams of Central America are smaller than their mighty river counterparts. Many are popular with aquarists; one of the best-known groups, the livebearers, is common in Central American streams. The geography of the surrounding land allows a number of unique streams, brooks and waterways that support thriving populations of fish.

Left: This stream in Carara National Park, Costa Rica is typical of the fast-flowing stretches of Central American streams. The rain forest grows close to the water's edge.

Above: Although the pike livebearer (Belonesox belizanus) only grows to about 10cm (4in), it is an experienced predator that catches small fishes with ease.

streams, waiting for an unsuspecting fish to arrive, at which point it uses its powerful jaw and sharp teeth to grab and hold its prey. All the fish in these streams are relatively small; few grow to more than 10cm (4in), so it is only the smallest individuals and young fry that regularly risk being eaten.

POPULATION CONTROL

A local population of fish can quickly rise or fall depending on the available food sources in the streams. The rapid change in a local fish population is due to the breeding habits of the livebearers. Unlike egglaying fish, the livebearers give birth to fully formed, free-swimming young. This gives the young fish a far greater chance of survival and also eliminates the need for parents to use up energy protecting eggs and defending breeding sites. Most livebearers give birth to between 20 and 100 young in one brood, although guppies and some mollies can produce up to 200 young. Livebearers mate readily and reproduce as often as once every four to eight weeks. In theory, a population of 20 female guppies, each producing 100 young every six weeks, could produce as many as 4,000 young in three months! Although most of the young would be eaten by other fish, including the

controlling mosquito populations. Another popular aquarium fish, the guppy *(Poecilia reticulata),* has also been introduced to some waterways for the same purpose.

As well as insect larvae, which are often found at the sides of the stream among marginal plants, there are many small aquatic invertebrates and detritus-feeders beneath the surface. These tiny creatures are preyed upon by small midwater fish, some opportunistic surface feeders, and catfish. Most catfish and bottom-feeders are scavengers that feed on whatever food sources they can find among the substrate. Normally, this consists of

small aquatic creatures, worms and, again, some larvae.

Algae is present in open-water areas that receive more hours of sunlight, although there are not many fish "designed" solely for eating algae. Many of the surface insect-feeders will graze large amounts of algae, although normally only as an alternative food when insect populations are low.

Few large fish inhabit the shallow streams, so there are not many predators under the water. The most common predator here is the pike livebearer *(Belonesox belizanus),* which will grow no larger than 10cm (4in). It hides among plants at the side of

These large cobbles are almost identical in shape and color the substrate and help to recreate a "natural" streambed.

parents, many will survive, given enough food and plenty of hiding places. Livebearers dominate the fish populations in these streams because of their high adaptability, breeding rates and the lack of predators. In larger rivers or waterways, they would do less well; as they are not highly camouflaged or used to avoiding predators, they would be quickly consumed by larger fish.

CREATING THE AQUARIUM

Although in nature, vegetation is found in only a few dense patches alongside the stream banks, these areas can be used to create an interesting and well-planted aquarium. The plants in this display must be carefully chosen, since only hardy varieties will survive in the hard, alkaline water. However, the aquarium is relatively simple to construct and many of the fish suited to the display are easy to care for, so this aquascape is ideal for beginners.

THE SUBSTRATE

The mostly lowland streams of Central America have not traveled far from their sources and have had little time to

Medium-grade pea gravel suits the streambed simulation and will support hardy plants.

pick up organics and soil debris from the surrounding land. The substrate, therefore, is mostly made up of rounded gravel and rocks. Only a few calmer areas have a muddy or sandy substrate and even these patches are relatively thin. In the aquarium, a substrate of medium-fine pea gravel can represent the natural streambed. In a display with a large number of plants, it may be worth using a combined substrate, with pea gravel as the visible top layer. Nutrient-rich additives will aid plant growth, but a heating cable to move nutrients about is not helpful. In hard, alkaline water, a heating cable will only cause useful nutrients to bind with minerals, making them unavailable to the plants.

To create a more natural-looking substrate, choose different grades of pea gravel and place larger cobbles and pebbles on top. These should be similar in color and type to the pea gravel. Blend the elements together by placing smaller pebbles around large cobbles. In this aquarium, a mix of light and dark cobbles creates some interesting contrasts, and an attractive foreground area in front of dense plant groups.

DRIFTWOOD

The vegetation around most Central American streams is bushy rather than densely forested because the soil is often relatively shallow and alkaline, which does not encourage strong growth. However, vegetative debris, including branches and roots, are commonly found near waterways. The driftwood in this aquarium is partially hidden by plants, but plays an important part in dividing areas of

Mature Echinodorus *species may require a finer rooting substrate and the addition of an iron-rich liquid or substrate fertilizer.*

CREATING HARD, ALKALINE WATER

Raising the pH and hardness of the water in the aquarium is relatively easy to achieve because it involves adding substances to the water rather than removing them. If your initial source of water is quite soft and/or acidic, use a proprietary chemical additive to introduce additional trace elements and minerals to the water. Alternatively, add calcareous rocks and substrates as these also release minerals over time and help prevent a drop in pH and hardness. Coral-based gravels or rocks, such as chalk, limestone, marble, ocean rock, and tufa, will all raise water hardness and pH.

Java moss (Vesicularia dubyana) can be planted on rocks or wood or simply left to cover open areas of substrate. Trimming keeps it neat.

water and prevent pH levels from dropping.

Ideally, the plants in a Central American stream display should be varieties that are naturally accustomed to hard, alkaline conditions. Given strong lighting and a good rooting substrate, they should do well. This aquarium features just five hardy and adaptable plant species, and all the plants of one species are placed together in separate areas of the aquarium. Grouping them in this way creates contrasting divisions and each group makes a bold impression.

Each of the plants here has a different leaf shape, from the fine, feathery *Cabomba* to the long-leaved, grasslike *Vallisneria*. There are two clear foreground and background planting areas, leaving plenty of swimming room for the fishes. Toward the front

the display. Several pieces are used together here, but appear as one long branch or root. The driftwood can hide heaterstats or filters, or simply add some extra interest to the aquarium.

PLANTS

Many of the fish suited to this display appreciate hard, alkaline water, but it makes life a little difficult for plants. Under these conditions, nutrients are not as easily available and plants have to work harder to obtain them. Additional fertilization with liquid fertilizers may help, although most of these nutrients will be removed by dissolved minerals in the water. To help the plants obtain nutrients, combine a substrate additive with the careful application of carbon dioxide fertilization. The problem with adding carbon dioxide is that it releases carbonic acid, which will lower the pH. A happy medium can be achieved by using carbon dioxide fertilization plus calcareous rocks or substrates that will help to "buffer" the

The leaves of this Hygrophila *species contrast well with other plants and look best when planted in a group.*

of the aquarium, there are some smaller cuttings of *Hygrophila*, as well as some Java fern *(Vesicularia dubyana)*, which will root on wood and rock rather than in the substrate. The foreground also feature some small *Echinodorus* plants.

THE FISHES

Most of the fish from this area that make interesting aquarium subjects are livebearers. Popular fish such as the guppy *(Poecilia reticulata)*, platy *(Xiphophorus maculatus)*, molly *(Poecilia sphenops)*, sailfin molly *(Poecilia velifera)*, and swordtail *(Xiphophorus helleri)* are peaceful and readily available. Most of these species are sold in a variety of color and finnage strains that differ significantly from their appearance in nature. The guppy is occasionally sold in its wild form, where males exhibit a number of brightly colored spots across the entire body. Females are less flamboyant; they have a much more subdued, pale brown body color. The enhanced finnage of male varieties is highly attractive, but does present some problems when fish species are mixed together in the aquarium, because the oversized fins make a good target for other fish to nip at.

Mixing male and female livebearers can also present problems in the aquarium because of their tendency to breed rapidly and regularly. Male livebearers constantly chase females, often to such a degree that the females become stressed and prone to disease if they are heavily outnumbered by attentive males. To prevent females from becoming stressed or a population boom occurring in the tank, it is a good idea to keep only males or females of any particular species. Be aware, though, that many females may already be pregnant when you buy them.

An interesting livebearer for the aquarium is the sailfin molly, so called because a mature male uses a heavily oversized dorsal fin both to display to females and as a territorial display toward other males. Male livebearers often use oversized finnage and color to attract mates. Another example is the swordtail, where males exhibit a long swordlike extension to the caudal (tail) fin for the same purposes.

Although livebearers are naturally hardy and adaptable, the intense breeding used to produce color strains and varieties often creates genetically weak fish that may be more prone to common diseases, such as bacterial skin problems, fungus, finrot, and whitespot.

Take care to choose healthy fish when selecting suitable varieties for the display aquarium.

The unusual pike livebearer *(Belonesox belizanus)*, sometimes called the pike topminnow, is a less common livebearer that does not suffer from the consequences of intense commercial breeding. It makes an excellent addition to the aquarium, but keep it only with fish of a similar size; anything less than half its size (5-6cm/2-2.4in) may soon become prey.

CATFISH AND OTHER FISHES

Although the livebearers dominate the Central American streams, a number of scavenging catfish are found toward the substrate. A fish of particular interest for the aquarium is the pictus catfish *(Pimelodus pictus)*. This small (10cm/4in) catfish is constantly active, searching for food in the gravel substrate and peaceful enough to be kept in groups with other fish. A few characins are also found in Central American waters, as well as some cichlids in deeper waters. However, most of these fish are rarely available and may not mix well with the livebearers due to the characins' fin-nipping nature and the cichlids' territorial and aggressive behavior.

Above: *The attractive pictus catfish* (Pimelodus pictus) *is constantly active in its quest for food in the substrate. Keeping a small group of these fish often creates the best effect in a display aquarium.*

Left: *The male guppy is one of the most popular aquarium fish and available in a number of color forms. The females are drab in comparison and many fishkeepers keep only the colorful males.*

Right: *In this small Gambusia* holbrooki, *the male's modified anal fin, called the gonopodium, is clearly visible. The gonopodium is used to fertilize females internally, and male livebearers will constantly chase females in the aquarium.*

Central American stream aquarium

This display leaves plenty of open swimming areas for the confident
livebearers and makes good use of cobbles and gravel to create the streambed.

*Vallisneria
will spread
quickly from
this area.*

*The bold appearance of this
group of Hygrophila is
softened only slightly by
foreground plants.*

*Java moss on the wood will move
with the water and makes an
interesting addition to the display.*

*A mix of cobbles and pebbles
creates a varied group of
rocks in this area.*

*Partly obscuring cobbles with
plants looks natural and appears
inviting to fishes seeking cover.*

Dark areas created by the wood
and plants will become welcome
retreats for fishes.

This piece of bogwood remains a
distinct feature even though it
is partially hidden by plants.

A thick, bushy group of **Cabomba**
catches the light well and provides
hiding spots for young fry.

Some randomly placed small
pebbles make the substrate look
like a natural streambed.

Foreground plants help to hide larger items
such as the driftwood, which in turn makes
a good background for the plants.

Grouping plants with
contrasting leaf shapes can
look dramatic.

Central American river

The landscape around the Meso-American landbridge (the area linking North and South America) is invariably rocky and volcanic. Many areas contain calcareous rocks such as limestone, which alter the water chemistry by removing dissolved organics and raising the pH and hardness. The soil around the rocky landscape is thin and there is little substrate in the rivers. In most areas the riverbed consists of exposed rocks and rubble, smoothed by the weathering actions of the flowing water. In calmer waters, some sandy substrate is banked up against larger rocks, and many fish hide and breed in these small pockets.

There are few major river systems in this region; indeed, many rivers are comparatively short from their source to the ocean. In the rainy seasons, the many streams that contribute to the rivers provide an influx of rainwater and at these times, the larger rivers increase in size and become raging torrents of fast-flowing water over exposed rocks. The annual increase in water flow often sweeps away any silt or fine substrate buildup, maintaining the rocky, barren appearance. In some places, the fast-flowing waters are interspersed with calmer areas on flat land that often form substantial pools.

In dry seasons, the river shrinks and becomes a gently flowing body of water in the center of the riverbed. In many places, there are large lagoons near the main river. These are often formed by volcanic craters, and although they appear to be separate from the rivers, they are normally connected underground, either through open caves or simply by the movement of water through the ground.

VEGETARIANS AND PREDATORS

Although there are few plants in many areas of the river, the shallow waters and exposed rocks are ideal locations for algae growth. The mouths of many of the catfish and cichlids found here are specially adapted to graze the tough algae from the rocks. Some fish graze the algae for the microorganisms that live within it, in much the same way as the cichlids of Lake Malawi.

Central American river habitats

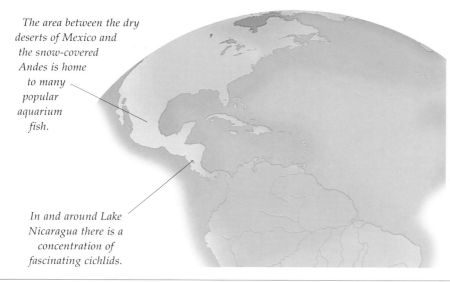

The area between the dry deserts of Mexico and the snow-covered Andes is home to many popular aquarium fish.

In and around Lake Nicaragua there is a concentration of fascinating cichlids.

The rivers of Central America are often clean and clear, flowing over exposed rock. They are home to many fish, including some of the popular cichlids. Unlike the shallower streams, the rivers support much larger fish species, which often have territorial and aggressive tendencies. These behavioral traits are both a joy and a burden for the aquarist who attempts to keep these interesting fish.

Algae provide a highly nutritious source of food but it is difficult to digest, and many fish prefer other forms of food. In the substrate among the rocks, many small aquatic animals, plant vegetation, and crustaceans form part of the diet of the Central American fishes. Where calmer waters are surrounded by terrestrial vegetation, you find small fish that feed primarily on mosquitoes and mosquito larvae. Some of these fish are the same species that inhabit the Central American streams, although the fish that live in the rivers are more alert to predators.

Many of the fish in these waters, particularly the cichlids, are predatory and carnivorous and spend their time hunting small prey. The cichlids have powerful mouths with which they can literally suck in their prey. Often these bigger fish will patrol the open waters searching for smaller fish, both on the surface and over the riverbed.

AGGRESSIVE BREEDING

The cichlids that inhabit the open waters are aggressive and territorial and regularly engage in bouts of strength, displays of body language, and occasional fights beneath the surface. This type of behavior is designed to ensure the survival of young fry. With so many predators in these waters and few hiding spots among the sparse aquatic vegetation,

Above: *This stretch of the Macal River in Belize is calm and surrounded by vegetation, indicating that both small insect feeders and large predatory fish live beneath the surface.*

Right: *Many cichlids are good parents that aggressively defend their brood. These are firemouth cichlids* (Cichlasoma meeki); *the male (foreground) is extending his gills as a defensive threat.*

most young fish would not survive unless protected by their parents. During the breeding season, male fish become brightly colored and attempt to attract a female by choosing and defending a suitable breeding site. The most aggressive males obtain the best breeding sites, thus increasing their chance of attracting a suitable female.

Once a pair is formed, they will both defend the site from any other creature that ventures too close. In some cases, a pair will form first and then select a breeding site together. The eggs are deposited by the female and fertilized by the male. Normally they adhere to a suitable rock or other smooth surface and when they hatch, the young fry stay close to their parents. Generally, the female spends more time looking after the young, while the male defends the territory. In many cases, cichlids will "hide" the young in their mouths should danger threaten.

The size of a territory depends on the species of fish, but often it may be over 3m (10ft) in diameter, although the young will be kept well within this boundary. Noticeable landmarks, such as rocks or wood, are often used to identify territories. Larger fish will even move objects around the substrate floor to define a territory or create a suitable breeding site.

Despite the cichlids' aggressive nature, physical contact fights rarely occur. Should two territorial fish, both in breeding condition, cross paths, they will display to each other, raising their fins and opening gill covers to appear larger and more threatening. Most disputes are solved by a complex behavioral display that decides which is the dominant fish. The loser of this noncontact fight will simply swim, or be chased, away. In the aquarium, it is not possible for the losing fish to swim away and this is why there are sometimes problems when stocking aggressive fish. A heavily dominant fish in the aquarium will continually chase other fish, which are unable to swim away. This situation is often called "bullying" in the aquarium. Bullying

can be reduced by providing plenty of hiding places and keeping a low stocking level of similarly sized fish.

A CENTRAL AMERICAN RIVER AQUARIUM

The main element of this display is the dark, bulky, and angular slate. There are other style options, but bear in mind that many of the larger cichlids can be quite destructive, moving smaller objects or destroying plants.

THE SUBSTRATE

The substrate used here is medium to large-grade pea gravel and is a fairly standard aquarium substrate. However, it is more than suited to this display because it is less easy to move than finer substrates and its smooth, rounded surface will not damage the mouths of the cichlids. Many of the Central American cichlids have a tendency to dig, an activity that may originate from breeding behavior, feeding methods, or sometimes even boredom. The substrate must also be deep enough to support the weight of the larger rocks and keep them firmly positioned. However, this can be difficult if fish begin to bury underneath or around any rocks. A

Large rocks can be used to form caves, but make sure they are firmly positioned so there is no risk of collapse.

good solution is to place a gravel tidy – a fine plastic mesh – just beneath the surface of the substrate. The fish will then be able to dig only as deep as the gravel tidy, preventing them from unbalancing rocks.

When setting up the aquarium, first place the majority of the substrate on the base of the tank, then put the gravel tidy in position and stand the large rocks on top of this. Once the final layer of gravel is placed on top of the gravel tidy and around the base of the rocks, the gravel tidy will be completely hidden from view.

ROCKS

The rocks used in this aquarium are large pieces of slate with a very bold, angular appearance. Other rock types

Left: *Sizeable rocks will look artificial against pea gravel in the aquarium. You can improve the effect by using small pieces of the same rock type around the base of the larger rocks to blend the two together.*

Like other varieties of Java fern, this Microsorium pteropus 'Windeløv' *is tough and should withstand the attentions of pugnacious cichlids.*

are also suitable and because the natural waters of these fish are hard and alkaline, you could even use calcareous rocks. Position the rocks so that they create hiding spots, gaps, and caves in which the fish can hide and possibly breed. Rocks with smooth, flat surfaces may also encourage breeding in some species. Remember that the rocks must all be firmly set in place so that they cannot be knocked over or moved by the fishes. Smaller rocks positioned above the substrate should be siliconed into place. Fragments of rock can be scattered along the aquarium floor, adding extra interest to the substrate. These smaller chippings

Smaller rounded slate pieces can be placed along the substrate.

should be the same type of rock as the larger pieces. If you do not have any suitable small rocks, carefully break a larger chunk into smaller portions.

WOOD AND PLANTS

In this aquarium there is only one small, almost unnoticeable piece of wood, which is there to act as a rooting medium for plants rather than for aesthetic purposes. However, wood can be used to good effect in this style of display, although it should not detract attention away from the bold rockwork. Furthermore, only one plant is used in the aquarium, a finely branched, small leaf variety of Java fern called *Microsorium pteropus* 'Windeløv'. Java fern is suitable because its tough leaves contain a distasteful chemical that protects it from the attentions of herbivorous or destructive cichlids. Other tough plants, such as large *Echinodorus*, *Anubias*, and *Sagittaria* species, are possible alternatives. In an aquarium housing only smaller species of cichlid, most hardy plants should be suitable.

THE FISH

The fish from Central America are mainly cichlids and many of them are available in the aquarium trade. Some of the bigger species can develop stunning coloration and often become the focus of the aquarium. Their behavioral traits often give individuals a strong personality, making them excellent display or "pet" fish. Do bear in mind, however, that if you wish to keep several of these fish you will need a very large aquarium. Fish such as the popular quetzal cichlid (*Vieja synspila*) can reach up to 40cm (16in) in the aquarium, and the boldly colored red devil (*Amphilophus labiatus*) will grow to 30cm (12in). These are sizeable examples, but there are also a few "giants" such as the jaguar cichlid (*Parachromis managuensis*), which has the potential to reach over 50cm (20in).

DEFENSIVE COLOURS

Many cichlids exhibit strong coloration and well-defined markings that occur only in mature fish. When young, many cichlids are a drab yellow-brown, but remember that this dull coloration is likely to change as the fish grows.

EQUIPMENT

Many larger cichlids are messy eaters that create large amounts of waste, so a good filtration system is essential. Large external filters containing plenty of mechanical filtration media are ideal. A few hardy scavenging catfish can be added to the aquarium to help remove some of the waste food matter. Because there is a danger of fish moving or knocking objects, the heater-thermostat is vulnerable to being knocked or cracked. A heater guard will prevent this from happening. These are made from a plastic mesh that fits securely around the heater-thermostat and are readily available from aquatic suppliers.

Often, it is the males that are more colorful, exhibiting breeding colors and strong dominant markings. A good example is the popular firemouth cichlid (Cichlasoma meeki), which is a relatively peaceful and small (15cm/6in) fish compared to many Central American cichlids. Its name comes from the deep red coloration that develops around the mouth area and the fish's habit of inflating its throat and gill covers as an act of aggression. Although normally peaceful, these fish will become highly territorial and aggressive when they are breeding.

Another fish named after its markings is the convict cichlid (Archocentrus nigrofasciatus), which has a series of black and gray vertical stripes across its body. The convict cichlid, a small species that grows to about 10cm (4in), is well suited to the aquarium environment. Given suitable conditions the convict cichlid will breed readily, preferably in a suitable cave, and is an excellent parent. Other smaller fish that reach up to 15cm (6in) include the Salvin's cichlid (Nandopsis salvini), and the colorful rainbow cichlid (Herotilapia multispinosa)

CATFISH AND OTHER SPECIES

Although the cichlids dominate this type of aquarium setup, there are a few other fish that could be introduced. Catfish can play an important part in this aquarium by eating algae and waste food matter. Most larger, tough catfish species will be ignored by the aggressive cichlids, although smaller catfish may be bullied. Algae-eaters, such as the popular plecostomus (Hypostomus and Pterygoplichthys species), will grow quite large and mix very well with cichlids. There are scavenging catfishes found in Central America, but African catfishes of the genus Synodontis can also be a very good choice for this type of aquarium. They are fairly fast and can hide among caves and rocks, away from the attention of aggressive cichlids.

For the open water areas, it may be possible to mix some larger barbs with the cichlids, as long as the cichlids are less aggressive species. An interesting South American fish is the banded leporinus (Leporinus affinis), which has an unusual "torpedo"-shaped body and enlarged dorsal and caudal fins. This tough herbivore will grow up to about 30cm (12in) and should mix well with peaceful, large cichlids.

Below: The plecostomus, or plec, (Pterygoplichthys spp.) has an armored body and will live quite happily with large, aggressive fish as well as more peaceful species. It can grow to more than 45cm (18in) and is capable of knocking over rocks. A large aquarium with carefully placed decor is essential.

Left: *This Leporinus* spp. *can be kept with the more peaceful cichlids and comes from the same natural habitats. It is a welcome addition to the aquarium because of its unusual shape and patterning.*

Below: *The intimidating, tough-looking Jack Dempsey* (Cichlasoma octofasciatum) *makes a stunning display fish, but be sure to choose any tankmates with care.*

Central American river aquarium

The theme for this aquarium and its inhabitants is "big, bold, and beautiful." Few plants will survive the attentions of the fish, so large rocks become the main decor.

Adding a little greenery draws some attention away from the rockwork. This variety of Java fern has feathered leaves. If they are eaten or torn by fishes the effect is less noticeable.

Large upright rocks can be siliconed to the aquarium glass.

Small slate pieces are scattered along the substrate and at the base of larger rocks. This helps to blend the rockscape with the substrate.

Large rocks can be carefully positioned to create caves.

*Algae-eating fish
will graze on the flat
slate surfaces.*

*Smaller pieces of Java fern
can be used to hide gaps
in the rocks.*

*Make sure that all the rockwork is
secured. Fixing rocks together with
silicone sealant is well worth doing.*

*A heater guard protects
the heater from both fish
and rockwork.*

*Cichlids may dig under rockwork. Placing a
gravel tidy beneath the substrate under rocks
prevents unwanted rockfalls.*

*Large-grade pea gravel is smooth
and rounded and will not damage
the fishes' mouths.*

Australian river

Several large river systems run throughout Australia. The best known is the Murray-Darling system, the fifth largest in the world. However, the Australian mainland has been isolated from contact with other landmasses and waterways for millions of years. The number of freshwater fish species in the waterways is therefore limited in comparison to similar-sized river systems in the rest of the world. The best-known fish are the beautiful family of rainbowfish found throughout Australia and New Guinea.

The fish that do live in Australia can be found in many different styles of habitat. Tropical rain forests, mangroves, lakes, seasonal pools, streams, fast-flowing and calm rivers, and estuaries occur throughout tropical, subtropical, and temperate areas. The rainbowfish – and other Australian fishes – are found in many of these habitats because a lack of competition has allowed them to spread into areas that would normally be inhabited by more specialized fishes. These fish are therefore hardy and adaptable species that cope well with changing conditions. It is more than likely that a number of fish species native to Australian waters have yet to be discovered. Many of the underwater habitats remain to be fully explored, and several pools and waterways are seasonal, changing every year.

Waterways created simply by rainfall often appear in different locations each year, and although these do not contain fishes, they are important homes for water-dwelling mammals, reptiles, and birds. Pools and creeks created by flooding often contain vast numbers of fish. Often, these pools are located in unusual geographic areas, where large, deep bodies of water are able to form. During times of flood or increased water flow, many fish begin to breed, providing an influx of young fry into the normally isolated pools and creeks.

HOT AND SALTY

The constantly changing habitats caused by flooding, isolated pools, and dry seasons, as well as the wide-ranging environmental conditions

Australian river habitats

Many popular aquarium fish, including the rainbowfish, live in the rivers of New Guinea.

The Murray-Darling River systems reaches the ocean near Adelaide in South Australia, although its collection area extends through New South Wales and Queensland.

Because of its unique geographical position, Australia encompasses many different ecosystems, from vast open deserts to cool temperate forests. Its rivers, lakes, and waterways are home to a large number of fish species spread throughout these ecosystems. The fish of Australia and New Guinea are hardy, colorful, and peaceful, making them ideal species for the aquarium.

throughout Australia, mean that the fish are highly adaptable. Virtually all native Australian fish can cope with temperature ranges between 15 and 35°C (59-95°F) and in extreme cases, such as the desert goby (*Chlamydogobius eremius*), can survive temperatures between 4 and 40°C (39-104°F). Although these temperatures are extreme, they do occasionally occur in open, unshaded waters.

There are also a number of brackish mangrove and estuarine habitats in Australia, but in some cases, high-salinity waters can also occur inland. Permanent pools supplied partially or completely by water seeping up through the underlying rock often contain a great deal of dissolved salts. These come from minerals in the rock, and constant evaporation from the surface continually increases salinity. When, or if, floods arrive, the highly saline pools experience an influx of fresh water, which greatly reduces the salinity, sometimes returning the pool to almost freshwater conditions. So, during a typical year, the fish that inhabit such pools must cope with a slowly rising salinity and a sudden annual drop. Many Australian fish can cope with sudden salinity changes of up to 15 parts per thousand – almost half the strength of seawater.

COOL AND CLEAR

The rivers are far calmer environments for the fish, annual temperature changes are much less severe, and the water is normally fresh throughout the year, except of course in estuarine or mangrove areas near the ocean. However, the rivers are not constant, but continually change size and shape throughout the year. At higher altitudes, often near the source of the river, the path is set and changes little over time. In these hilly areas, the river cuts through bedrock, forming many waterfalls and pools through the undulating landscape. It is typical to find large pools at the base of small or large waterfalls in these higher ground areas. Many of the pools are formed

Above: The landscape of the Northern Territories is often dry and scrublike. In this area, open grassland is briefly interrupted by patches of trees at the edge of a waterway. Beneath the clear surface is a wealth of aquatic life.

Left: The desert goby (Chlamydogobius eremius) is one of the most adaptable fish in the world and can easily cope with dramatic changes in temperature and salinity.

Left: Pieces of driftwood with unusual shapes will help to create cave formations and hiding spots in the aquarium. To avoid the water from becoming discolored, use chemical filtration.

THE SUBSTRATE

Most Australian waterways have an exposed, rocky base or a sandy, muddy substrate. In the aquarium, you can use silver sand, together with a few sprinklings of a larger substrate, such as pea gravel, for a more natural appearance. Regularly disturb the silver sand to prevent compaction and stagnation; it may need to be replaced occasionally. As an alternative, a similar sandy effect can be achieved with a small-grade, yellow-brown, lime-free substrate. This is a much more favorable planting medium if you are planning to include a large number of plants, and can be mixed with other, nutrient-rich substrates.

ROCKWORK

The rocks used in this display are large pieces of slate, which contrast with the sandy substrate and create a bold appearance. For the best effect, these

when two different rock types meet, because the continual flow of water erodes different rock types at different rates. When the river crosses from a "hard" rock to a "soft" rock type, small waterfalls are created as the softer rock is eroded more quickly than the harder one. Eventually, large pools form beneath the waterfalls.

Further downriver, the volume of water is greatly increased and the river takes a winding path toward the ocean. In these areas the path of the river is not set, but changes over time. If the river were viewed from overhead through a number of decades, it would appear to move in a similar fashion to a snake moving quickly across sand. As the water moves around the twists and bends in the river path, it moves faster on the inside of bends than on the outside. This causes the inside riverbank to be eroded and become steep and overhanging. In contrast, the outside bends experience a gentle water flow and often become the repository of silt and debris, resulting in an ever-increasing sandbank.

FINDING FOOD

In the rivers, pools, and creeks there are few sources of food for fish. Small aquatic animals, invertebrates, and crustaceans exist, as they do in most waterways, and bottom-dwelling fish and catfish actively search them out. Since few locations are surrounded by

dense forest, fruits, seeds, and forest debris food sources are rarely available. In most cases, the fish are opportunistic feeders, feeding on a range of food sources throughout the year.

For many fish, insects and their larvae often form a large proportion of the diet. In the pools beneath waterfalls or in areas with a collection of dense vegetation, you will find many terrestrial animals, such as small or large mammals, birds, and marsupials. All of these attract insects, which often congregate around the water surface. Any that fall in will be quickly eaten by the small fish beneath the surface.

AN AUSTRALIAN RIVER AQUARIUM

Because the rivers of Australia pass through so many different environments, it is difficult to create an Australian biotope aquarium that is not regional, i.e., based on one particular area. The problem is further compounded by the fact that there are few native Australian aquatic plants available in the aquarium trade. However, the basic elements found in most Australian waterways, such as a sandy base, fallen tree branches, and large-leaved aquatic plants, can be combined to form a suitably "Australian" environment suited to the native fishes to be kept in the aquarium display.

Grasslike plants, such as this Sagittaria sp., *will grow well in the sandy substrate and represent semi-aquatic or marshy vegetation.*

Java fern will root on pieces of wood and can be used to add vegetation to the upper levels of the display.

rocks should be partially obscured by plants or wood that will tone down the appearance of the rocks and create a more natural-looking display. Any inert rock could be used in this display to create different effects. For a sandier, and slightly brackish look, choose sand-colored rocks, such as sandstone or Westmorland rock. Lava rock is suitable for a darker, riverbank overhang look; and a downstream pool or fast-flowing river could be created using cobbles and pebbles. Because many of the fish are accustomed to hard, alkaline conditions, you could even use some calcareous rocks, such as ocean rock or tufa rock.

Here, smaller pieces of rounded slate are used along the substrate, often half buried and placed near the larger rocks. When smaller pieces are used in this way, they should always be the same type as the larger rocks. Using highly contrasting rock types often looks slightly unusual and unnatural.

WOOD
The wood in this display represents fallen branches or old tree roots. For this effect, a style of driftwood often called "jati" wood is particularly useful. Select pieces that resemble roots or branches and use angled lengths to create caves and hiding spots. A few medium-sized pieces are useful, but a single, very large, carefully selected piece could achieve a more dramatic effect. Broken pieces can also be scattered across the substrate.

PLANTING
The number of plants included in the display depends on the amount of decor. If there is a strong focus on recreating tree roots or a rocky substrate, you need only a few plants. Alternatively, an Australian pool could feature several floating plants and a few fully submerged "traditional" ones. In this design, there are a number of traditional aquatic plants. Although these are mostly American or African species, they are used to represent the type of vegetation that might be found in an Australian riverbank or pool. Large Amazon swords (*Echinodorus* spp.) are a prominent feature and are ideal for representing riverbank vegetation. Their large leaves

Jati wood has a "raw" appearance and imitates newly broken branches or tree debris.

provide cover and hiding places for many of the fish in the aquarium. Toward the opposite ends of the tank, *Vallisneria* and *Hygrophila* species introduce some variety in the leaf shapes. The foreground plants consist of a few oval-leaved cryptocorynes and some *Sagittaria* species. A similar plant, *Lilaeopsis novae zelandiae* (New Zealand grassplant) is also suitable for the foreground area.

CHOOSING FISHES
Native Australian fish are often available in aquarium stores, although there is less variety compared with African, American, and Asian species. The rainbowfish group is the most common. Although many of these originate from New Guinea rather than Australia, they are close enough to be included in this style of aquarium. Certain catfish and goby species are Australian in origin, but many of these prefer slightly brackish water. However, it would be relatively easy to create slightly brackish water that would suit both the rainbowfish and the brackish species of goby and catfish. Virtually all the Australian, or Australasian, fishes are active and peaceful (with the possible exception of some gobies, which are

occasionally territorial), so there should be few compatibility problems. However, some catfish can grow to significant sizes; the shark catfish (*Hexanematichthys graeffei*) may reach up to 25cm (10in) and will require a large aquarium. At this stage, it will be easily capable of eating any small tankmates.

BOTTOM-DWELLERS

A number of catfish, goby, and gudgeon species are common throughout Australia and the three groups each have differing behavioral traits and appearances. The catfish are often found in brackish waters, and many freshwater varieties are related to similar brackish species, having ventured upstream from their original brackish water habitats over thousands of years. The best known of these catfish is the shark catfish, so called because of its metallic silver color and sharklike body shape and finnage. This peaceful fish is constantly active during the day, foraging among the substrate for items of food. It is particularly useful in an aquarium with a sandy substrate, as it constantly disturbs the top layer, helping to prevent stagnation and the formation of algae.

Gudgeon will also disturb the substrate. Although these bottom-dwellers are less active than the shark catfish, they are no less interesting. Two readily available species are the common gudgeon (*Gobio gobio*) and the purple-striped gudgeon (*Mogurnda mogurnda*). These two species will grow no bigger than 10cm (4in), although some other native Australian gudgeon can grow as large as 40cm (16in). In the wild, gudgeon like to hide among tree roots and vegetation, so they appreciate the same conditions in the aquarium.

Gobies are also good examples of smaller bottom-dwellers. The desert goby, a native Australian fish, will grow no bigger than 6cm (2.4in). They make excellent aquarium fish and their quirky behavioral traits and unusual

*Above: In common with many other rainbowfishes, the coloration of the banded rainbowfish (*Melanotaenia trifasciata*) will improve as it ages.*

*Right: The Celebes rainbowfish (*Telmatherina ladigesi*) is a midwater and surface-swimmer with unusual and eye-catching finnage. It remains relatively small and can be kept in fresh or brackish aquariums.*

darting motions make them interesting to observe. If gobies are given plenty of hiding places in the aquarium, this will boost their confidence and they will actually spend more time out in the open. A number of similar goby species that are not native to Australia can be found in aquarium stores and these can be used as welcome replacements for Australian species.

RAINBOWFISHES
Rainbowfishes are found only in Australasia and make good aquarium fish for beginners, as well as

experienced aquarists. When young, many of them have dull colors and are therefore often overlooked in aquatic stores. However, as they mature, they develop deep coloration that can rival some marine fish. The rainbowfish are generally peaceful, hardy, active, easy to care for, and will grow to no bigger than 10cm (4in).

Popular varieties include the banded rainbowfish (*Melanotaenia trifasciata*), which has horizontal red-and-blue stripes, and the bosemani rainbowfish (*Melanotaenia bosemani*), which is one of the most colorful, sporting a solid

Above: The purple-striped gudgeon (Mogurnda mogurnda) *is an interesting fish that sports attractive markings and has an unusual behavior in the aquarium.*

yellow-orange color toward the rear and an iridescent green-blue around the head area. The New Guinea red rainbowfish (*Glossolepis incisus*) is often dull when younger, but males become a stunning deep red color as they mature. Other interesting rainbowfish include *Melanotaenia fluviatilis, M. splendida,* and the Celebes rainbowfish (*Telmatherina ladigesi*).

Australian river aquarium

Large-leaved Java fern and Echinodorus species placed behind the driftwood and rock pieces imitate the vegetation found at the water's edge.

Large Echinodorus species dominate this area of the aquarium.

Rainbowfish often swim in open water and will enjoy the cover provided by these tall stems.

Substantial slate rocks have a bold appearance and hide the stems of the taller background plants.

Cryptocorynes will grow well in a sandy substrate and soften the division between the large decor and the substrate.

Many small fish and bottom-dwellers will find this area a welcome retreat.

This Java fern fills open space
and catches the light in the
center of the aquarium.

Hygrophila *species*
introduce a variety of
leaf shapes.

The striking effect of large rocks
can be softened by careful
planting around the edges.

Grasslike plants, such as this
Sagittaria *sp. will spread
across the substrate.*

A few rounded slate pieces and a
sprinkling of pea gravel create
a more natural substrate.

European river

Rivers throughout the European continent are all relatively similar in appearance and formation. Generally speaking, they begin in moderately mountainous or hilly regions, before progressing to a lengthy waterway that winds through open countryside and occasionally forested regions. The surrounding land in most areas is flat and sparsely vegetated, but on the riverbanks, many taller reeds and bushes provide some welcome cover for smaller river fish.

A typical river can be divided into three distinct areas: the open water in the middle of the river, the reed-filled or shaded riverbank, and small stretches of shallow water over rocks and gravel substrates. In each area there is a relatively small diversity of life compared with similar regions in tropical rivers and highly vegetated swamps, lakes, and streams. Many European fish species tend to stick to particular regions of river that suit their individual needs. Because of this, any two stretches of the same river may harbor a completely different group of fish and/or plant species.

LIFE ON THE EDGE

For the smaller inhabitants of the river, the thick reedbeds and overhanging banks at the side of the river provide hiding places, breeding spots, and sources of food. Many of the smaller fish found here rarely venture out into open water, unless conditions are clear and shallow, and predators easily visible. The reedbeds and other vegetation "trap" debris from the river, much of which is eaten or broken down by small animals, bacteria, and filter-feeders. This process results in a nutrient-rich mulm that feeds the lush green vegetation above the water.

The small bugs and creatures that live here are a food source for the fish that dart among the reeds and search the substrate for food. Tiny animals are

European river habitats

Isolated landmasses often contain a reduced number of species, but some species are native and found nowhere else.

The rivers in central Europe contain similar fish species, although each has its own distinct habitats.

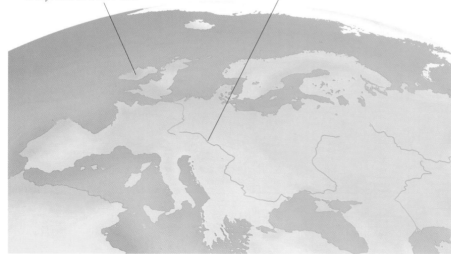

The rivers of Europe flow through open land, rather than vast tropical rain forests. In these temperate climate conditions, underwater life is often less diverse in any particular area, but no less interesting. River life for the fish that inhabit these waters is dangerous at the best of times, with many predators and other dangers lurking beneath the surface.

also useful sources of food for young fry, which are abundant in the riverbanks from late spring. The fry here are far safer from predators than in the open river, although for many fish, young fry are an ideal and highly nutritious source of food. The fish among the riverbanks are often accompanied by other animals; small rodents, ducks, birds, and even otters rest, breed, or feed in the dense reedbeds.

Not all riverbanks are accompanied by dense vegetation; many are barren but frequently interspersed with overhangs, large tree roots, or patches of rock and vegetation. In these tiny habitats, the same small fish take advantage of every possible hiding place or feeding site. Minnows, sticklebacks, bitterlings, and weather loaches are typical inhabitants of these riverbank regions, along with juveniles of larger species, such as roach, rudd, dace, goldfish, and perch.

SWIMMING WITH THE BIG BOYS

In the open waters in the middle of the river, there are few hiding places and this is where the larger fish can be found. Not all of them are predatory by nature, although most would not pass the opportunity of a meal if it should swim across their path. Rudd and orfe, often sold as ornamental pond fish, feed on insects at the water surface and in muddy substrates on the riverbed. Other fish, such as carp species, perch, and the notorious pike, feed almost exclusively on other fish. The pike is a typical example of a well-adapted and highly evolved predator. Its elongated body shape and streamlined head allow it to sit motionlessly for many hours, even in flowing water, waiting for its next meal to arrive. Unsuspecting fish may not notice the stationary, well-camouflaged pike, even in clear,

Above: A typical European waterway is shallow, with highly vegetated banks, home to a number of small fish. Larger species can be found further downriver, where the water becomes deeper.

Right: The rudd (Scardinius erythrophthalmus) is an opportunistic feeder that searches for food sources, including insects, plant matter, fry, and substrate-dwelling creatures.

open water. As its prey approaches, perhaps searching for food in the substrate, the pike very slowly turns to face it. Without needing to chase, the pike swiftly opens its mouth and sucks in the unwary fish before clamping down its sharp teeth and rendering its prey immobile.

Other predatory fish are better designed for fast movement and will chase prey into a corner or rocky crevice before executing a "snapping" maneuver, sucking in their prey much like the pike.

A QUIETER LIFE IN THE FAST LANE

In many places the river is less deep or divides into shallow waterways, often coursing over rocks and gravel substrates. The water here is fast flowing, well oxygenated, and clear. Unusually, many plants can be found

Below: The unusual bullhead (Cottus gobio) can be found hiding under rocks in many European rivers, lakes, and streams. Its quirky appearance and interesting patterning make it a good aquarium fish.

along the river, although they are often well spaced. Larger predators rarely lurk beneath the surface of these shallow waters, so smaller fish can safely come out, pick small creatures from the substrate, and feed from insects at the surface. Minnows and sticklebacks, normally found in the densely vegetated riverbanks, are equally at home in this environment, where life is relatively stress-free due to the lack of larger fish. Substrate-dwellers can also be found here.

This shallow area of the river is also home to some unusual species that occur throughout Europe. A few gobies and blennies, usually found in marine environments, have traveled upriver from the sea, becoming freshwater species over thousands of years. Most notably, the aptly named river goby (*Gobius fluviatilis*) and river blenny (*Blennius fluviatilis*) can be seen darting around the riverbed, searching for small items of food. Along with these you may see another goby species, the colorful bullhead, or miller's thumb (*Cottus gobio*), the stone loach (*Barbatula*

Above: The stone loach (Barbatula barbatula) is typical of the many European loach species. The barbels and downturned mouth indicate that this fish is a scavenger and naturally feeds off substrate-dwelling creatures. Be sure to provide hiding spots in the aquarium for it to feel secure.

barbatula), and scavengers from the *Misgurnis* family, which includes the weather loach (*M. anguillicaudatus*).

Despite the lack of underwater predators, there is still some danger that fish may become a meal for another species. Small birds often perch on overhead branches by the side of these shallow regions, waiting for small fish to come into view. At this point, they swiftly dart down to the river and catch or "spear" a fish with stunning accuracy, before returning to the branch to consume their meal.

BREEDING IN THE BUSHES

A particularly fascinating aspect of European fishes is their breeding habits, which rival those of the most interesting tropical species. As food sources become abundant in the spring and the fish are fully active, mature adults start to prepare for breeding. Many fish from these rivers have a highly developed sense of sight and smell, which they use, among other things, to select a suitable mate. Females in good breeding condition often release hormones into the water that attract the attention of males.

Once established in the aquarium and partially hidden by other decor, this synthetic wood will appear entirely natural.

Males of some species will show enhanced colors and try to attract willing females to breed. Other fish, particularly some carp species, almost "bully" females into breeding by constantly chasing them, attracted by the scent of hormones. Once the female has been chased into an area of dense vegetation, normally in a shallow riverbank location, the male will wrap himself around the female and literally squeeze the eggs from her. The eggs are deposited on a leaf or sometimes a suitable rock or piece of wood, and the male then releases his milt to fertilize the eggs. There is virtually no parental care after this; since many thousands of eggs are released, the chances of some young surviving are high.

Other species lay fewer eggs and concentrate heavily on parental care. In these cases, both male and female(s) (there is often more than one female to any male) are willing participants. Of particular interest is the stickleback, which will often breed in the aquarium. The male stickleback bears

Rounded pebbles are used in large amounts in this display and are welcomed by bottom-dwellers.

much of the burden of breeding. To begin with, a male in good condition will select a suitable breeding site and create a "nest" from plant material and debris, fixing it together with a specially produced fixing or cementing substance. When the nest is complete, the male – now an intense red breeding color – will attract a number of females into it to lay eggs that he will then fertilize. The male stickleback is intensely territorial and constantly guards the nest from any intruders, including those several times his size.

A EUROPEAN RIVER AQUARIUM
Because of the different habitats in any particular part of the river, the possibilities for creating an aquascape are diverse. For an interesting aquascape with a mixture of fishes, you can adopt a general approach that incorporates elements of the open water, shallow, and riverbank habitats. A loosely based design allows you to include a number of different substrates; for example, open river areas are often muddy, while sandbanks are sometimes present at the sides of the

river. This design uses a basic substrate of silver sand, which will be welcomed by scavengers such as loaches. For added interest, the substrate is covered in many places by groupings of small pebbles, pea gravel, and larger cobbles. Grouping these smaller stones around larger rocks not only creates "microhabitats," but also mimics the natural environment. Use rounded cobbles and pebbles; in nature the constant, yet gentle, flow of the river would weather any exposed rocks until they were worn smooth.

RIVERBANK ROOTS
Because there is little vegetation in this type of display, the middle and upper parts of the aquarium can be taken up with selected pieces of driftwood. In many places in a river, broken wood and exposed tree roots create welcome hiding spots for fishes. This is the effect being recreated here. Driftwood with a particularly rootlike appearance can be placed horizontally across the substrate to imitate wood debris. Smaller, curved pieces that emerge and return to the substrate as if they were part of a tree's root system are also effective. A few synthetic "wood" pieces are particularly useful in this situation; many are designed to look like broken branches or roots. In this aquarium, the

thick branchlike piece in the center is in fact artificial, but once it is covered with a little algal growth, it will look completely natural.

LIMITED PLANTS

In this aquarium, there are only two species of plant: elodea (*Egeria densa*) and hornwort (*Ceratophyllum demersum*). Neither requires a good rooting substrate, as they obtain most of their nutrients through their leaves rather than their roots. In nature, they often flourish as floating species, although in the aquarium they look more attractive when planted in a traditional manner.

A larger number and/or variety of plants could also be used in a European display, although they may detract from the bold rocks, substrate, and wood. Many tropical plant species survive well at lower temperatures. Particularly suitable species include hairgrass (*Eleocharis acicularis*), umbrella plant (*Hydrocotyle verticillata*), Japanese cress (*Cardamine lyrata*), and some species of *Ludwigia*, *Sagittaria*, and *Echinodorus*. Many plants sold as pond "oxygenators" or marginal species can also be used. Parrot's feather (*Myriophyllum* spp.), and creeping Jenny (*Lysimachia*

Hornwort (Ceratophyllum demersum) *can be used as a floating or rooted stem plant.*

nummularia) are particularly well suited and both occur naturally in European locations.

Floating plants are common in many European rivers and are either large-leaved species such as water lilies, non-native water lettuce, or water hyacinths, or smaller-leaved plants such as azolla and duckweed. However, once again, bear in mind that in the aquarium, floating plants may detract from the rest of the display and overcrowd the aquarium, although they could be used to good effect in small quantities. Many floating plants are very fast growing and may need to be regularly thinned.

Virtually all the plants suited to this type of display are relatively hardy and will not need specialized or nutrient-rich substrates. If there only a few, they will obtain enough nutrients from the fish waste and enough light from a single fluorescent tube. However, if there is a large number of plants or their health begins to decline, you may need to add a liquid fertilizer.

SELECTING THE RIGHT FISH

Many of the fish species that originate from European rivers can grow to quite a substantial size and are particularly active under the warmer conditions of the aquarium. You will need a tank measuring 150cm (5ft) or more to house them. Fishes that grow to over 30cm (12in) include roach (*Rutilus rutilus*), rudd (*Scardinius erythrophthalmus*), carp (*Cyprinus carpio*), orfe (*Leuciscus idus*), and sometimes dace (*Leuciscus leuciscus*). Goldfish (*Carassius auratus*) can exceed 35cm (14in) in ideal conditions, but unfortunately they are often underprivileged and the most neglected of all fish due to their popularity and hardy nature.

Many of these larger fish are quite destructive and less likely to behave

Elodea is a common plant with a number of similar varieties. It is a hardy plant with few needs.

naturally in a small enclosed environment. Both in terms of size and behavior, the smaller European species often make more practical and interesting aquarium subjects. Many loach species, including the popular weather loach (*Misgurnis anguillicaudatus*), are well suited to the lower reaches of the aquarium. The weather loach is so called because of an unusual sensitivity to pressure. A change in atmospheric pressure will cause the weather loach to become restless and frequently take gulps of air from the surface. Many aquarists who become aware of the fish's behavior, use it as a "living barometer" to recognize signs of an oncoming change in weather. Other suitable substrate-dwellers include the stone loach (*Barbatula barbatula* or *Noemacheilus barbatulus*) and the sailfin sucker

(*Myxocyprinus asiaticus*). This is not a true European species, as it is found largely in China, but its stunning finnage and bold coloration make it a popular aquarium fish. Bullheads (*Cottus gobio*), river blennies (*Blennius fluviatilis*), and river gobies (*Gobius fluviatilis*) are very interesting bottom-dwellers. Their unusual darting movements and lively personalities make them ideal for the aquarium, but they are rarely offered for sale.

The minnow (*Phoxinus phoxinus*), bitterling (*Rhodeus amarus*), and stickleback (*Gasterosteus aculeatus*) are excellent choices for the midwater ranges. Some slightly larger, although not true European species, such as varieties of pumpkinseed or sunfish, could also be used in this aquarium.

*Above: The roach (*Rutilus rutilus*) looks very much like the tropical tinfoil barb and its behavior is also similar. In the aquarium, these fish may eat plants and grow to over 30cm (12in), so provide them with adequate living quarters.*

Right: The wonderful Myxocyprinus asiaticus *is proof that many coldwater species are just as unusual and colorful as tropical fishes. This species requires a large aquarium with plenty of caves to hide in.*

European river aquarium

In this display, the aquarium floor is covered with items of decor and is only briefly interrupted by small patches of vegetation.

Use plants sparingly in this aquascape. Some of them will grow quickly and require regular trimming.

This aquarium has a large open swimming area for fishes.

Mixing large cobbles with pebbles and pea gravel creates a good effect around the base of larger stones.

This large piece of "wood" is synthetic but looks natural among other items of decor.

Silver sand is a good substrate to pile up against rocks or in which to partially bury smaller pebbles.

Place some plants in areas of bright light for a dramatic effect.

Driftwood is carefully placed along the rear of the aquarium to create an interesting background.

Hornwort (Ceratophyllum demersum) *can be planted or used as a floating plant.*

Banking areas of substrate against wood or rocks creates a more natural, undulating riverbed appearance.

Large rocks look impressive emerging from the sandy base. Algae-eaters will rest on them.

Fill gaps between larger rocks with small pebbles.

European lake

For many European river fish and animals, only certain parts of the river are suitable to live in. This may be due to the location of food sources, hiding spots, or breeding sites. So, although a river may be home to a number of species, they are often found only in certain areas, leaving some stretches of the river relatively barren and devoid of life. However, larger European lakes are often far more varied in their environment; there are many rocks, broken woods, shallow and deep-water plants, and fertile substrates, all of which form the basis of a range of microhabitats. In this calm, diverse environment, many of the plants, animals, and fish that find themselves in the lakes are inclined to stay, breed, and sustain a population. A gathering of species in a small area is an ideal habitat for the aquarist to observe and recreate in the aquarium.

SUNLIGHT AND NUTRIENTS

The nutrient content of a lake will generally increase over time, due to the recycling of wastes in an enclosed environment, the continual addition of nutrients from surrounding topsoil and rainwater run-off, and the production of biomass through photosynthesis by plants and algae. Therefore, the substrate in most established lakes contains more nutrients and organic mass than the substrate of the rivers that supply or drain from the lake. Although the same organics and nutrients are introduced into a river, the constant flow of water will remove them until they are eventually deposited in the sea.

European lakes are often relatively shallow, having been formed by the movements of sweeping glaciers during the Ice Ages, rather than through the volcanic or tectonic plate

The European lake habitat

The lakes of southern Europe are warm and shallow, often drying up in the long, hot summers.

Northern European lakes abound with life in spring and summer, but freeze solid in the winter months.

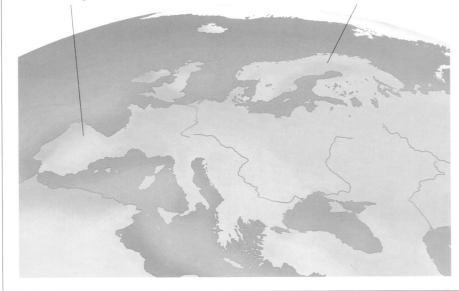

The lakes found in the temperate regions of Europe are home to a wide variety of animal and plant life drawn from the surrounding areas. In many cases, the lakes have a richer and more diverse underwater life than the rivers and streams that feed them.

movements that gave rise to many of the tropical lakes. These shallow lakes, especially those in open rather than forested areas, receive a great deal of sunlight during the summer months, which penetrates down to the not-so-deep lake beds. As soon as spring arrives, the many seasonal aquatic plants in the beds spread rapidly, transforming the underwater appearance of the lakes.

BUGS AND LARVAE IN PROFUSION

Sunlight and nutrients also encourage algae to grow rapidly in the calm lake environment. Single-celled algae are particularly common and often turn the lake water a murky green during early spring, before the aquatic plants begin to thrive and out-compete them. Single-celled algae and other floating organic materials provide a good food source for many open-water filter-feeders. Mussels and water fleas (daphnia) thrive on the open-water algae, as do water boatmen, dragonfly larvae, and tadpoles, all of which are vital food sources for some fish. Larvae, worms, snails, crustaceans, and small invertebrates all thrive in the fertile lake bed and form the diet of many small lake fish. Larger fish species, such as larger carp or rudd, not only feed on these substrate-dwellers but also on larger items, such as plants and small fish or young fry. In some cases, the tables are turned on the fishes; small fish are often attacked and slowly eaten by some larger larvae, frogs, and other creatures.

The small minnow (Phoxinus phoxinus) is found throughout Europe and is a useful insect feeder as well as a welcome food source for predatory species.

Above: *A calm, clear lake in southern Finland – typical of many in Europe. In the shallows, reedbeds harbor many aquatic creatures.*

PLANT LIFE IN THE LAKE

Often, the edges of the lake are either devoid of any plant life or packed with marginal creeping plants, taller rushes, and reedlike plants. The distinction between these two extremes relates to the depth and type of substrate. In many lakes, the flow of water is generally in one direction and, depending on the direction of its borders, a lake often has distinct areas of built-up muddy substrate and weathered, eroded areas.

Sticklebacks embark on a complex sequence of establishing territories, nest building, and displays of color and movement, while bitterlings have a unique method of breeding, involving the freshwater (or swan) mussel. When a pair is ready to spawn, the female bitterling lays her eggs through a long ovipositor (a tube that extends from the vent) into the inhalant area of the mussel. The male then releases his sperm close to the inhalant area and it is drawn in by the mussel, fertilizing the previously laid eggs. Once the fry have developed and are free swimming, they emerge from the mussel having been protected through such an important stage of growth. As is often the case in nature, this is not an example of one species taking advantage of another, but a process that is beneficial to both organisms. Mussels regularly eject tiny, microscopic young mussels called glochida, although only a few of these develop into fully formed mussels. Because of the activities of the bitterling, many of the glochida attach themselves to the skin of the fish and receive a "free ride" to other locations in the lake or river, widening their distribution and thereby their chances of survival.

Areas with a gravel or rocky substrate contain few nutrients and so are home to only the smallest and hardiest plants, whereas areas with deep, muddy substrates are perfectly suited to storing nutrients and ideal for plants to root in. Toward the center of the lake, the substrate is fairly uniform – a mix of fine mud, cobbles, and gravel. Many plants will grow here, normally evenly distributed, without any dense groupings. Popular pond plants, often sold as "'oxygenators," such as elodea (*Egeria* spp.), hornwort (*Ceratophyllum demersum*), and parrot's feather (*Myriophyllum proserpinacoides*), are commonly found in these open areas. Other popular aquarium or pond plants, such as water cabbage (*Samolus parviflorus*), creeping Jenny (*Lysimachia nummularia*), hairgrass (*Eleocharis acicularis*), and many species of water lily are also found throughout European lakes.

Some lakes surfaces are partially covered not only by lilies, but also by floating plants, such as water lettuce (*Pistia stratiotes*), water hyacinth (*Eichhornia crassipes*), *Azolla* spp., and smaller species of duckweed (*Lemna*)

LIFE AT THE BOTTOM

The plants that grow in the open-water areas of the lake are vitally important to

Above: The male stickleback's red color will intensify when the fish is in breeding condition. Observing the behavior of these common European fish in the aquarium is a fascinating pastime.

many of the animals that live in and around them. Smaller fish, such as sticklebacks and minnows, will use the plants as breeding spots and places to hide in, as well as somewhere to hunt for food items. Many other lake fish also hunt among the plant life, including bottom-dwellers such as weather loaches (*Misgurnus anguillicaudatus*), gudgeon (*Gobio gobio*), and larger predatory fish, most notably pike (*Esox lucius*), perch (*Perca fluviatilis*), and, occasionally, the even larger but scavenging sterlet or sturgeons (*Acipenser* spp.).

The majority of lake-dwelling fish are small species that live on tiny worms and bugs in the substrate and plant life, but some predatory omnivorous species, including many carp and pumpkinseed species, feed on smaller fish, as well as vegetation and larger invertebrates. However, not even these sizable fish are safe in the lake, because in the often shallow water, they become easy prey for animals above the surface. Otters and large birds commonly hunt them,

while smaller birds sit patiently on overhanging branches, keeping an eye on the shoals of small fish that congregate in areas of shade.

Beneath the surface of the lake, a balance of fish species form part of a complex food chain where almost all but the largest fish are both hunters and the hunted. A number of fish in the lakes have developed behavioral and physical methods of avoiding prey. Many fish, notably the sticklebacks (Gasterosteidae family), have developed spines along the back, which can be erected as a warning or to deter any predators that may have learned

This collection of rounded cobbles, pebbles, and stones can be used to recreate the weathered rocks found in many European lakes. Use different-sized stones together in the aquarium for a more natural effect.

not to eat such tricky and painful prey. Because of this "kill-or-be-killed" situation, many smaller coldwater species have interesting behavioral traits that are ideal for close observation by the aquarist. Quirky movements, shoaling, establishing territories, and specialized hunting habits are all commonplace in smaller European fish species.

A SEASONAL AFFAIR
The diverse life found in such lakes varies throughout the year and is largely seasonal. During spring, the water begins to warm up, and plants and algae grow rapidly, beginning the complex food chains that support fish and other species. In the late spring and summer, food sources are at an optimum level and this is when the fish begin to hunt and breed actively. Daphnia, worms, and larvae are abundant in all areas of the lake and form important foods for both the adults and the young fry. Toward the fall, the adults are no longer breeding and although the majority of fry will have been eaten by other fish, those that are left are now larger, quicker, and wiser. They have grown significantly, having fed on the abundant summer food sources. As the water begins to cool, plants stop growing and fish feed

less, as they no longer need energy for breeding and establishing territories. With the approach of winter, food sources become scarce and plants die back, further reducing any available foods. The lack of food during winter months does not greatly affect the fish, because as temperatures drop, they enter a state of slower metabolism, similar to hibernation. During this time they find warmer areas under banks, rocks, or debris on the lake bed, where they move and feed very rarely. As all the fish enter this state, there is little need to be fully alert for predators, which will also be feeding very rarely.

A EUROPEAN LAKE AQUARIUM
The substrate of a European lake may vary from a muddy bottom to a mixture of cobbles and gravel, although the latter is far easier and more interesting to recreate. Many of the suitable plants require little rooting medium and often prefer to assimilate nutrients through their leaves rather than their roots. A simple pea-gravel substrate is suitable both for the plants and to recreate the natural

lake bed. Try a mixture of different grades or a medium-grade substrate with sprinklings of smaller and larger grade substrate on top. To add to the effect of a mixed substrate, use small pebbles and cobbles across the surface. The aquarium should contain plenty of open space to mimic the expanse of the lake and to allow plenty of swimming room for fishes, although plants can take up some of the open water space. To achieve this effect, limit the decor to a few bold objects, such as large boulders or driftwood. Make sure that any large boulders are firmly placed in the substrate and unlikely to move or fall. Smaller broken driftwood pieces can also be scattered along the substrate for a more natural appearance.

Creeping Jenny (Lysimachia nummularia) is a common aquarium and pond plant, often sold in the pale yellow-green "Aurea" form.

SUITABLE PLANTS

In the open waters of the lake, plants are found not in any one place, but scattered across the lake bed. In the aquarium the plants should not be heavily grouped by type, but mixed around and placed randomly. However, placing plants generally around the back and sides of the aquarium will achieve a more traditional aquarium display, which some people prefer. Tall stem plants, such as elodea (*Egeria* spp.) and parrot's feather (*Myriophyllum proserpinacoides*), are ideal for this display, as is hornwort (*Ceratophyllum demersum*), which, although it is really a floating species, can be planted as a stem plant. Smaller stem plants can be planted among or in front of these taller species. An ideal example is creeping Jenny (*Lysimachia nummularia*), often sold in its cultivated form 'Aurea'. Its pale green leaves contrast well with other plants. Although only present in a few European locations, hairgrass (*Eleocharis acicularis*), which is widespread in tropical regions, would be a worthy addition to this type of display. It can be scattered around the aquarium floor to represent the smaller vegetation that is commonplace in patches of the lake bed.

Ceratophyllum demersum is a typical temperate lake plant. Its fine, needlelike leaves will benefit from a gentle water flow that removes debris suspended in the foliage.

Right: Myriophyllum spp., commonly known as "parrot's feather," is a hardy and attractive plant that will grow above the water surface. Many of the hardy coldwater plants will grow quickly in the aquarium and may need regular trimming.

Many temperate plants from outside Europe, most notably from North America, can be used in this style of aquarium to create more diverse planting arrangements. Plants of particular interest include the umbrella plant (*Hydrocotyle verticillata*) and Japanese cress (*Cardamine lyrata*), which have unusual round leaf shapes and a slightly "messy" appearance. Suitable, common, non-European aquarium plants include the helzine (*Micranthemum* spp.), *Ludwigia* spp., *Lobelia cardinalis*, and some *Echinodorus* and *Sagittaria* species. Floating plants, such as *Salvinia* spp.

and Amazon frogbit (*Limnobium laevigatum*), add some shade and cover for the fish. Substantial floating plants should be used only in larger aquariums. Many marginal plants sold for ornamental ponds can also be used underwater in this type of aquarium, although be sure to remove any soil in which they are potted to prevent muddying the aquarium water.

THE FISH

Since it can be difficult to obtain a wide variety of temperate fish species, a little research may be required to obtain good sources of fish. Many of the larger carp, tench, and rudd species can be quite timid and easily

Egeria spp. will grow quickly in cool water and may need regular trimming.

Left: *The common gudgeon (Gobio gobio) is found throughout central Europe and will appreciate an aquarium with rocky areas and patches of dense vegetation. These fish are peaceful, hardy, and well suited to the aquarium.*

frightened, and are suitable for only very large tanks (some of these fish may grow more than 45cm/18in long). Smaller fish, such as bitterlings (*Rhodeus amarus*), sticklebacks (*Gasterosteus aculeatus*), clicker barbs (*Pseudorasbora parva*), dace (*Phoxinus* spp.), and minnows (*Phoxinus phoxinus*) are ideal, as is the commonly available weather loach (*Misgurnus anguillicaudatus*), which makes an ideal scavenging fish. Bitterlings and sticklebacks are particularly interesting in the aquarium due to their unusual and interesting breeding habits.

Many non-European fish, often from North America or China, can be kept in this style of aquarium. The shiner (*Notropis lutrensis*), black-banded sunfish (*Enneacanthus chaetodon*), medaka (*Oryzias latipes*), stone loach (*Barbatula barbatula*), and sailfin sucker

Right: *The predatory perch (Perca fluviatilis) is an experienced hunter and uses its vertically striped body as camouflage, hiding among the aquatic vegetation. Any smaller fishes that stray too close will be quickly eaten.*

(*Myxocyprinus asiaticus*) are all interesting aquarium fish that originate from similar habitats. Less habitat-specific fish commonly sold as tropical aquarium fish include many small barbs and corydoras catfish.

INVERTEBRATES
Adding some common invertebrates to the aquarium makes for a truly interesting and realistic display. The two most suitable are snails and freshwater mussels (*Unio* species and *Anodonta* species). Take care with snails, as in certain conditions they breed rapidly. Generally speaking, larger species of snails do not breed as quickly (or in such quantity) as smaller species. Ramshorn snails, often sold for ponds, are ideal for a European aquarium. Mussels will move around the aquarium but are generally static although still interesting creatures to observe in the aquarium. These "filter-feeders" obtain their food by filtering

water from the environment. Suitable food for them is rarely obtainable in an aquarium, so feed mussels occasionally on small frozen foods. Daphnia and plankton-based foods often sold for marine aquariums are ideal.

The shells of these snails have become covered in algae, although the snails themselves are excellent algae-eaters.

CHECK BEFORE YOU BUY

Before buying (or collecting) any fishes native to Europe and the USA, check out the legal situation. In the UK there is effectively a ban on keeping species that could escape and thrive in the wild, interfering with the indigenous fishes. These include the pumpkinseed and topmouth gudgeon. In the USA, interstate movement of some fishes is prohibited for much the same reason.

A European lake aquarium

*This aquarium is a "jumble" of different elements that together create
an exciting environment suited to a number of temperate fishes.*

*Mixing together three different stem plants
(Myriophyllum, Egeria, and Lysimachia)
creates a varied planting area.*

*To create a more natural
appearance, place some
plants individually.*

*Freshwater mussels are quite at
home here and will move around
the aquarium of their own accord.*

*The cobbles and plants
complement each other
in this area.*

The fine leaves of these plants may be used by sticklebacks to build nests during breeding.

If there is enough room above the surface, this parrot's feather (Myriophyllum) will grow out of the water.

Bogwood is used to represent driftwood and debris, and also provides hiding spots for the fishes.

Large cobbles add a "solid" element to the aquarium among the jumble of other decor.

These large snails are good algae eaters and a visually interesting addition to the display.

Flooded Amazon forest

The floods occur due to an influx of water from the many mountain streams and river tributaries that flow into the Amazon River. In midwinter and early spring, a combination of increased rainfall and melting snow and ice in the mountains produces a massive increase in the volume of water reaching the main river. In the lowland or flat areas, the river cannot hold such a vast amount of water and soon bursts its banks, overflowing into the surrounding land. At the height of the floods, vast areas of rain forest, often covering over 100,000 square kilometers (39,000 sq miles) become submerged. In many places the flooded forest may be as much as 10m (33ft) deep.

The forest is able to survive such floods because many terrestrial animals either head into the trees or toward patches of higher land. Mature trees are large enough to withstand the floods and smaller vegetation either dies, adapts, or simply braves the watery environment until it recedes. Many plants take advantage of the conditions by dropping fruits and seeds while the forest is flooded. The seeds are then transported by the water to another location, where they will germinate as soon as the flood recedes. Although many of these seeds may be eaten by fish and other aquatic creatures, they often stand a better chance of survival than against terrestrial scavengers.

NOTHING IS WASTED

The flooded areas of the forest contain plenty of organic debris, largely resulting from dead or dying vegetation. This "waste" is quickly broken down by animals and detritus-feeders, many of them so tiny that they

Flooded forest habitat

The Amazon River Basin is massive, with many large tributaries. It is the sudden increase in water volume of these tributaries that causes the floods.

Because the Amazon River has tributaries on both sides of the equator, it collects water from areas with two distinct rainy seasons. As a result, some areas of the river may flood twice a year.

Many large river systems periodically flood, but none as regularly or on such a massive scale as in the Amazon River Basin. In some regions, widespread forest floods are an annual occurrence that often last for up to six months or more. Many fish exploit this "new world" and take advantage of the abundant food sources provided by the flooded forest.

Above: *In South American regions, the flooded forest is called the igapo. Floods are a good time to collect fruits and seeds from treetops just above the water surface.*

are hard to see with the naked eye. This abundance of minuscule creatures constitutes an ideal source of food for newly hatched fry, and many fish breed during the flood periods.

Fishes belonging to the popular tetra group are widespread in the Amazon Basin and most breed just as the floods begin. They are triggered into breeding by a rise in water level and a slight drop in temperature, both of which predict the oncoming flood. A male will chase a female into a dense patch of vegetation at the riverbank, where she deposits eggs for the male to fertilize. When the young fry hatch, they are swept into the flooded forest, where they feed on the abundant detritus feeders. Some of the tetras are relatively easy to breed in the aquarium if you create similar conditions.

FRUITS AND NUTS

The fishes of the Amazon have a keen sense of smell, which some of them use to locate fruits and seeds in the wide expanse of the flooded forest. As they are about to drop their seeds, certain plants release traces of biochemical substances into the water. The fish sense these chemicals and head toward the best trees, lying in wait for the falling fruits and seeds.

Many of the larger Amazonian fishes are also herbivorous. The most notable examples are the pacu (*Colossoma* and *Myletes* spp.), which can grow to over 60cm (24in) in length, and the silver dollar (*Metynnis* spp.), which can reach 30cm (12in). Even unlikely candidates such as the piranha will feed on suitably sized fruits when these are abundant in the flooded areas.

A WATERY FATE

Many forest insects seek refuge in the trees when the floods arrive, but some will be unable to escape or become stranded on small outcrops of higher land. They become a major source of food for some fish, which use their lateral line systems and eyesight to sense vibrations and locate such prey. The arowana is specially adapted to take advantage of the abundance of insect life. This massive fish, which can grow to over 1m (39in), has eyes at the top of its head that enable it to see above and below the water surface simultaneously, spotting insects as they fall. The arowana will even jump out of water to catch insects or knock them off small branches. In extreme cases, arowanas have been seen taking small birds, bats, and other mammals.

CAUGHT IN A TRAP
The relative luxury of the flooded forest and its abundant sources of food do not last forever, and toward midsummer, the water begins to recede almost as quickly as it arrived. Within just a month, the water level drops rapidly, exposing the land once again and leaving many pools of different sizes surrounded by dry land. Most of the fish make their way back to the river in the receding waters, but many are stranded in the pools. Some pools will remain until the next floods, and the fish in them may also survive this period of isolation.

However, fish that remain in pools destined to dry out can do little to avoid their fate. Some catfish have evolved methods of crossing dry land; if they become trapped in a receding pool, they venture out across the land to find a route back to the river. Others can burrow into the soil and cocoon themselves in a mucus coating, entering a stage similar to hibernation, until the surrounding land becomes waterlogged again.

A FLOODED FOREST AQUARIUM
Two principal elements in a flooded forest aquarium evoke the natural environment: overhanging vegetation, and forest debris across the substrate.

The natural substrate is a mixture of dark soil and plant debris. Although using soil in the aquarium can present a number of problems, the effect can be recreated with a fine substrate, such as silver sand or lime-free quartz gravel, plus a sprinkling of peat or a dark, nutrient-rich substrate designed for aquatic plants. Small amounts of dark gravel or even crushed coal add to the effect. Forest debris can be represented by small pieces of broken driftwood strewn across the aquarium floor.

Some of the flooded areas will be covered by large patches of floating plants, but many are clear and the surface is

Black gravel helps to create a darker and more textured substrate.

This planting medium resembles the mulm that accumulates on the flooded forest floor.

broken only by overhanging branches and terrestrial plants. This effect can be created with synthetic plants sold by florists. For the best effect, stick to the green-leaved varieties, rather than some of the more exotically colored or flowered stems. Alternatively, suitable species of houseplant or marginal bog plants can be planted above the aquarium and allowed to extend their branches or leaves into the aquarium. Floating plants with long roots, such as water lettuce (*Pistia stratiotes*) or water hyacinth (*Eichhornia crassipes*), also add to the effect of vegetation above water.

DRIFTWOOD
Driftwood plays an important part in this type of aquascape. Pieces that represent tree roots or broken branches are particularly useful and can be

Pieces of bark are ideal for this display. As bark is very buoyant, silicone them to a piece of glass before placing them on the floor of the aquarium.

106

placed in any area of the display. Cork bark is highly effective in the aquarium, although it is extremely buoyant and does not easily become waterlogged. To overcome this problem, silicone pieces to a piece of glass or a heavy object such as a larger rock.

Other types of wood, such as twisted roots, can represent tree roots or branches. Some pieces of artificial decor are designed to look like tree stumps and are ideal in this display. Others can hide items of equipment, such as filters, heaters, or pipework.

GRASS AND BUSHES

On the flooded forest floor, much of the vegetation will be made up of terrestrial plants. Some will die, but others can withstand the underwater conditions during the floods. In the aquarium, most true terrestrial plants will quickly die and rot, but certain semiterrestrial plants, many of which originate from areas that periodically flood, are suitable and sold for aquarium use. Common semiterrestrial plants include the grasslike *Acorus* (Japanese rush) and *Ophiopogon* (fountain plant), as well as the wider-

The unusual color of this Alternanthera reineckii *blends well with the wood and debris in the aquarium.*

Artificial plants can be used to good effect in this display. These fabric leaves have a distinctly tropical look and can represent overhanging foliage.

leaved *Syngonium* (stardust ivy), *Dracaena* (dragon plant), and *Spathiphyllum wallisii* (peace lily).

Grasslike plants are very effective when spread across the foreground to mimic the patches of grass found on the forest floor. In this aquarium, the grassy effect is created by *Lilaeopsis novae zelandiae* (New Zealand grassplant). *Eleocharis acicularis* (hairgrass), *Echinodorus tenellus* (pygmy chain sword), and some smaller *Sagittaria* species make good alternatives.

Larger, bushy plants, such as *Heteranthera zosterifolia* (stargrass), also evoke the forest undergrowth. Stargrass can be trimmed to different lengths, with smaller stems at the front to create an even bushier effect. Other plants with prominent stems and bold leaf shapes can represent terrestrial vegetation. The popular *Hygrophila* group of plants has a number of species that almost resemble tree branches.

A number of *Echinodorus* species grow near the original river, and some may spread outward during the flood. In this aquarium, a few, or even just one larger *Echinodorus* could become a specimen or focal plant, either in the center or toward the back of the aquarium.

SELECTING THE RIGHT FISH

The flooded forest regions of the Amazon are home to virtually any of the fish that inhabit areas of the river and its tributaries that flood. Some of these fish are more interesting to aquarists than others, although some can grow quite large. Piranhas *(Serrasalmus)*, pacus *(Colossoma* and *Myletes* species), arowanas *(Osteoglossum* spp.*)*, and silver dollars *(Metynnis* spp.*)* will all grow to between 25 and 100cm (10-39in). To keep these fish, provide an aquarium measuring at least 180x60cm (72x24in), although 250x90cm (98x36in) would be even better.

Larger fish are also more destructive and it may be difficult to keep plants with them, although Java fern (*Microsorium pteropus*) and *Anubias* spp. may be tough enough to survive. Despite their notoriety, it is possible to keep groups of piranha with other similarly sized fish, although there may be occasional fin nipping. As piranha increase in size, they normally become more docile, so it may be worth growing a group of piranha until they are about 15cm (6in) before introducing similarly sized fishes to the aquarium.

For most aquariums, the wide choice of smaller fish may be more appropriate. The most common groups of fish from these areas are the tetras, which are almost all relatively small, growing to only about 5cm (2in). Tetras are shoaling fish, so always keep them in groups, preferably six or more of any one species. The tetras are ideal for the midground area of the aquarium, and colorful species such as the cardinal tetra *(Paracheirodon axelrodi)* or rummy-nose tetra *(Hemigrammus bleheri)* will contrast well with the darker substrates and driftwood. More somber-colored tetras, such as the black widow tetra *(Gymnocorymbus ternetzi)*, may not look as bold in the aquarium but can add to the overall effect and are well worth considering.

The hatchetfish group of fish *(Carnegiella* and *Thoracocharax* species and *Gasteropelecus sternicla)* are ideal for the surface areas of the aquarium. Their unusual body shape is due to an oversized muscle connected to the pectoral fins that allows them to jump out of the water to great heights from an almost still position. They use this ability largely as a means of escaping from predators, but if a fish in the aquarium is suddenly shocked (say by

a door opening or other vibration), it may also attempt to jump. A tight-fitting lid is a sensible precaution.

Angelfish may also spend a great deal of time toward the upper reaches of the aquarium and are ideal for this display. They have a reputation for eating small fish such as cardinals, but if they are grown alongside the cardinals (or other fish), this should not be such a problem. At 3-5cm (1.2-2in), fully grown cardinals are usually too large for an angelfish to eat, but do not introduce any fish that do not reach at least 3cm (1.2in) in length.

Along with the angelfish, discus *(Symphysodon* spp.*)* will also do well in this aquarium. However, they do require ideal water conditions, so beginners are best advised not to attempt them. Both angelfish and discus grow quite large, but they are relatively slow-moving and make a bold additions to the aquarium.

Several interesting catfish make good subjects for the aquarium floor. *Corydoras* catfishes are ideal for this display, even though they are often

found further upstream in tributaries of the Amazon that do not become flooded. These small fish constantly scavenge in the substrate searching for items of food. This activity is particularly useful in the aquarium, not only because the fish remove food waste, but also because they constantly disturb the substrate, which prevents algae from forming.

Two very interesting and similar catfish groups are the *Farlowella* and *Rineloricaria* species, often called twig or whiptail catfish. The *Farlowella* species have a very long, thin, twig-colored body that provides a very effective means of camouflage. As these fish do not move around much – indeed, they often remain motionless – the camouflage effect often works just as well on humans as on fish, which adds further interest to the aquarium.

Below: The arowanas (Osteoglossum *spp.) are common in the flooded forests and make interesting aquarium fish. Since they eventually reach up to 1m (39in), they are suitable for only the largest aquariums.*

Left: *This* Rineloricaria *species is a good algae-eater with a unique and unusual shape. These peaceful fish will appreciate the hiding spots provided by the wood and vegetation in this aquarium.*

Below: *Altum angels (Pterophyllum altum) have a deeper body than the traditional angelfish and make quite stunning aquarium fish. In good conditions, they may regularly breed.*

Below: *The* Farlowella *group of catfish, often called twig catfish, are impressively camouflaged and rarely spotted by other fish. Even when touched, they may remain motionless, maintaining the impression of a twig.*

From above, the effect of the sticklike color and body shape is even more dramatic.

Flooded Amazon forest aquarium

A scattering of wood and darker substrates along the base of the aquarium, plus a mass of surface vegetation, combine to create the impression of a flooded forest.

The red undersides of these **Alternanthera** leaves add extra color to the display.

The dark feathered roots of the water hyacinth help to block light and provide hiding spots.

Plants such as this **Hygrophila** species have leaves similar to those of terrestrial vegetation.

The cork bark along the center of the aquarium is a main item of decor and helps to create the forest floor appearance.

Grasslike plants should be separated and planted out in a random fashion.

These Echinodorus *spp. have bold, rounded leaves; use them sparingly as specimen plants.*

Smaller floating plants, such as these water lettuce, will mix in among other surface vegetation.

Artificial plants make effective representations of overhanging foliage.

Sprinklings of black gravel and a mulmlike planting substrate recreate the debris-ridden forest floor.

Jati wood has a rough, "fresh" appearance and makes interesting hiding spots for bottom-dwelling catfish.

Small, bushy plants, such as this Heteranthera zosterifolia, *are well placed behind and around large pieces of driftwood.*

111

Amazon acid pool

Whether or not a pool dries out often depends on its position in the forest. Pools on higher ground and exposed to the sun soon evaporate or simply seep away through the soil. Lower-lying pools may be close enough to the natural water level – and often near the main river, where the surrounding soil is also waterlogged – that they do not seep away. In some places, exposed rock or clay will hold water in the pool, while overhanging vegetation may reduce the light level and hence any evaporation.

The pools that do remain often have a substrate of dead vegetation from the forest and this is continually replaced by new forest debris from the surrounding area and from overhead vegetation. The mass of organic material produces humic and tannic acids that soon alter the chemistry of the pool. Tannic acids will heavily discolor the water, much like a teabag does, turning it a dark yellow-brown.

A MINIATURE HUNTING GROUND

As in the flooded forest, the organic and vegetative debris in the acid pools provide an ideal breeding ground for the tiny detritus-feeding animals and bacteria on which other small creatures will feed. These tiny animals form the main diet of the fish that live in the acid pools, and also of young fry.

The availability of food and relative protection from predators make the pools ideal places for many fish to breed. The drop in pH, often accompanied by a rise in temperature, act as an environmental trigger for fish breeding. The rise in temperature occurs in most pools, but especially in those with little overhead vegetation or a few open spots where direct sunlight reaches the water surface. In a small, calm body of water, such as an acid pool, direct sunlight will significantly raise the temperature of the water. In some cases it can reach up to 33°C (93°F). This is significantly higher than

Acid pool habitats

Most acid pools occur around the Amazon River and its larger tributaries. In these areas flooding occurs regularly. Only larger pools or pools lying on thin or claylike soil will survive all year. The high temperatures in this tropical region cause the pools to heat up rapidly.

After the flooded forest returns to normal, many pools of water remain, isolated in the forest. Some of the smaller or shallower pools will dry out, but deeper or lower-lying ones will remain until the floods return. In most of these a mass of organic vegetation acidifies the water to pH levels of 5 or even less. Many fish thrive in such "harsh" conditions and are free to feed and breed without risk of predators beneath the surface.

POOL CHEMISTRY

The large amount of dissolved organic matter in the pools binds with dissolved salts or minerals, effectively removing them from the water. This has the effect of reducing the hardness to almost zero. Humic acids are produced by rotting wood and plant debris, and with virtually no water hardness, these acids will lower the pH level to about 4-5. As the majority of freshwater fish live in water with a pH of between 6 and 8, a pH of 4-5 is quite a significant drop (see page 41). Many fish would not survive such harsh conditions, but the fish that live in these pools physically adapt to the change by retaining a higher salt (mineral) concentration in the body and producing large amounts of dilute urine. Higher salt retention is accompanied by a higher retention of other chemicals. In the aquarium, this means that under low hardness and pH conditions, these fish are particularly sensitive to chemical treatments and water pollutants such as ammonia, nitrites, and nitrates. A high standard of water quality and biological filtration is therefore essential when keeping these adaptable, yet sensitive, fish.

Above: *The tea-brown color of the water in this pool is a result of tannic acids produced from dead plant matter. A number of fish will thrive in these acidic waters.*

the temperature of the initial floods, where melt- and rainwater average about 22-24°C (72-75°F). The rise in water temperature speeds up the metabolism of all the organisms beneath the surface, and combined with a high amount of organic matter, causes blooms of microalgae and infusoria that are just visible to the naked eye. These microblooms may be too small for some larger fish to take advantage of, but

they are the ideal size for fry and young fish to feed on.

SLOW AND STEADY IS THE KEY
The warmth and high-nutrient, low-oxygen conditions of the acid pools might at first seem to be ideal for plant growth, but a number of factors prevent dense blooms of aquatic plants. The low hardness means that some mineral nutrients are hard to obtain, and the high temperature will increase healthy growth only if light levels are also high. In many cases, the high temperature causes plants to grow rapidly, but they cannot obtain

sufficient nutrients and sunlight to photosynthesize and produce energy. Many plants simply wear themselves out in such an extreme environment.

A few smaller, naturally slow-growing plants do, however, thrive in partially shaded areas. A slow growth rate allows plants to conserve nutrients, and since there are only a few herbivorous fish, they are unlikely to be eaten. Some "traditional" aquatic plants will grow in areas of direct sunlight, providing welcome hiding spots for fishes. Sometimes, semiterrestrial plants left over from before the floods continue to grow underwater.

AN ACID POOL AQUARIUM

A typical acid pool has a very dark orange-brown appearance, often with only a few patches of aquatic vegetation, but in the aquarium, extra plants create a more interesting display. Driftwood naturally stains the water a tea-like color (although this can be removed by a chemical filter medium, such as activated carbon). Alternatively, for a more authentic feel, simply allow the water to become discolored. In fact, with careful use of lighting and/or spotlights, discolored water can become quite an effective design element. To add to the overall dark and discolored atmosphere, use substrates and decor with "autumn" colors, such as red, black, and brown. This approach need not be restricted to the substrate and wood; brown or red-leaved plants are also highly effective.

These red chippings will enhance the acidic "autumn" colors of the aquarium display.

Floating plants, such as these water lettuce, will break up the overhead lighting and provide cover for small fishes.

THE SUBSTRATE

The natural substrate of an acid pool is similar to that of the flooded forest, consisting of a mix of fine mud and sediment, scattered with debris from the forest. In the aquarium, use silver sand or a lime-free substrate on the base, with a different material on top or mixed in with it. A sprinkling of darker substrates, such as black quartz or colored gravel, along with reddish colored substrates, should produce the desired effect. When using colored substrates, apart from black, it is best to use subtle or natural-looking colors.

The silver sand in this aquarium makes an effective substrate, but it will need regular stirring to prevent any compaction and the development of stagnant areas.

THE WOOD

Driftwood plays a large part in this aquarium design, and represents forest debris as well as providing some planting areas. The driftwood should be of the natural, rough-looking variety, and not precleaned and smoothed. This rough driftwood, often called jati wood, will release tannic acids and stain the aquarium water to a greater degree than many types of wood, but as we have seen, discolored water adds to the overall effect.

How you arrange the wood is not overly important, as long as it is aesthetically pleasing. A few vertical pieces can represent exposed or broken tree roots, while pieces laid diagonally or horizontally across the foreground look like branches swept into the pool. Small, broken pieces of wood scattered across the bottom add authenticity.

Driftwood will produce tannic acids, changing the colour of the water. Although sometimes undesired, the effect is ideal for this display.

PLANTING

Although the range of plants found in natural acid pools is restricted by the harsh environment, you can use virtually any plants in the aquarium. The selection should be a combination of aesthetically pleasing species and a representation of the type of plants found in the pools. In this aquarium, two dense groupings of *Hygrophila* and *Heteranthera zosterifolia* (stargrass) represent the plants that naturally grow in open, sunlit areas. To add to the effect of the driftwood, choose plants that root on the wood rather than in the substrate. *Anubias* species are ideal, and will spread slowly across the wood. To attach the plants, either wedge them into cracks in the wood or tie the main root (rhizome) to the wood using black cotton.

The distinctive Anubias spp. are hardy plants that are tolerant of many conditions, and will also grow on wood.

The foreground areas of the aquarium can be interspersed with the occasional small plant to add a little variation. In the flooded forest aquarium, grasslike plants represent some forest vegetation, although in the acid pools much of this would have died off. Small plants with wider leaves, such as some dwarf *Echinodorus* species, are ideal for the foreground of this aquarium. A few floating plants across the surface will be particularly appreciated by some of the small tetras or surface-dwelling fish in the aquarium. This display features the adaptable water lettuce *(Pistia stratiotes)*, but you could also use *Azolla*, *Salvinia*, or *Riccia* species.

THE FISH

When the floods first recede, many fish are found in the acid pools, but as the water becomes highly acidic and temperatures rise, only a few will survive. Many tetras are suited to these conditions, as well as a few scavenging catfish and larger species, such as angelfish and discus. Tetras are shoaling fish, so always keep them in groups of six of more. Often, a more impressive display can be created using just a few species of tetra, but in larger numbers. A 90cm (36in) tank

Hygrophila sp. have an attractive bushy appearance and also look similar to terrestrial vegetation

with good biological filtration could easily support a shoal of up to 30 small tetras, along with a few other fish.

SCAVENGERS AND ALGAE-EATERS

A sandy substrate will need constant disturbance to prevent compaction, stagnation, and the formation of algae. Most of substrate maintenance will be done by the fishkeeper, but a few scavenging catfish will continually agitate the very top layer, preventing algae growth. Many *Hoplosternum* species or the slender armored catfish *(Callichthys callichthys)* are found in the Amazon acid pools. These hardy catfish have poor vision, but use sensitive whiskers (barbels) instead to search for small aquatic creatures and insects among the muddy pool substrate. Many of the catfish found in the acid pools, including these two examples, have additional breathing organs and are able to take gulps of atmospheric air from the water surface. This adaptation is particularly useful in the acid pools, where the calm surface, high temperature, and abundance of organic detritus often causes oxygen levels to drop dangerously low.

Although not often found in the acid pools, the *Corydoras* catfish species are native Amazonian fish that would be ideal for this style of aquarium. These

115

small catfish are also shoalers that need to live in small groups. Their constant activity makes them a great fish for disturbing substrates and removing any waste foods. There are many different species and varieties of corydoras catfish, and since almost all will shoal together, a group could consist of several different species.

Algae-eating fish are less common in the acid pools, as algae rarely forms in sufficient quantities in such a harsh environment. However, in the aquarium, a small amount of algae will always grow on the plants, glass, and decor. Although this can be regularly removed by the aquarist, algae-eating fish have a very useful role to play and a few varieties are ideal for this display. Since larger algae-eaters may be destructive in the aquarium and often have a bad habit of "attacking" the skin of fish such as discus, which produce

an unusual mucus layer, smaller algae-eaters are preferable. Otocinclus (*Otocinclus affinis*) and the clown plec (*Peckoltia*) are normally safe to keep with any fish.

MIDWATER SWIMMERS
Many tetras are well suited to this aquarium, notably the red-eye tetra (*Moenkhausia sanctaefilomenae*), cardinal tetra (*Paracheirodon axelrodi*), and the neon tetra (*Paracheirodon innesi*). Many tetras can be quite timid, but if kept in shoals and given plenty of hiding places, they soon become active, confident aquarium fish. The darker substrate, dense patches of plants, and floating cover in this aquarium make an ideal environment for these fishes.

There are, of course, other midwater swimmers suited to this aquarium. The small but attractive pencilfishes are one group. They often have a striking

Above: *The trailing plant roots provide excellent cover for these fishes. These small shoaling cardinal tetras will thrive in a dark acidic environment with plenty of hiding spots. The stunning colors of these fishes can be seen at their best only against a dark substrate or background.*

horizontally striped pattern along the entire length of the body. The penguin fish (*Thayeria boehlkei*), Harrison's pencilfish (*Nannostomus harrisoni*), dwarf pencilfish (*Nannostomus marginatus*), and Beckford's pencilfish (*Nannostomus beckfordi*) are all ideal species. In nature, pencilfish are found in numerous shallow brooks, streams, and pools in the Amazon region.

SURFACE DWELLERS
Although tetras and midwater fish occasionally venture toward the surface and hide beneath the floating plants, a

greater surface presence can be created using the hatchetfish group of fishes. The silver hatchetfish *(Thoracocharax stellatus)* is one example; its unusual body shape will create a focal point of interest in the display.

LARGER FISH

The popular angelfish *(Pterophyllum scalare)* and beautiful discus *(Symphysodon spp.)* are also excellent choices. Keep larger fish such as these in groups of four to six. Both angelfish and discus are cichlids and exhibit some territorial and aggressive behavior, although this is normally only directed at other fish of the same species. Keeping these fish in groups should limit such aggressive behavior.

Above: The eyes of this slender armored catfish are small in comparison to its body size. This indicates that the fish uses other senses, including touch and smell, to find food and move around its environment.

Left: This penguin fish is part of the pencilfish family. These peaceful midwater fishes are found in many small pools, streams, and waterways throughout the extensive Amazon region.

Below: Bottom-dwellers such as this Megalechis thoracata *are found in many acid pools. In nature, they hide beneath debris in the substrate. In the aquarium, they are amusing to watch and appear clumsy due to their poor eyesight.*

Amazon acid pool aquarium

Color plays an important role in this aquarium: the brown wood, red chippings, and yellow sand combine with driftwood-stained water to recreate the acid pool environment.

Open areas provide swimming spaces and also dark patches that enhance the appearance of some fish colors.

These red chippings add color to the substrate and reduce the contrast between the driftwood and the sandy substrate.

Pieces of driftwood placed in the substrate imitate broken branches and forest debris.

The generous leaves of Hygrophila provide cover for large and small fishes.

Larger driftwood pieces will release tannic acids, staining the water an acidic tea-brown color.

The trailing roots of floating plants help to break up the overhead lighting and also provide cover for surface-dwelling fish.

Placing bushy plants among larger driftwood pieces creates more natural-looking vegetation.

Wood-rooting plants such as these Anubias can be planted in the center of the display, creating unexpected patches of vegetation.

Dense groups of plants should be placed in areas of brighter light. This Heteranthera zosterifolia can be trimmed to any size.

119

Downriver Amazon

The Amazon River system is vast and could be divided into many separate habitats for fishes. The downriver areas contain a large number of the fishes that have become popular additions to the aquarium, although not all of these may be found together in the same areas of the river in nature. The main river has two typical areas: the open water environment where larger fish can be found, and the shallower riverbanks that provide cover and hiding spots for smaller fish. Due to the size limitations of most aquariums, it is the smaller fishes that are often of most interest. The riverbanks also provide a more appealing environment, full of overhangs, vegetation, and tree roots, to recreate in the aquarium. Many of the fish that live here have highly developed camouflage techniques, which prove vital in such an open environment populated by many different species.

RIVER PATROL

The open waters and massive expanse of the river have become an ideal habitat for large predators to develop. Many grow to over 1m (39in) long and each one has its own way of hunting fish. A number of large catfish occupy the deeper areas, including well-known fish such as the tiger shovelnose (*Pseudoplatystoma fasciatum*), which grows to over 1m (39in), and the redtail catfish (*Phractocephalus hemioliopterus*), which can reach up to 110cm (44in). The tiger shovelnose is so called because of its tigerlike silvery brown camouflage color and long, flattened nose. Lying motionless on the substrate, it uses its long barbels to sense food items such as other fish. When they approach, a burst of immense speed enables the tiger shovelnose to capture and swallow its prey.

The attractive redtail catfish is often farmed as a food fish by native

The Amazon River

The Amazon River stretches over a vast area. In downriver stretches it may be many kilometers wide, although most fish can still be found near the edges.

Some of the tributaries that contribute to the Amazon River are massive in their own right and have similar environments.

As the numerous tributaries flow into the Amazon River, it becomes larger and more diverse. In downriver Amazon, the waters are clear and home to many fish species. Large predators roam in the open waters, hunting for a meal, while smaller fish seek out the relative safety of the riverbank. In this varied habitat, a whole celebration of fish can be found; festive cichlids, clown plecs, banjo catfish, royal panaques, and talking catfish all make regular appearances.

Left: The wide Amazon River contains a mass of water, although most fish are found in the shallows at the edge, where abundant vegetation provides food and safety.

are the peacock bass *(Cichla monoculus)*, which grows to 1m (39in), the blue-flecked cichlid *(Nandopsis umbriferus)*, reaching up to 60cm (24in), and the oscar *(Astronotus ocellatus)*, growing to 45cm (18in). With their distinct personalities, oscars are one of the most popular larger aquarium fish, although they are often clumsy and destructive. In the Amazon, they feed on other small fish, as well as large fruits, vegetation, and seeds.

WALLFLOWERS
Many Amazonian fish species use camouflage, both to help them hunt prey and to hide from hunters. In an environment where there are many species of fish, both large and small, it can be quite an advantage to remain hidden. Bottom-dwellers are the best camouflaged, since they can blend in with the substrate. The closely related royal farlowella *(Sturisoma panamense)* and royal panaque *(Panaque nigrolineatus)* sport horizontal stripes across the body that appear like markings on wood when viewed from above. These algae-eaters spend much of their time grazing of tree roots or wood debris in the river.

Amazonian people. It can become quite tame in the aquarium, regularly taking food from its owner's hand. The redtail catfish often swims in open water in search of prey, and like many large predators, may feed only once or twice a week, spending the rest of its time resting on the bottom, digesting its food in peace.

Other large Amazonian catfish include the ripsaw catfish *(Oxydoras niger)*, which grows to 80cm (32in) and sports a series of sharp spines along its side and caudal area. The common

bacu *(Lithodoras dorsalis)* is an unusual fish that reaches up to 90cm (36in). In nature this fish is not a predator, but a scavenger that feeds on crustaceans and plant matter, including fruits. However, in the aquarium such a large fish may easily consume other, smaller fishes if it is hungry.

Large cichlids and characins also roam the open waters. Notable cichlid examples

The twig catfish *(Farlowella acus)* has developed its camouflage even further by evolving a long, thin body just like a twig, even fooling many a customer in aquatic shops. In many cases, if this fish is disturbed by another fish or animal that may be a potential predator, it lies motionless and rigid, just like a twig.

The banjo catfish *(Bunocephalus coracoideus)* has a brownish mottled pattern and a highly indented "rough"-looking body. When it

Body shape and color enable the banjo catfish to become hidden among river debris.

sits motionless on the substrate it blends in with wood and leaf debris, and other fish cannot distinguish between the two.

Catfish are good camouflage artists although many fish have slight camouflage adaptations. Fishes that live among plants often have vertical stripes that blend in with plant stems. Virtually all midwater-swimming fishes have a darker topside and a pale, silvery underside. From above, the darker color blends in with the substrate, while from below, the lighter underside is hard to see against the sunlit surface waters. Another bottom-dweller, the unusual freshwater stingray *(Potamotrygon* sp.)*, has a pale sandy brown-colored body that is highly compressed horizontally, allowing it to blend in with sandy substrates. Often these fish partially bury themselves, completing the camouflage effect.

One of the most stunning examples of camouflage in Amazonian fishes can be seen in the aptly named leaf fish *(Monocirrhus polyacanthus)*. The leaflike body shape and coloration of this attractive species are so effective that it can hunt small fish by "floating and hovering" above them in the vegetated riverbank. Smaller fish in this area idly swim past the leaf fish, assuming it to be another piece of vegetative debris, only to be swiftly sucked in by the leaf fish's powerful protrusive mouth.

Pieces of driftwood such as these are useful for adding structure to the aquarium display and making clear divisions between planting areas.

A DOWNRIVER AMAZON AQUARIUM
An open-water environment for the larger predatory fishes is one possibility, but the aquarium would need to be a minimum of 2m (6.5ft) long to accommodate the fish, and many aquarists would consider this an impractical, not to mention expensive, undertaking.

However, the riverbanks populated by the smaller Amazonian species are an ideal area of habitat to recreate in the aquarium.

The attractive but relatively simple display shown here is well suited to the smaller fishes, who appreciate the cover provided by the large echinodorus plants that are commonly found in downriver Amazon areas.

Above: In some areas, sunlit shallows of the Amazon are crystal clear and brimming with plants. This underwater jungle is as full of life as the surrounding rain forest and home to hundreds of fish species.

SUBSTRATE
The natural substrate consists of fine gravel, soil, or sand. In this design, we have used silver sand, along with a sprinkling of pea gravel and a few small pebbles, but a fine lime-free substrate is another alternative. The light-colored sand and pale green plant leaves give the aquarium a very bright, open look. For a more "dark and moody" design, choose a darker substrate, or mixture of substrates, together with larger pieces of dark wood. Regularly disturb the sand to prevent compaction and stagnation; you may need to replace it occasionally.

To clean the sand and remove algae and debris, methodically siphon the surface, using a clear siphon tube. Every time you siphon away the silt and waste buildup, you will inevitably also take away a small amount of sand, so top it up periodically.

DRIFTWOOD
In this design, there are a number of medium-small pieces of jati wood in the midground area. These help

to create a division between the foreground and background plants, which are similar in color and would otherwise blend into each other and become less defined. The driftwood also hides the relatively uninteresting stem portions of the larger background echinodorus plants. As an alternative, consider twisted roots, which evoke exposed tree roots along the riverbank.

PLANTS

In this aquarium, there is plenty of open-water swimming space, combined with an entire background full of hiding spots among the taller *Echinodorus* species. This is achieved by using only small foreground plants and large background plants, with little or nothing in the midground/mid-height range. Small catfish will find hiding places among the driftwood,

The tiny green leaves of Micranthemum umbrosum *create an attractive foreground feature.*

while dwarf cichlids can establish territories in the foreground areas. Larger fish or tetras can use the open-water areas for swimming and the heavily planted background for hiding and/or breeding. In the foreground, there are grasslike plants, including the commonly available hairgrass (*Eleocharis acicularis*) and pygmy chain swordplant (*Echinodorus tenellus*). Under good conditions, these plants spread rapidly across the foreground. Depending on the fish in the aquarium, it may be worth thinning the foreground plants occasionally to ensure that there are plenty of open substrate areas for catfish, or even stingrays, to inhabit.

Toward the center of the foreground is a group of *Micranthemum umbrosum*, often called helzine. This attractive little plant has numerous small, pale green, rounded leaves borne on stems that should grow no taller than 20cm (8in), but may occasionally reach up to 30cm (12in). To stop the plant from becoming too large, it can be regularly trimmed and the cuttings replanted in the substrate. All these foreground plants will require bright lighting and would benefit from the addition of a nutrient-rich substrate or suitable liquid feed additive.

This Echinodorus 'Rose' *will develop a deeper reddish color if provided with bright light and plenty of nutrients.*

The taller echinodorus swordplants toward the rear of the aquarium are made up of three varieties: *Echinodorus* 'Rose', *Echinodorus palaefolius* var. *latifolius,* and *Echinodorus* "Red Flame." Under good conditions and bright lighting, some of these will develop attractive reddish or mottled brown-red leaves. Many *Echinodorus* species, including those used here, can

Below: Hairgrass (Eleocharis acicularis) *can be planted around the base of larger plants and among driftwood and rocks to create a thin "lawn" across the substrate.*

potentially grow quite tall, often over 60cm (24in), and will quite happily produce leaves above the surface. To prevent this, periodically remove the largest leaves. Occasionally trimming the roots and replanting can also help to keep the plants short. Most *Echinodorus* species will do well in reasonable light and a good source of iron, so an iron- or nutrient-rich substrate additive will be beneficial.

SELECTING FISHES
A large number of popular aquarium fish originate from the Amazon region and also inhabit the downstream Amazon areas. Stocking this style of aquarium with fish, therefore, presents many possibilities. Larger tanks can house any fish, but including large catfish and cichlids may be an attractive option. The dwarf cichlids are a highly interesting group to observe in the smaller aquarium, and these can be kept with some tetras and smaller catfish species. Fish of special interest, such as freshwater stingrays, twig catfish, leaf fish, and even arowanas, can create a unique aquarium display.

CATFISH
Larger catfish, such as redtail catfish and shovelnoses, are really suited only to massive tanks and you should not buy them, even when they are small, unless the aquarium is truly large enough to house them once they are fully grown. Reasonably large catfish, such as the plecostomus (*Hypostomus* spp.), which grow up to about 45cm (18in), can be kept in good-sized, but not massive tanks. As they are algae-eaters rather than predators, these large, peaceful fish can be kept with much smaller species. Plecostomus make good tankmates for other large fish, such as oscars or arowanas (*Osteoglossum* spp.).

Medium-sized catfish suited to this display include the bristlenose (*Ancistrus* spp.), which is similar in appearance to the plecostomus and makes a good, smaller alternative. The beautiful royal panaque (*Panaque nigrolineatus*) is a peaceful specimen fish, as is the well-camouflaged royal farlowella (*Sturisoma panamense*). The closely related twig catfish (*Farlowella acus*) is another unusual species, well suited to the aquarium. This algae-eater moves very little in the aquarium, often remaining stationary for long periods of time. However, this does not make it uninteresting; the occasional "moving stick" impression will surprise many human visitors observing the aquarium. Other fish with an interesting appearance are the talking catfish, or striped dora (*Platydoras costatus*) and the banjo catfish (*Bunocephalus coracoideus*), although both may eat much smaller fish, such as some tetras.

In smaller aquariums, or those containing small fish, consider the popular and peaceful *Corydoras* species catfish. They are often found in smaller tributaries and streams that connect to the Amazon River, although some extend as far as the downriver Amazon regions. A number of *Corydoras* species

are available and almost none grow any bigger than 5cm (2in).

The *Brochis* genus of catfish resemble the corydoras, but grow to about 10cm (4in). Another suitable choice is the small, attractively mottled or striped brown clown plec (*Peckoltia* spp.). This peaceful and gentle algae-eater can be kept in groups in the aquarium.

CICHLIDS
The dwarf cichlids are ideal aquarium fish that inhabit the lower portion of the aquarium. In common with most cichlids, they are territorial, but only defend small territories when in breeding condition. Many dwarf cichlids breed easily in the aquarium and it is highly interesting to watch them pair up, select a site, defend, and "clean" a suitable area in which to lay eggs, and then defend and protect the young. Common dwarf cichlids include the yellow dwarf cichlid (*Apistogramma borellii*), cockatoo dwarf cichlid (*Apistogramma cacatuoides*), agassiz's dwarf cichlid (*Apistogramma agassizi*), and the stunningly colored ram (*Mikrogeophagus ramirezi*). Another dwarf cichlid, the checkerboard cichlid (*Crenicara filamentosa*) is an attractively patterned fish and a good challenge for the fishkeeper. This fish can sometimes

be a little timid, but given the right conditions and environment, should thrive in the aquarium.

Some slightly larger cichlids are well suited to the upper areas of the aquarium. Severums *(Heros severus)*, festive cichlids *(Mesonauta festivus)*, and angelfish *(Pterophyllum spp.)* will all appreciate the open water and dense planting provided by this display. The severums and angelfish can sometimes become territorial and aggressive, so to keep a group of them together, you will need a reasonably large aquarium. By contrast, the festive cichlid is one of the most peaceful cichlids; it rarely bothers, or is bothered by, other fish. This makes it an excellent tankmate for a large number of fish.

TETRAS AND "ODDBALLS"
For aquariums without large catfish or cichlids, which may be predatory, the midwater areas can be occupied by a shoal of tetras, and there

are many Amazonian species to choose from. To add extra interest, you can keep some of the more unusual Amazonian fishes – often grouped with other unusual fish and labeled "oddball" species. Two notable examples are the leaf fish *(Monocirrhus polyacanthus)* and the freshwater stingray *(Potamotrygon spp.)*. The leaf fish is relatively easy to care for, but is predatory so do not keep it with smaller species. Freshwater species of stingray vary in size; many are capable

of reaching up to 60cm (24in), although this includes the long "whiplike" portion of the body. They are peaceful but should be handled with care; most freshwater stingrays have a tail barb containing a toxin that can give you an extremely painful sting.

Below: There are a few species of freshwater stingray (Potamotrygon spp.) and all are native to Amazonian waters. A graceful fish and an aquarium oddity, the stingray is well worth observing.

Left: The striped dora (Platydoras costatus) is also called a "talking catfish" and can emit loud grunting noises when stressed or attacked. Handle these fishes with care, as the body is covered with sharp spines.

Downriver Amazon aquarium

Large Echinodorus *plants have a bold appearance and one or two is usually* *enough. In this display,* Echinodorus *plants are certainly the dominant features.*

Use larger-leaved Echinodorus *at both ends of the aquarium to create a "surround" for the display.*

Echinodorus tenellus *is a similar foreground plant to hairgrass yet it mixes well at the front of the aquarium.*

Small pebbles and a sprinkling of gravel create a more natural substrate.

*Hairgrass (*Eleocharis acicularis*) will spread across the sandy substrate if given enough light.*

Driftwood is used along the center
of the aquarium and provides
many hiding places for catfish.

Different leaf shapes and
sizes add variety to the
background plants.

An open-top aquarium is best for this type
of display. These large Echinodorus will
soon grow beyond the surface.

The paler leaf color of **Micranthemum
umbrosum** *picks up the aquarium
lighting well and acts as a focal point.*

Many varieties of **Echinodorus**
*can be used. This plant has
attractive mottled markings.*

Congo whitewater river

The Congo River, previously known as the Zaire River, stretches for over 4,320 kilometers (2,700 miles) and passes through several distinct habitats before finally reaching the Atlantic Ocean. Although fish of interest come from almost all of these distinct habitats, the rapids are a particularly interesting habitat to recreate in an aquarium. The Congo has one of the most extensive stretches of rapid water in any river, with 32 individual whitewater rapids in the space of 320 kilometers (200 miles). The concentration of rapid water in this area is due to the surrounding terrain, which has a thin soil layer above the underlying rock. Over a long period of time, the river has carved through the rock, weathering it in some places but not others and removing virtually any trace of topsoil. The result is an undulating surface of solid rock and boulders that frequently alternates between steep, rocky slopes (the rapids) and moderately flat stretches of calmer waters. Although this habitat is extreme, there are many hiding spots around the large rocks and boulders and stretches of quieter, but still fast-flowing, water. These are home to fish that have become highly adapted to life in the raging waters.

MINIMAL SUBSTRATE
Despite the lack of any deep topsoil on the surrounding dry land, the substrate of the rapids is not completely covered by bare rock. Although the water is fast moving, large boulders and calmer stretches of water protect the bottom of the river from the loss of all its

Congo whitewater habitats

The Congo River begins in the African Rift Valley and extends westwards toward the Atlantic Ocean. Many rapids occur along the length of the river and some create natural barriers that even fish cannot cross.

The mighty Congo River lies at the heart of the world's second largest river system. Much of the Congo is surrounded by tropical rain forest, and in lower portions the waters are calm and sandy. Further upstream, however, the Congo carves through solid rock, twisting and turning to create whitewater rapids that appear inhospitable to any life. Nevertheless, fish are found in these turbulent stretches, thriving in the highly oxygenated water.

current. A buildup of nutrients is not possible in the thin, mobile substrate, and this, combined with a high oxygen level, means that the environment of the rapids is highly unsuitable for most plants. A few aquatic species grow sparsely in the calmer areas between rapids, but this remains a difficult environment and the attentions of herbivorous fish keep any vegetation to a minimum.

A few species of aquatic plant have managed to adapt to life in the rapids, most notably the African fern *(Bolbitis heudelotii)*, and the *Anubias* group of plants. This is because they attach their roots to rocks rather than in the substrate, and obtain the majority of their nutrients through their leaves. To combat the high oxygen levels and lack of nutrients, these slow-growing plants recycle much of their energy into collecting more nutrients rather than growing quickly. This method works well in an inhospitable environment, because fast growth is normally used by plants to "outcompete" other species, but in the environment of the rapids there is little competition. The thick, tough leaves of these plants also resist too much damage from the herbivorous fish in these waters.

MINIMAL VISIBILITY...
The heavy turbulence and flow of water in the rapids lifts much of the sandy substrate into the water body, along with any soil from the surrounding landscape. This creates water with high levels of suspended particles and very low visibility. Even in calmer areas the water will appear muddy, as there is rarely time for it to settle before the river reaches another rapid. Such low visibility makes life hard for many fish, as they cannot rely on their eyesight to find food and for navigation. Instead, they are highly adapted to using the senses of smell and touch, and the lateral line system. In some species, eyesight is very poor compared to other fishes, showing that even good eyesight would be of little help in this environment.

substrate. The heavy weathering of rocks and pebbles, combined with dusty, sandy soil in the surrounding areas, gives the riverbed a mixture of sand and gravel-like substrate. In most cases, the substrate is piled up against rocks, moved into this position by the flow of water. Depending on the geology of the surrounding area, rocks are normally either smooth and rounded boulders, cobbles, and pebbles, or rough and jagged. Brittle rocks such as slate make up the jagged rocks, broken apart or carved away by water movement, while stronger rock types are smoothed and eroded by the water movement, and become rounded.

Above: A fast-flowing current cascading over small rocks creates small-scale whitewater conditions in this forested stretch of river – home to adapted fishes.

Both rock types create "microhabitats" in which fish can rest from the torrent of water, find food, and often breed.

MINIMAL PLANTS
In this fast-flowing environment, the substrate is constantly moved around and relatively thin, so it does not offer a good rooting medium for most plants. Any that do manage to root quickly find the substrate shifting beneath them and are soon swept away by the

...BUT PLENTY OF FOOD

In most waterways, the organic content of the water, resulting from animal and plant waste, is broken down by bacteria and small animals, and then taken up by plants as nutrients. This is the start of a food chain that supplies many fish. In the whitewater rapids, a lack of substrate to house the bacteria and organisms that decompose waste, and the almost total absence of plants, means that considerable quantities of organic waste remain in the water. This is ideal for "filter feeders," such as many crustaceans, worms, sponges, shrimp, and other invertebrates that make up the diet of the fish that inhabit the rapids. In addition, there are snails that feed off algae and debris, and many scavenging species (including small fish and crabs).

So although at first this appears to be an environment that would support little life, in fact, there is plenty of food for fish. Other than predatory, carnivorous species, most search along the riverbed rather than in open water and find their food in the substrate or in rock crevices. Their enhanced sense of touch and smell means they can easily locate food in the low-visibility environment.

...AND PLENTY OF FISH TO EAT IT

The fish found in the rapid waters belong to various families and are highly diverse, although they all live very close together. Most fish have specific adaptations to the fast-flowing environment, particularly the many scavenging or algae-eating catfish. Algae-eating catfish from this area have powerful suctionlike mouths that firmly attach the fish to rocks, allowing them to graze in areas where the flow is far too strong for many other species. Both algae-eating and scavenging catfish have powerful fins, often oversized, that can be used for defense, to wedge themselves firmly between rocks and to aid maneuverability

Above: Peckoltia *spp., often called "dwarf plecs," are well suited to a fast-moving and rocky environment. Unlike similar algae-eaters, these fish are peaceful and stay small.

through the turbulent waters. These catfish all feed from the riverbed or from rocks and have little reason to head toward the surface. In many cases, the swimbladder – normally used for buoyancy – is much smaller or even absent. Some small loaches and gobies are also found in the faster-flowing waters, darting along from place to place – often a more efficient way of moving around in these conditions. Few fish in the rapids spend much time swimming against the current for long periods, as this would waste valuable energy. Instead, most adopt odd darting or hopping motions, moving quickly between calmer spots behind rocks or along the riverbed. Some tetras live in the calmer areas between rapids, including the common Congo tetra (*Phenacogrammus interruptus*) and the larger, herbivorous banded African tetra (*Distichodus sexfasciatus*). Here, you will also find some cichlids, notably the buffalohead cichlid (*Steatocranus casuarius*).

A CONGO WHITEWATER AQUARIUM

The most notable feature of an aquarium based on this habitat should be the flow of water. The turbulence created by the rapids leaves the water highly oxygenated and fast flowing. To recreate this in the aquarium the water

Large angular pieces of slate can be complemented by smaller slate chippings scattered across the aquarium floor.

should be well aerated, with plenty of flow provided by a combination of filters, powerheads, and airstones. Spraybars can be used on external filters to introduce bubbles and visible water movement along the rear of the aquarium. For extra water movement, hide powerheads among the rocks. Powerheads can also be used at the surface, where a venturi effect can add

Right: Debris collecting on a sandy substrate is easily removed using a siphon. Over time, the sand will need replacing.

to the impression of water movement. For the best effect, all the pumps should have their outputs in the same area of the tank. This will create a strong flow in one direction and also allows calmer areas to develop in other areas of the aquarium.

The decor should be relatively sparse and all the rocks should be of the same type, normally either jagged rocks, such as slate, or large cobbles and pebbles, but not a combination of the two. Use a few very large rocks together with several medium to small ones, and bank the substrate up against large rocks in the direction of the water flow for the best effect. The odd piece of driftwood or twisted root will create an impression of forest debris, but more than this would detract from the barren, open-water appearance. The substrate can be a mix of materials; a base mix of silver sand or lime-free quartz works well with jagged rocks, while pea gravel will match an aquarium with cobbles and pebbles. The substrate can be enlivened a little by a sprinkling of different-sized, but similar, substrates on top of the main substrate. Plant life is limited in the natural environment of the rapids, but an aquarium often looks a little empty without a touch of vegetation. *Anubias* and *Bolbitis* species should do well in the otherwise harsh conditions. Attach them

to rocks or wood with black cotton, which will eventually break down and disappear or can be removed once the plants have rooted. The fish and plants for this aquarium are relatively hardy and do not place heavy demands on water quality. A pH level between 7 and 7.8 is ideal; under normal conditions the lack of organics in the substrate and the high oxygen levels will stabilize the water at around this level without any additional help. Maintain the water temperature at 24-27°C (75-80°F).

THE FISH

Many fish from the rapids are suitable for this aquarium and most are relatively compatible. Bear in mind that some of the larger fish are carnivores and will eat smaller species. A mix of bottom-dwellers (catfish and loaches), rock-dwellers (cichlids), and open-water swimmers (tetras and barbs) will create a lively display in which all the areas of the aquarium are occupied. Scavenging catfish from this region

The tough crinkled leaves of Crinum natans *are unusual and well equipped to cope with strong flows of water.*

include many of the *Synodontis* species, including *Synodontis alberti, S. shoutedeni, S. angelicus,* and *S. brichardi.* As well as these catfish, other native fish include the open-water swimming Congo tetra *(Phenacogrammus interruptus)*, butterfly cichlid *(Hemichromis thomasi)*, African glass catfish *(Eutropiellus debauwi)*, and the rock-dwelling *Distichodus* species, including *Distichodus sexfasciatus, D. lusosso,* and *D. affinis.*

There are, of course, many more fish suited to this aquarium from similar habitats in other areas of the world. Algae-eaters suited to the fast-flowing environment include the large Plecostomus *(Hypostomus* spp.), and the smaller clown plecs *(Peckoltia* spp.), Chinese hillstream loach *(Pseudogastromyzon cheni)*, Siamese flying fox *(Crossocheilus siamensis)*, algae loach *(Gyrinocheilus aymonieri)*, and bristlenose *(Ancistrus* species).

Midwater swimmers include many barbs, danios, and some tetra. Particular fish of interest include the White Cloud Mountain minnow *(Tanichthys albonubes)*, danios *(Brachydanio* spp.), the silvertip tetras *(Hemigrammus marginatus)*, and the rainbowfish *(Melanotaenia species)*.

Above: The African fern (Bolbitis heudelotii) *will root to rocks or wood and actually prefers a moderate flow of water.*

Below: The slow-growing Anubias *can survive many harsh conditions, including the fast-flowing environment of this aquarium. Reasonable lighting and a few nutrients are all this plant requires.*

The thick, leathery leaves of Anubias are often avoided by plant-eating fishes.

Right: *The Congo tetra (Phenacogrammus interruptus) can be found shoaling in calmer spots between the rapids in nature. In the aquarium, these fish will also enjoy a little water movement.*

Below: *The flying fox (Epalzeorhynchus siamensis) is a hardy algae-eater that will become a useful addition to the aquarium. Although relatively peaceful, it is territorial and keeping more than a few of these fish together may cause problems.*

Left: *This fish (Distichodus sexfasciatus) has attractive red finnage and bold stripes along its body. Although it can be aggressive and will devour most plants, it is a good fish for larger aquariums.*

Congo whitewater aquarium

Airpumps, powerheads, and an external filter are combined to create the impression of waterflow in this dramatic aquarium design.

Airstones and powerheads can be hidden behind the rocks. Placing a powerhead so that its flow "intercepts" the air bubbles is particularly effective.

Using some airline without an airstone will produce these large, rising bubbles.

This large piece of slate divides the aquarium into distinct areas.

The single, uniform color of slate makes a good background for fish, plants, and other decor.

Slate chippings along the aquarium floor represent rock debris. They also lend a more authentic appearance to the sandy substrate.

Bolbitis *species will appreciate the strong water flow in this aquarium. Using wood provides a medium on which to introduce plants to the aquarium.*

Several plants, including Bolbitis heudelotii, Anubias barteri *var.* nana, *and* Vesicularia dubyana *are used together on this one piece of wood for a dramatic and bold effect.*

This small **Crinum natans** *will soon grow up to the water surface.*

Some slate pieces are laid horizontally, as though they had fallen or broken away from the underlying bedrock.

The sandy substrate will need regular stirring to prevent compaction and the buildup of anaerobic conditions.

West African streambed

Small pools, streams, and larger puddles are formed annually throughout Africa and may occur in rain forest or temperate forests, as well as in open savannahs and high mountainous areas. The forest pools may be permanent waters but many, including those found in other environments, dry out every year. In open areas near patches of forest, a number of small streams may flow across the landscape, constituting a haven for larger terrestrial wildlife. The streams often collect in natural dips through the landscape, creating small pools or "waterholes." These oases are surrounded by patches of thick bushes, grass and, occasionally, some larger trees. Despite the annual nature of some of these streams and pools, they often support small fish and the most interesting are the tiny killifish, which make excellent specimens for a display aquarium like the one featured here.

SMALL BUT BEAUTIFUL

The killifish are a group of beautifully colored fish that rarely grow large, mainly because the habitat they occupy is often too small to warrant a larger size. Killifish are not only found in Africa, but in many small waterways throughout the tropical regions. Most inhabit small pools or large puddles in rain forest regions or in open savannahs. In some places, killifish can be found in larger streams or even rivers; one is the largest of the killifish, *Orestias cuvieri,* which can reach up to 30cm (12in). However, the killifish of Africa, where some of the most stunning specimens are found, are all

Some of the streams and waterways found in many parts of tropical Africa, completely disappear in the dry season, while in others only small patches of water are left. Despite the annual nature of these streams, they do contain a number of small fishes, principally the attractive killifish.

West African streambed habitat

In areas around Lake Chad and the River Niger there are many marshes and these are home to numerous small fishes.

The desert scrublands are dry for most of the year, but killifish can be found in occasional small pools and streams.

136

The pools and streams in which the killifish are found vary a great deal in water quality and temperature. In some areas, killifish can be found in temperatures up to 38°C (100°F) and in salinities several times above normal seawater. These conditions are extreme, however, and not typical. For the large majority of killifish, soft-medium hard water with a pH of 5.5-7 will be suitable.

small species; the largest is *Lamprichthys tanganicanus*, which reaches up to 13cm (5in). As the name suggests, this fish is found along the shores of Lake Tanganyika, where there is plenty of room for growth. In comparison, some of the dwarf killifish may never reach more than a few centimeters long. These fishes are more likely to be found in small pools, streams, and puddles in open landscapes. Apart from the killifish, a few other species are found in the streams and pools of Africa. Occasionally, fish from connecting rivers or permanent streams can be found nearby, although the annual nature of the waterways ensures that they do not stay for long.

A BUSY LIFE
Not all the killifish are annual species; some are found only in permanent waters and the "non-annuals" make up the largest group of species. These fish can live for up to five years and so may make better aquarium subjects for the fishkeeper who is not planning to breed or replenish the aquarium's stock continually. However, breeding the killifish is relatively easy and adds an extra element of interest to keeping these fishes. In nature, the annual killifish must be born, grow, and breed,

Above: This small pool, which may be connected to streams or a natural spring, provides a valuable source of water for terrestrial animals. Beneath the surface there may be many small fish, which feed primarily on insects and live for only a few months.

Above: This Nothobranchius *species may grow to only about 5cm (2in) but can be quite aggressive in the aquarium. The eggs it lays in pits buried in the substrate will survive dry conditions for long periods.*

all within a nine-month period. Often, the pools are habitable for less than nine months, and this is the longest that most annuals will live for, even in permanent waters. The annual killifish are able to reproduce as little as four weeks after they are born, although it normally takes up to five months before they are fully grown.

When a male is ready to breed, he will approach a suitable female and display his finnage and colors. The courtship display also involves an odd-looking shimmering motion that is similar to an aggressive stance toward another male. If the female accepts her mate, she will move closer; if not, she will simply swim away. Once a pair is established, the male will push the female toward the substrate, where the eggs are deposited. Even when the water in the pool evaporates, the muddy bottom remains moist and the eggs begin to develop. When the rains return and the pool begins to fill, the eggs will hatch. The young fish must immediately cope with a harsh environment. The new water from the rains is often very low in oxygen content due to the respiration of bacteria and decomposing organisms that feed upon an abundance of organic debris. However, it is these organisms that supply the fish with their food sources. As the young grow, they begin to feed on larger aquatic animals and eventually move on to insects and insect larvae.

The breeding habits of the semi-annual or nonannual killifish are similar, although many of these fish will lay their eggs on the leaves of plants, rather than in the substrate. The eggs are still able to withstand drying, although in most cases they develop and hatch while remaining continually underwater.

CREATING A WEST AFRICAN STREAMBED AQUARIUM

The style of display chosen for this example is a paludarium, which has areas of interest above and below the water. This allows you to incorporate an above-ground waterfall or small trickling stream, as well as semiterrestrial bog or marginal plants. In fact, the main feature of this display is the small, trickling waterfall, which adds an interesting element of water movement, as well as recreating a natural setting. If the aquarium is large enough, the above-ground element could be extended to accommodate tropical lizards, frogs, or even some snakes. Such a display is surprisingly easy to create and contains only a few basic elements.

SUBSTRATE

The substrate is made up of lime-free and pea gravel. This is a good mixture for creating steep slopes and deeper areas, and should stay firmly in place with the aid of larger driftwood pieces and plant roots. It also makes a good substrate for the plants, many of which have their roots only partially submerged below the waterline. A sprinkling of black quartz gravel gives the substrate a little more texture and a darker feel. Brightly colored small fish such as the killifish will appear at their best only against a dark background and substrate. Paler substrates will detract and reduce the appearance of color on any small fish.

The raised area is created by banking substrate up against larger driftwood pieces. When the aquarium is first constructed, a steep bank such as this may be prone to slipping. In this design, a large amount of hairgrass (Eleocharis acicularis) is used throughout the aquarium, but especially on the raised areas. Once this plant becomes established, its roots will help to keep the sloping substrate in place.

CREATING A TRICKLING WATERFALL

The waterfall is relatively easy to construct and consists of a large piece of cork bark positioned at a slight angle on top of the raised area. Cork bark is a useful material; it has grooves along which the water can flow and fall into the aquarium from a number of different areas. The cork bark must be firmly wedged into position, so place substrate or heavier

The unique substrate in the display is a mixture of large and small pea gravel and black quartz on a base of lime-free gravel.

The driftwood in the display is used to construct the waterfall and raised area, as well as to hide pipework.

and into the underwater environment. Again, this mimics a natural setting where the "pool" is seasonal and covers terrestrial vegetation.

The light green, fleshy leaves of the floating water hyacinth contrast well with the olive green-brown, finer leaves of the hairgrass. The trailing roots of floating plants also provide cover and hiding spots for small killifish. The underwater area is relatively barren and the floating plants add greenery to this area of the aquarium, as well as filling up the above-water area.

Marginal plants add a little variation to the raised area. Any species could be used here, although it is better to use a selection of different leaf types. This design features a reedlike *Hemerocallis* species, which is similar in appearance to some *Sagittaria* species, along with individual *Ranunculus lingua* and *Alisma parviflora* marginal plants.

Water hyacinth (Eichhornia crassipes) *grows well in the aquarium but do not place it close to strong lighting, which may burn the leaves.*

Hairgrass (Eleocharis acicularis) *is used both above and below the water and represents the natural grasses that grow at the side of streams and pools.*

driftwood pieces on top of some areas of the bark. The water flow is provided by the outlet of an external filter, so no additional pumps are needed. To obtain the desired flow pattern, carefully position the outlet and then disguise it with plants and driftwood.

PLANTING

Three groups of plants are used in this design: the floating water hyacinth *(Eichhornia crassipes)*, the grassy hairgrass *(Eleocharis acicularis)*, and a few marginal bog species. Hairgrass has an important function in this design and is used both above and below the water. On the raised area, it will grow

as a marginal plant and help to hide pipework and/or cables. It also imitates a marshy area around the stream, as might be found in nature. A realistic effect can be achieved by extending the hairgrass down through the water level

Hemerocallis *(featured in this display) is often sold as a marginal pond plant, but will also grow in shallow water in the aquarium.*

SELECTING THE FISHES

Choosing the right mix of killifish for the aquarium can sometimes be a little difficult. Many of the more colorful species can be aggressive and territorial, although damage is not often done and bullying is rare. Any aggression normally occurs between males, whereas females are generally peaceful. However, the females are often far less brightly colored than the males, and in some species the females are difficult to identify, showing color and body shapes almost identical to the males. In some killifish species, the males will continually fight if two are kept together, yet in a group, they are rarely aggressive. In most cases, killifish are not shoaling species, so a community of different fish may be a good choice. To reduce the chances of any harmful aggression, choose species of a similar size and nature.

KILLIFISH SPECIES

There is a vast array of killifish species and while some are more readily available than others, a few species stand out and are always available. Therefore, it is often best to follow the genus names and take a "lucky dip" when buying fish or research the exact species for sale beforehand.

The killifish can be divided into three groups: annual, semiannual, and non-annual species. The annuals rarely live for more than nine months and must either be continually replaced or bred to maintain a high stocking level. However, the semiannuals and non-annuals will live for several years in the aquarium.

Annual species include fish from the *Cynolebias*, *Nothobranchius*, and *Pterolebias* groups. Of these three, the *Nothobranchius* species, which often have red or blue markings, are the most colorful, and native to African waters. They are lively, but males can be aggressive. Most *Nothobranchius* species rarely grow to more than 5-6cm (2-2.4in).

The semiannual and nonannual species include *Aphyosemion*, *Roloffia*, *Aplocheilichthys*, and *Epiplatys* species. Many of the *Epiplatys* species originate in African waters and all are relatively peaceful, yet timid, and can be kept in aquariums with plenty of hiding spots. The *Aphyosemion* species are also found mainly in Africa and some, although not all, of these fish are also peaceful and can be kept in groups. *Aphyosemion* species are all brightly colored and make stunning display specimens.

OTHER FISHES AND ANIMALS

Although the killifishes themselves will make a stunning display, adding other species can help to create a more varied aquarium. Small catfish are one option, although this often means that any eggs

will be quickly eaten. Any additional fish should be small, but hardy and peaceful. Some smaller barbs or even tetras may be well suited, as well as anabantoids, including the gouramis. In larger aquariums, the above-ground area of the display can be extended to make an ideal habitat for water-loving frogs, newts, crabs, or even lizards. If such animals are to be introduced, make sure they are not species that are likely to eat or harm the small killifish.

Below: The playfair's panchax (Pachypanchax playfairi) *is easy to keep and breed. During spawning, the male's scales may appear to rise, which is often mistaken for a symptom of disease.*

Left: Epiplatys sexfasciatus *is a semi-annual species that may live for several years in the aquarium. Its unusual elongated jaw and striped camouflage suggests that it may have predatory feeding habits.*

Below: *The stunning and detailed markings, which are common in many killifish, can be clearly seen on this* Aphyosemion *species.*

West African streambed aquarium

*The main features of this display are the above-water element and
the dense vegetation that combine to form the West African streambed.*

*Water hyacinth (Eichhornia
crassipes) has a bold, leathery
leaf. Both the roots and leaves
provide valuable hiding places.*

*Wood that emerges from below the
water helps to fill out some of the above-
water areas and links the two zones.*

*The highly undulating substrate
helps to reduce the sudden impact
of the banked area on the right.*

*Hairgrass here represents a marginal plant that
has become submerged during flooding. In this
area, small groups are spread out and divided.*

The leaves of Hemerocallis *resemble those of the much larger reeds found in nature, but these would be unmanageable in the aquarium.*

This piece of wood helps to hide pipes and the source of the waterfall that flows over the cork into the aquarium.

Covering the above-water area with hairgrass mimics the typical African streambed surroundings.

This attractive piece of driftwood supports the waterfall and stream bank.

Right: *The overhanging stream waterfall looks particularly effective when viewed at an angle. Smaller fish will hide underneath the overhang.*

Lake Malawi

Lake Malawi can be best described as a freshwater ocean rather than a lake. At up to 80km (50 miles) wide and 560km (350 miles) long, it is not possible to see across the lake to the opposite side in most places. The lake is so large that it experiences slight tides caused by the gravitational pull of the moon. The volcanic nature of the lake's surroundings have produced a shoreline that alternates between rocky outcrops and sandy areas. The fish that inhabit the lake can be divided into two groups: the rock-dwelling fish, or "Mbuna," and the open-water fish, often called "Haps." Of most interest to the aquarist are the rock-dwellers. These can be found all around the lake, often only near the surface, where food is readily available around the large

rounded boulders and cobbles that make up the typical rocky areas. In any particular rocky area, swarms of fish thrive beneath the surface.

The lake water is often slightly hard and alkaline, the result of dissolved minerals from the underlying rocks, and water conditions remain stable over long periods, as in the ocean. While rivers, streams, and other freshwater habitats are affected by annual weather and vegetation changes, the water quality within the lake is unchanging due to the immense volume of water, which extends to over 700m (2,296ft) in depth. For this reason, and because of their attractive colors, the fishes of Lake Malawi are sometimes confusingly described as "freshwater marine" fish.

The Rift Valley lakes

Lake Malawi is one of the Rift Valley Lakes situated in East Africa. The surrounding landscape is rocky and dry, but in the shallows beneath the surface there is an environment filled with masses of tropical fish.

The Rift Valley Lakes of East Africa are home to a number of fish species, but are dominated by the native cichlids. Of the three great lakes – Victoria, Tanganyika, and Malawi – Lake Malawi is the least touched by human activity and harbors hundreds of cichlid species found nowhere else in the world. The crystal-clear water of the lake laps against alternating rocky and sandy shorelines, and the shoals of beautifully colored fishes can be clearly seen just beneath the surface.

Left: The masses of fish living in the shallow rocky waters bring life and color to an otherwise barren environment. The cichlids that live here have a complex system of territories and social behavior.

Left: *The bright* yellow Pseudotropheus saulosi *provides an excellent example of the stunning coloration typical of the cichlids found in Lake Malawi.*

these were outcompeted or preyed upon by the cichlids. The cichlids continued to adapt to the environment and now dominate the lake's fish species. At the current count, over 600 species of cichlid native to Lake Malawi have been described, although these all descend from a small number, probably in the tens, that originally inhabited the lake. This vast diversity of fish species is the result of a combination of fish behavior and the geological changes that the lake has experienced throughout its lifetime.

Cichlids are territorial by nature, and many of the rock-dwelling cichlids that inhabit the lake will stick to a particular rocky outcrop, never venturing out across sandy areas to find new habitats. Throughout the lake's history, the water level has constantly changed, and each time this happens, a rocky outcrop may be split into two areas, divided by an open sandy region, and sandy areas may become rocky outcrops. This causes a group of fish to become divided, and in time a particular species may also evolve separately, becoming two distinct species. Genetic similarities also allow crosses and hybrids to become commonplace, and this also creates new species.

EVOLUTION

Among freshwater lakes, Lake Malawi's ecosystem is unique and home to only a small diversity of species. However, masses of fish congregate around the rocky outcrops and large shoals swim in the open waters. On the other hand, the lake houses only five true aquatic plants, a few snail and crab species, and very few invertebrates. The reason for this can be found in the formation of the lake, which occurred when the earth's tectonic plates pulled apart a rift in the earth's crust. The term "Rift Valley

Lakes" describes the three great lakes along the rift in East africa.

Lake Malawi is fed by a few small streams, but apart from these has no source and only one outlet – the river Shire. This geographic isolation means it has become virtually impossible for many river species to travel upstream into the lake or downstream from other rivers. However, fish are very adaptable and, in evolutionary timescales, can alter their physiology to thrive in such barren environments. It is likely that thousands of years ago there were many species in the lake, but

TAKE A CLOSER LOOK

Because of the comparatively low number of aquatic animals and invertebrates in the lake, and a lack of surrounding terrestrial vegetation, it is difficult to see how such a large number of fish could be supported. The answer lies in the rocky outcrops, where algae grows in abundance over the surface of smooth boulders near the surface. The rock-dwelling cichlids constantly graze on the algae, so much so that the algae never grows more than 1cm (0.4in) long, and often far less. However, it is often not the algae

OVERCROWDING

Unlike many territorial fishes, the cichlids of Lake Malawi constantly change territories to secure new feeding sites. This means that if a particular territory is too difficult to protect, a fish may simply move elsewhere. In the aquarium, this behavior can be used to control and reduce aggression. If the aquarium is heavily stocked, even slightly overcrowded, then a dominant fish will be unable to retain a territory. Dominant fish will still occur and there will be plenty of chasing, but normally overcrowding will prevent "bully" fish from holding sway, thereby preventing damage or undue stress to other fishes. This method is not harmful to the fish because in the natural environment of the lake it is not uncommon to find masses of different species all inhabiting the same small area.

that the fish are consuming as a food source, but the many tiny creatures that live among the algal "fuzz." The collective name for these creatures and the algae in which they live is "aufwuchs," and many cichlids have specially adapted mouths that enable them to graze the aufwuchs and pick out items of food. The cichlids often use territorial aggression to keep a good patch of aufwuchs to themselves, grazing it in a methodical manner. In effect, the fish could be described as "underwater aufwuchs farmers."

MOUTHBROODING

Territorial behavior is also used during breeding, an event for which the cichlids have developed a highly specialized method of caring for and raising young. Most cichlids are good parents and care for their eggs and fry by defending territories and chasing away any predators until the young are large enough to swim off on their own. Due to the difficulty of guarding their

young in an environment with a vast number of fishes (potential predators) in a small area, the cichlids of Lake Malawi have taken their protection a step further. Without any suitable hiding spots, females will hold the eggs and the young inside the mouth, away from the eyes of predators. In many cases, the eggs are actually fertilized inside the female's mouth and she will keep them there until they have hatched and are free-swimming.

After a female has chosen a suitable mate, she will take in the male's milt (sperm) before laying her eggs. She then takes the eggs into her mouth and again ingests the male's milt. This breeding method ensures that the maximum number of eggs is fertilized and predators have little chance of stealing the eggs. The eggs often take more than 10 days to hatch fully and the young spend little time outside the female's mouth for up to one month after hatching. During this period, the female will not feed, surviving on energy reserves stored within her body. In fact, the young will leave the mother's mouth only when they are simply too big to fit inside together. However, they remain close to their mother, often within a 10cm (4in) radius, for a few months while they grow and usually leave by accident after straying a little too far.

A LAKE MALAWI AQUARIUM

Unlike many biotope displays, a Lake Malawi aquascape has only two main elements: the rockwork and the fish.

Above: The popular and colorfully patterned Melanochromis auratus *should be mixed carefully with other fishes due to its territorial and aggressive temperament.*

WATER QUALITY

Within the lake, water conditions are very stable compared with many other freshwater habitats. Although cichlids are hardy and tolerant of slight changes, it is important that water quality remains stable in the aquarium, too. This can be difficult because the fish are messy feeders with large appetites and produce a great deal of waste. Taking this into account, along with the application of overcrowding methods, and the result is a large increase in biological waste. To avoid any problems, you must use large filters. Ideally, use one or more external filters designed for larger aquariums and include plenty of mechanical and biological media. The water conditions in the natural environment are slightly hard and alkaline, and these conditions should also be created in the aquarium. Water can be kept hard and alkaline through the use of calcareous rocks or substrates such as tufa or ocean rock and coral sand, normally sold for marine aquariums. Alternatively, use proprietary "trace element" liquid additives. Some of these are specifically designed to reproduce Rift Lake conditions in the aquarium.

The construction is relatively simple, but you must take care when using such a large number of heavy rocks.

Water quality and fish behavior are further considerations; housing a large number of fish together, all with aggressive tendencies and messy eating habits, will require good filtration and careful selection. Although a few catfish are found in the lake, none is commonly available from aquatic retailers and few are well suited to the aquarium. There are some alternatives, but the fishes of Lake Malawi are more than able to create a stunning and active display on their own.

SUBSTRATE

Silver sand is ideal for this style of aquarium and looks identical to the type of sand found in many areas of the lake. The sand substrate should be quite deep to support the weight of the rockwork, and it may be worth using a gravel tidy to prevent the rocks from sinking toward the glass base of the aquarium. Over time, the sand will naturally move and is liable to be dug up and moved by the attentions of the cichlids. This activity can be reduced by

These rounded boulders are identical to those found in the lake.

placing a medium-grade (3mm/0.12in) substrate underneath a gravel tidy and adding sand on top. The fish will not be able to dig below the gravel tidy, so most of the substrate should stay in place. Using a larger substrate beneath a gravel tidy and only a thin top layer of silver sand will also prevent any problems of compaction and stagnation, which can occur with very fine, sandy substrates.

It is important to avoid substrates larger than 4-5mm (0.16-0.2in) because the weight of rockwork could concentrate pressure into one area, or one piece of substrate, thus increasing the likelihood of cracking the base of the aquarium .

ROCKWORK

The type of rocks found in Lake Malawi are identical to the large rounded stones used in this display. Many Rift Lake aquarium displays contain lava or tufa rock, and although these rock types do not represent the natural environment, they are excellent for creating rockscapes because they are porous and therefore very light and easy to stack together. In fact, the fish are probably just as happy with tufa or lava rock as they are with the more authentic rounded boulders or cobbles.

For an interesting display, make a selection of different-sized stones. Apart from two very large rocks, most of the pieces in this display are about 20cm (8in) in diameter or less. Smaller pebbles and cobbles are also used along the aquarium floor and to fill some "gaps" in the larger rockwork, helping to create a natural rockfall appearance. The size of the rocks depends on the size of the aquarium. Ideally, in aquariums up to 150cm (5ft), the largest one or two rocks should be a quarter to a third of the aquarium's length.

A 120cm (4ft) tank could therefore contain one or two 30-45cm (12-18in) rocks, with the rest measuring 20-25cm (8-10in) and less. Position the larger rocks first and surround them with a steep collection of medium-sized rocks. Then add smaller cobbles and pebbles.

It is vital, of course, that the rocks are built up in a stable fashion so that they are unlikely to fall and damage the aquarium. Silicone sealant can be used to fix the rocks in position before the aquarium is filled, but you must still ensure that they are stable.

THE FISH

Because there are currently over 600 listed Lake Malawi cichlids, it is difficult to choose specific fishes for the aquarium. Although some are regularly available from aquatic retailers, it is not uncommon to find new species or color strains on a weekly basis. Fishes in the best-known group, the *Metriaclima* species, are often called zebras due to the vertical stripe pattern that appears on many of the fish. Zebras, along with most mbuna, will grow to about 15cm (6in).

There are many color varieties and body forms of the cichlids. Notable examples include the *Cyrtocara* species, such as the blue dolphin cichlid (*Cyrtocara moorii*), so called because of its unusual dolphinlike head shape and the large hump that males develop; *Melanochromis* species, with their bold horizontal stripes; and the *Aulonocara* species, which develop a stunning, reflective metallic blue coloration around the head area. Although most of the cichlids will attain similar sizes and have similar temperaments, it is always worth checking before making a purchase. A particularly large and aggressive fish will cause problems, even in a crowded aquarium (see panel). Males are normally the most aggressive fish, and two males of the same, or similar, species should be kept together only in a very large aquarium. Although a few cichlids can be kept in any combination, it is best to keep one male to at least two or three females.

Lake Malawi aquarium

A good aquascape does not depend on a complex design involving plants, wood, substrates, and rocks, as this simple yet striking display proves.

The gaps created by rockwork will become welcome hiding spots for the cichlids.

Try to imitate a rockfall in some areas by filling gaps with smaller cobbles and pebbles.

Use a gravel tidy (plastic mesh) to prevent digging cichlids from undermining the rocks.

Smaller pebbles help to fill gaps and blend the large boulders and sandy substrate.

Rocks that are broken in half can be used to give the impression of partially buried boulders.

Construct the rockscape with care and use silicone sealant to fix rocks together.

A mixture of shapes and tones can be used to create a varied rockscape.

Although these cobbles look randomly placed, they are all in stable positions where they are unlikely to fall.

Silver sand recreates the natural lake bed.

Use the largest stones as a base to place smaller stones on.

The sand is deeper in this area to support the heavier rocks.

A darkened cave

A cave environment is a loose term that applies to any reasonably large body of water covered by an overhead land mass. A darkened cave could be simply an underground opening no bigger than a house, where light is still able to penetrate the shaded water that connects to nearby waterways. In these pools, fishes from the adjacent river or stream feed on "conventional" foods, such as insects, crustaceans, and substrate-dwelling creatures. Alternatively, a cave environment might extend for some distance beneath the ground. In this situation, sunlight never reaches the water and pockets of air provide the only source of oxygen. The fish in these areas are highly adapted to the conditions and rarely find their way out into the nearby rivers. In some cases, the waters in

these caves enter through tiny channels that run through the rockwork. The original access through which fish would have arrived in this cave environment may have long since disappeared. Throughout the world, over 40 fish species normally live exclusively in caves, but many more are found as occasional visitors.

THE FORMATION OF CAVES

A number of geological processes can form caves, although the large majority are formed either by erosion, lava flows, or tectonic activity. Erosion often occurs when two rock types are found together near a river or waterway. "Soft" rock will erode quickly, breaking down into minerals that are dissolved and taken away by the movement of water. However, harder rock can

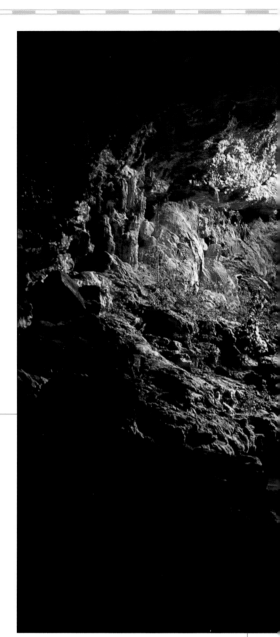

Cave habitats

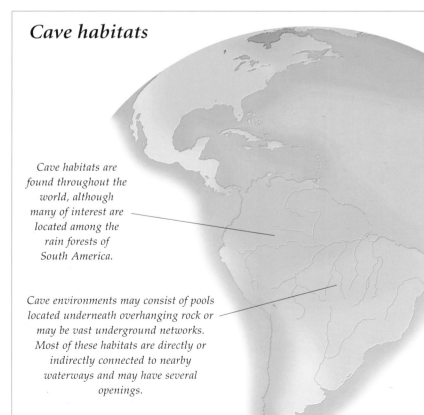

Cave habitats are found throughout the world, although many of interest are located among the rain forests of South America.

Cave environments may consist of pools located underneath overhanging rock or may be vast underground networks. Most of these habitats are directly or indirectly connected to nearby waterways and may have several openings.

The hidden underwater habitat of the caves is a harsh environment where food is hard to find and the senses of its inhabitants are tested to their limits. Yet a number of fish are found here; some are just visitors, while others are highly specialized species that spend their entire lives in virtual darkness.

lava flow. As the lava, or magma, flows across the ground, the uppermost surface, which is in contact with the cool atmosphere, and possibly rain, will lose heat first and harden as rock. However, lava continues to flow below the surface, pushing its way through a self-made channel underneath the newly formed rock above. As the lava flows begin to slow down, the environment inside the channel is incredibly hot and often empties before the lava sets. The empty channels left behind form the cave environment, which may eventually fill with water from the surface or from nearby waterways.

Tectonic activity occurs in the same locations as eruptions and lava flows, and is caused by a buildup of pressure when two tectonic plates come together. However, when two plates pull apart, they literally "rip" the earth's crust, forming dips and lakes on the surface. Caves can also be formed by this ripping, and are often found close to places where lakes and pools appear, creating ideal conditions for the eventual introduction of aquatic life, including fishes.

NATURE'S BLINDFOLD

In the cave environment, light may be partially or totally blocked out. In general, most large cave systems experience more areas of total darkness than of shade or partial light. Good eyesight is useless in this situation and many fish and other cave animals have developed in the opposite direction, partially or even completely losing the sense of vision. A large proportion of an animal's brain is used to process the information it receives from the senses. It could therefore be said that the senses are "in competition" for brain capacity. A cave-dwelling animal with poor or no eyesight can thus use its brain power to increase the effectiveness of other senses, such as hearing, touch, or smell. Many of the fishes found in caves have very small eyes in comparison to their body size, and some, such as the aptly named

Above: This view of the Rio Frio Caves in the Cayo District of Belize shows a pool of water extending into the gloom and eventual darkness of the cave system. Even here, fish and other creatures flourish.

withstand the action of the water for a far longer period and remains relatively intact over thousands of years. If the rocks are arranged in a certain way, the softer rock will erode, forming a cave surrounded by harder rock, and over

time the cave becomes gradually larger. The water movement need not be extreme; a gentle flow will start the process and simply being saturated with water can be enough to erode soft rock. Rainwater may pass through channels in the harder rock overhead and as it percolates through the softer rock, erosion slowly occurs.

Many caves are formed through the flow of lava after a major volcanic eruption or as the result of a continual

151

blind cave fish, appear to have no eyes at all. Unusually, these fish are born with eyes which, as they mature, slowly become covered by skin and scales. The eyes are still present and may be sensitive to sudden changes in light, although they are no longer used. The blind cave fishes employ sound and smell or taste to locate food items, and the lateral line system enables them to detect objects and move around the cave. It is quite a novelty to keep a blind cave fish in a community aquarium, where it often darts around rapidly without ever banging into the glass, other objects, or fish, and is often the first to reach food, despite being almost totally blind.

THE CAVE UNIFORM

Because sight is unimportant, and there is little or no light, colors also become irrelevant. The fish and animals found in the total darkness have, over time, lost all their pigmentation and markings and become natural albinos. Without any pigmentation, the fish appear a pink, fleshy color that varies only slightly due to different fat and muscle quantities between species. Some crustaceans also live in caves, mainly a few crab species, and these have also often lost their pigmentation. These creatures, however, often appear pure white, caused by the calcium compounds from which their "shells," or exoskeletons, are made.

A FINE BALANCE

For complex animals such as fish and crabs to inhabit any ecosystem, they must have a suitable and readily available source of food. Virtually all complex animals are part of a food chain that begins with vegetation, or more accurately, the sun. Plants and algae derive their energy from the sun and from nutrients. In turn, the plants become food for other animals, which produce waste on which bacteria and tiny animals feed, providing sustenance for other larger species, and so on. Eventually, a complex food chain can be created, with hundreds or often thousands of animals and organisms in any given ecosystem or habitat.

The virtual darkness of the caves, however, prevents any form of vegetation from growing, so at first glance it is difficult to see how complex creatures could live in the caves. The answer lies in microscopic bacteria that live on raw materials unconnected to sunlight and vegetation. Some of these bacteria live on the minerals found in the surrounding rock. Most notably, bacteria and other microorganisms can thrive on sulphur, which often occurs in volcanic, or "young," rocks. These bacteria and microorganisms are then fed upon by tiny animals such as amphipods or tiny shrimps, which become food for the larger animals, including fish.

Some terrestrial animals may live in caves that have occasional openings at the surface. Bats are a particular example. They are found in many cave environments, venturing into the outside world only at night. Bats often form colonies of thousands and produce vast amounts of waste from droppings, as well as the occasional dead youngster. This waste may fall into the waters below, providing vital nutrients on which more bacteria, microorganisms, and, directly or indirectly, the fish can all sustain themselves. Some caves also have regular visits from small birds and insects, which may appear on purpose or simply by accident, providing more sources of energy and food.

FINDING FOOD

As we have seen, cave fish rely on senses other than sight to locate food sources. Many cave fish have heightened senses of smell, touch, and hearing that are vital in the dark environment. Most cave-dwelling fish have a larger number of sensory receptors for smell, often combined with enlarged inhalant nostrils. Some species have a sense of smell two to three times more sensitive than in other fish – even more than many predatory species. However, the most valuable adaptation, seen in all fish, is the lateral line system, which can detect changes in pressure from the surrounding water. Some fish with a highly developed lateral line system, such as many cave fish, are able to sense the movement of objects nearby, such as food items or predators, by localized pressure changes in the water.

A similar sense is used by some fish in the form of an electrical field. When an electrical field is passed through a substance, such as water, rock, or even another animal, it encounters resistance, which varies depending on the density of the object. Fishes that have developed the ability to generate electricity from muscle movements can create their own electrical field around their body. When the field passes through rock, for example, the fish can "recognize" the change in that part of the electrical field, and thus knows that there is rock in that area. Electrical fields can tell the fish where objects are, in much the same way that radar works, although the lateral line system also does this. The electrical fields are mainly used for locating prey, which may not be so easily detected by other means.

Subtle color substrates such as this black gravel can be used to create a dark and mysterious environment.

Lava rock is highly porous, making it very light and easy to break into pieces. It is ideal for constructing rockscapes.

A CAVE AQUARIUM

In the deep recesses of the cave environment, there is little but water, darkness, and vast open space, which do not make a good aquarium display.

However, toward the cave mouth or near surface openings, daylight may enter and a few plants may grow. This display is designed to convey the impression of a cave wall and a gloomy environment, while still creating a vibrant and interesting aquarium.

THE SUBSTRATE

There are various options for the substrate in this aquarium, but the aim is to achieve a dark surface that matches and continues the effect of the rockwork. In this display silver sand makes an ideal support for the light, porous lava rock. However, silver sand is quite pale in color, so a top layer of black-colored gravel has been added, which is similar in color and texture to the rockwork. In this example, the pale silver sand is mostly hidden, but the small patches that are visible actually draw attention to the darker rocks and gravel. Any dark substrate would be suitable, but ideally it should match the type of rock used to create the "cave" walls. A good

Plants should be used sparingly in this design. Small Cryptocoryne species are ideal for planting among the overhanging rockscapes, where they will flourish.

method, especially with light, porous rocks such as lava rock, is to continue the rock wall across the substrate. In this way, the bottom of the aquarium will be taken up by the same rocks as appear in the rock wall, and you will not need any substrate material, or only a small quantity to complete the display.

CREATING THE CAVE WALL

Any type of inert rock is suitable for the rock wall and overhang, although lava rock, as used in this aquarium, is by far the easiest and most practical to work with. Lava rock is incredibly porous, making it very light and easy to stack. Even when used in large quantities, it poses no problems of excess weight or potential danger of structural damage.

And, of course, the dark red-gray color of lava rock provides a visual feel that is ideal for this display.

The rockscape should be constructed in stages, well before the aquarium is filled with water. First, silicone together the rocks that make up the back and side walls, then silicone them to the aquarium glass and leave them to dry. To create the overhanging areas, lie the aquarium on its back on the floor. The overhangs can then be constructed vertically and fixed in place before the aquarium is returned to its normal position. Leave the silicone to dry for a few days. In this display, the overhang extends around the two sides and back of the tank and out to the front in the middle. With suitable lighting, two brighter patches will simulate openings in the cave ceiling surrounded by shady areas.

THE PLANTS

Although the aim of this display is to recreate a barren environment, it may appear a little too bare without a few plants. The plants in this display are carefully located so that they enhance the cave effect, not detract from it. Lava rock is actually a good supporting medium for some species of aquatic plant, such as *Anubias* spp. or varieties of fern, and a few smaller species, such as the cryptocorynes used here, all of which will root and thrive in lava rock. The cryptocoryne varieties are all low-growing, smallish plants placed around the "openings" in the cave overhang, where the light is easily accessible. This conveys an interesting impression of the division between the "overground" and "underground" worlds. Toward the substrate, again in the areas of light, you can place slightly taller plants, such as the *Vallisneria americana* used here. Its elongated twisted leaves catch the light well and when placed individually rather than grouped, they create the impression of opportunistic growth.

THE FISH

A number of cave-dwelling fish exist, but only a few of these are available in the aquarium trade. To create an interesting aquarium, it is possible to cheat a little and use albino varieties of common fishes that would not normally be found in caves. They will represent the cave fishes, which often lack pigments. Albino varieties of fish such as tiger barbs (*Puntius tetrazona*), glowlight tetras (*Hemigrammus erythrozonus*), bristlenose catfish (*Ancistrus* spp.), and corydoras catfish species are often available.

A few true cave fish can be found, the best-known one being the blind cave fish (*Astyanax fasciatus mexicanus*). This hardy, adaptable, and active species normally grows no bigger than 8cm (3.2in). Some species of molly (notably *Poecilia sphenops* and *Poecilia mexicana*) can occasionally be found in smaller cave environments and these peaceful fish will make excellent additions to the aquarium. The mollies are available in a number of colors, although pure black varieties may look best in this aquarium, contrasting well with the other, albino, fishes.

Well-known species of cave-dwelling catfish, including the albino clarias (*Clarias batrachus*) and the similar blind cave-walking catfish (*Clarias cavernicola*), are prohibited in the U.S. Alternatively, you could consider some *Hoplosternum* species. Although they are not cave-dwellers, they do have

Below: The albino clarias catfish (Clarias batrachus) *uses its sensitive whiskers, or barbels, to feel its way around and "taste" possible items of food. These fish (Clarias spp.) are prohibited in the U.S.*

small eyes and very limited vision, a feature found in many true cave-dwellers.

Two highly interesting groups of creatures are the swamp eels and the salamanders. The swamp eels are not true eels but look very similar and are found in many natural cave habitats. The most common variety is *Synbranchus infernalis*, although others are sometimes available. The salamanders, notably the cave-dwelling salamander *(Proteus anguinus)*, also called the white salamander, are extremely unusual and interesting amphibians to keep. In its natural cave environment, this salamander does not develop eyes or pigment, but when placed in daylight for extended periods, eyes quickly develop and the skin becomes a brownish color. This fish is an example of how far evolution will allow species to adapt to harsh environments, such as the darkened cave. It is said that it frequently lives for more than 100 years and is able to survive for several years without food. Salamanders often use electrical fields to navigate, communicate and locate food. Any salamander species would be suitable for this style of aquarium.

Above: The electric catfish (Malapterurus spp.) can generate an electrical field around its body to locate objects and stun prey. Many cave-dwelling species can produce small electrical fields, but few are as powerful as those created by this catfish.

Left: The olm (Proteus anguinus) is a cave-dwelling salamander with a distinctive albino appearance and pink external gills. The lack of pigment and absent eyes are evident only when it is kept in constant darkness.

A darkened cave aquarium

Creating the rockscape is the most time-consuming and challenging aspect of this display. The finished result is a unique and magical design.

Small fishes and catfish use gaps in the rockwork as hiding spots.

The cryptocorynes placed around the overhangs represent terrestrial vegetation above the cave.

Overhanging rocks will block out the light in many areas of the tank, creating a dark environment.

Larger rocks form the base for the tall rockscape. Although the lava rock is light, it must be siliconed together.

A small **Vallisneria** species is placed in areas where light can penetrate the overhanging rocks.

Not all plants will live and grow in the rockwork. Smaller species are best, although a little trial and error may be needed.

The two openings in the overhang are ideal spots to place small plants.

A pocket of gravel in the rockwork will encourage plants to take root and grow.

The effect of blocking out the light in some places is to highlight other spots and draw attention to the plants.

The sandy bed provides support for the rockwork, while a covering of black gravel continues the dark atmosphere of the display.

Smaller pieces of lava rock can be placed along the substrate to imitate fallen rocks.

157

Southeast Asian stream

The rain forests of Southeast Asia and the Indonesian islands contain a diverse array of animal and plant life. However, the landmass over which these rain forests occur is highly fractured and, unlike the rain forests of South America and Africa, large river basins cannot be formed in the smaller island regions. Nevertheless, heavy rainfall during the rainy season, combined with the forest's ability to retain water, ensures that throughout the year there are many streams, pools and waterways throughout the forest. Although these streams are mostly permanent, the rainy and dry seasons do create a fluctuation in water level. In a shallow stream, this often means that a drop of only 30cm (12in) may reduce the diameter of the stream by more than 2m (6.5ft).

The continual forest growth ensures that the surrounding soil is rich in organic nutrients, although it is often relatively thin. Combined with an iron-rich clay composition in many places, this makes the streambed substrate ideal for plant growth. The strong vegetation both above and below the water harbors a number of small animals and insects that make ideal food sources for smaller fish species. The relatively shallow and continually moving water reduces the number of larger fish found in many areas and there are few predators beneath the water. In fact, the numerous bird species that inhabit the forest canopies present a greater risk than anything beneath the surface. The highly adapted fish in these streams wisely adopt camouflage, shoaling techniques, and the dense streambed vegetation to avoid such predators.

PLANT SURVIVAL
The high-nutrient content of the streambed, continual replenishment of nutrients from forest runoff and a relatively shallow environment are ideal for many aquatic plants. On the other hand, certain conditions are hostile to many plants, so the aquatic vegetation in these streams is limited to those species that are uniquely adapted to survive in this environment. For example, the thin substrate prevents tall plants from growing in many areas, whilst overhanging vegetation reduces the intensity of light, and a continual water movement introduces oxygen and reduces carbon dioxide levels. So although nutrients are readily available to the plants, only slow-growing species that require less carbon dioxide and sunlight for photosynthesis can take advantage of them.

In many streams, the cryptocoryne group of plants dominates the aquatic vegetation. These small plants are highly adapted to thrive both in shaded and open water areas and, due to their

Southeast Asian streams

Streams found in the Asian mainland are often connected to larger rivers.

In the rain forests of Southeast Asia the many streams and waterways are rich in aquatic vegetation and fish species. There are few large fish; instead, the underwater world is dominated by the smaller rasboras and barbs that hide among the abundant cryptocoryne beds and in the welcome shade of the overhanging forest vegetation.

The Indonesian islands abound with streams, swamps, and rivers surrounded by rain forest. Some fish species are found only on specific islands.

relatively slow growth, are not adversely affected by a lack of carbon dioxide. At the stream edges, the *Cryptocoryne* species often have brown leaves and are particularly abundant in slow-moving areas or where underground springs provide nutrients. In these ideal locations, the plants will cover every available space, creating a miniature underwater jungle where many small fish and scavenging species can be found. In the center of the streams, where direct sunlight reaches the surface for a longer period during the day, many green-leaved plants will grow in patches of calm water and/or deeper substrate among rocks, stones, and forest debris.

GROWING FAST AND SLOW

Although cryptocorynes are certainly a dominant group of plants in many streams, a large number of *Aponogeton* species can also be found among the aquatic vegetation. Both *Cryptocoryne* and *Aponogeton* species are ideal for the Southeast Asian streams due to their ability to adapt to changing water levels. As the dry season arrives and the water level begins to recede, many plants enter a dormant, or "rest," period and survive as marginal plants above the surface. Some *Aponogeton* species lose all their leaves when the streambed recedes, but the roots, including bulbs and/or tubers, remain. As soon as conditions are suitable, they will produce new leaves and regrow.

Small and slow-growing cryptocorynes dominate many shallow areas in Southeast Asian streams and rivers.

Above: *This small river in Borneo shares the same fish species found in the numerous streams connected to it. This area is well shaded but a clearing can be seen in the distance where bright sunlight reaches the surface. Plants thrive in both shaded and sunlit areas.*

Many fern species flourish by the sides of the streams, including the popular aquarium plant Java fern (*Microsorium pteropus*). Many of these ferns grow on tree trunks or rocks, where other plants cannot root. When water levels are high, they grow prolifically, but when the stream falls, these hardy plants must obtain water from the humid air and morning dew and their growth is heavily reduced.

In many places, bamboo grows rapidly in moist areas and at the edges of streams. The giant bamboo often found in these regions, can grow up to a staggering 115cm (45in) a day and many small areas of the forest are dominated by patches of this highly unusual plant.

UNFUSSY EATERS
For many fishes, the surrounding forest provides a large proportion of their diet, which consists largely of insects and some fruits and seeds that fall or are washed into the river by the rains. The shallow, densely planted streambeds are ideal locations for many insects and insect larvae. A continual influx of forest debris also ensures that there are many small organisms within the streams to break down organic matter. These are also important food sources for bottom-feeders, young fry, and midwater-swimming fish. Many of the fish in the streams are opportunistic feeders that take whatever food sources are available. In particular, the loaches

and the similar cyprinids, including popular species such as the red-tailed black shark (*Epalzeorhynchos bicolor*), ruby shark (*Epalzeorhynchos frenatus*), and horse-faced loach (*Acantopsis choirorhynchos*), will feed on any small creatures they can find along the streambeds. When these food sources become scarce, they will feed on the algae that grows in open sunlit areas.

AN ASIAN STREAM DISPLAY
The main aim of this display is to create an impression of the dense planting that occurs at the edges of the streams. A large number of cryptocorynes are used to achieve this effect, interspersed with a few *Aponogeton* species for added interest and contrast. Jati wood and bamboo define different areas of the aquarium and make a large, bold statement in otherwise empty background areas. The densely planted stretches are ideal for smaller shoaling fish to swim and dart about in, while bottom-dwellers such as loaches will enjoy the hiding spots provided by the decor and the various substrates.

THE SUBSTRATE
The combination of different substrates in this display creates the impression of a streambed. The basic substrate is a medium-grade pea gravel, and this is mixed with a finer, lime-free gravel, pebbles, red chippings, and broken driftwood pieces. These help to create a slightly darker "autumn" color of

substrate. In the Southeast Asian streams, the substrate would often be a dark reddish brown color, caused by the iron-rich clay substrate and a buildup of forest debris. The pebbles and driftwood pieces also help to give the substrate a more interesting texture and streamlike appearance. Because of the large number of plants in the aquarium, it may be worth including a nutrient-rich substrate additive beneath the planted areas. Despite the hardy nature of the plants, carbon dioxide fertilization and liquid fertilizers may be beneficial and may make the difference between plants that thrive and those that merely survive.

JATI AND DRIFTWOOD
Several small pieces of jati wood are used in this aquarium, although most are partially obscured by the plants. The pieces are arranged in a line across the aquarium, about two-thirds of the way back, as if they were broken fragments of an old tree root or tree stump. Using the wood in this way allows you to establish a clear demarcation between the background and the open foreground space. Placing plants around the wood reduces the impact of the demarcation and creates a more natural setting for them. The larger piece of jati wood in the heavily planted corner of the aquarium serves mainly as a support and rooting medium for the plants in this area.

Driftwood helps to keep the water slightly soft and acidic, which is ideal for the fish that will inhabit the aquarium. It may also discolor the water and although this staining can be

Left: The red-tailed black shark (Epalzeorhynchos bicolor) *exhibits the simple yet bold and striking coloration typical in fishes from this area of the world.*

Various sizes of bamboo can be used in the aquarium to produce a very Asian feel to the display.

removed using chemical filtration media, slightly yellow-brown "tea-colored" water may actually enhance the natural look of the display.

BAMBOO

Two sizes of bamboo appear in this aquarium, although you could use a mixture of sizes if you can find them. The smaller bamboo cane can be cut to different lengths and positioned almost randomly throughout the aquarium. Over time, it will begin to rot in the

The unusual leaf shape of Cryptocoryne balansae *adds variety to the display.*

water, at which point it may start to develop a slightly slimy coating and turn dark brown. The cane can be varnished before use to prevent this from happening, although since it is inexpensive, it may be easier simply to replace the cane every few months. Replacing the cane has the added benefit of continuously changing the display. The larger pieces will rot far more quickly if untreated and may prove expensive to replace on a regular basis, so cut these into lengths such that the inside of the cane is fully accessible and treat the wood as described on page 32. The wood may need a couple of coats of clear polyurethane varnish to ensure that it is fully sealed. Avoid colored varnishes, as they may contain chemicals that are harmful to fish and plants. Once the varnish has fully dried, the bamboo should be safe to place in the aquarium.

Because bamboo is a dry wood – unlike driftwood, which is already water saturated – it is highly buoyant. To overcome this problem, silicone the wood to a flat rock or piece of glass and place this underneath the substrate. An easy, but crude, alternative is simply to wedge a large cobble or rock inside the base of the bamboo to weigh it down underwater.

The thin, fragile-looking leaves of Aponogeton boivinianus *belie the hardy and adaptable nature of the plant.*

PLANTING

The main element of this display – the large number of *Cryptocoryne* species – creates a dense, miniature, underwater jungle. Choose the cryptocorynes on the basis of a mix of different leaf sizes and colors. Plant some of these individually to maintain a natural appearance, but place others in groups for a more dramatic impact. Of particular interest in this display are the two contrasting groups at either end of the tank. One is a tightly planted cluster of small, pale olive green-colored cryptocorynes that covers some of the foreground area, while the other is made up of larger, green-leaved crypts that extend up toward the surface. These larger crypts are carefully placed around a vertically positioned piece of jati wood used as a "scaffold." The roots of these plants are, therefore, not

161

planted in the substrate but remain in pots positioned up to three-quarters of the way up the aquarium. Although keeping plants in pots is not ideal, most cryptocorynes will not suffer, and providing there is adequate liquid fertilization, they should remain healthy and growing. The same effect can be created, but more permanently, using a larger bamboo piece as a "planting container." Fill a section of bamboo with a fine planting substrate or a mix of lime-free gravel and nutrient-rich substrate additive. Cut holes into the side of the bamboo, just large enough to hold a few plants. With the plants in position, stand the bamboo vertically in the aquarium, with the rooted plants coming out of the top and the specially created side planting pockets.

A few *Aponogeton* species, namely *A. madagascariensis, A. boivinianus*, and *A. crispus*, are also included in this display. These plants can be positioned on their own as "specimen" plants toward the foreground or mixed in among the cryptocorynes. Many of the aponogetons have unique leaf shapes that add a little variety to the

cryptocoryne-dominated display. Some *Hygrophila* species could also be added to this aquascape, although in most cases *Cryptocoryne* and *Aponogeton* sp. are enough for an impressive display.

SHOALING FISH

The small stream-dwelling fish from Southeast Asian regions normally consist of small barbs or rasboras. Both these groups of fish are relatively peaceful and active, although some can be prone to occasional fin-nipping. In most cases, this behavior can be controlled by keeping the fish in shoals. The popular tiger barbs (*Puntius tetrazona*) are especially renowned for fin-nipping, although when kept in groups of six, seven or more, this behavior is much less evident. In nature, these fish stay in groups (shoals) and have regular "play fights," in which a type of social hierarchy is established. Fin-nipping occurs during the process of establishing this social order. When the fish are kept in small numbers, they are unable to carry out these "play fights" and vent their mis-placed aggression on other fishes. Tiger barbs are available in a number of

color morphs, which although they are not natural colors, look quite attractive in the aquarium environment. Other suitable small barbs include the cherry barb (*Puntius titteya*), whose males wiil turn a stunning deep red color, and the small five-banded barb (*P. pentazona*), a peaceful fish suited to any small community aquarium.

Two popular rasboras for the aquarium are the harlequin rasbora (*Rasbora heteromorpha*) and the larger scissortail rasbora (*Rasbora trilineata*). All these small shoaling fish will spend their time in the midwater range of the aquarium, darting among the dense plants. Several of the loaches are

Above: *The horse-face loach* (Acantopsis choirorhynchos) *is an active scavenger, but peaceful enough to keep with other loaches. The fish has an ability to bury itself in the substrate to escape danger.*

Right: *A peaceful nature, small size, and striking color make the cherry barb* (Puntius titteya) *an excellent aquarium fish. The males will turn a deep cherry red color in the right environment.*

Above: *The flying fox (Epalzeorhynchos kalopterus) is a very good algae-eater, although it may be aggressive toward its own kind and sometimes other loaches. Provide plenty of hiding spots for this fish*

suitable for the lower areas of the aquarium and are also useful for controlling algae. Good algae-eaters include the sucking loach (*Gyrinocheilus aymonieri*), flying fox (*Epalzeorhynchos kalopterus*), and Siamese flying fox (*Crossocheilus siamensis*). Similar fishes (sold as "loaches") include the red-tailed black shark (*E. bicolor*), the ruby shark (*E. frenatus*), and horse-faced loach (*Acanthopsis choirorhynchus*). Unfortunately, of all these loaches, the horse-face is the only one peaceful enough to be kept in groups. The others are all territorial and aggressive toward each other, although not toward different groups of fish, such as barbs, tetras, catfish, and rasboras. In most cases, unless the aquarium is over 120cm (4ft) long, it would be wise to keep only one loach – except, of course, the horse-face loach, which can be kept in groups and with other loaches.

163

Southeast Asian stream aquarium

*A mixture of structured grouping and random placing of a
variety of plants makes this display a true underwater garden.*

*These cryptocorynes are
carefully positioned above
each other rather than
planted in the substrate.*

*The larger bamboos
are weighted down
with a few large
cobbles.*

*Smaller-leaved plants are
closely planted to create a
bushy effect.*

*The substrate is a mix of gravels
and small pebbles, creating the
appearance of a streambed.*

*Some plants are placed individually,
such as this* Aponogeton
madagascariensis.

A mix of **Cryptocoryne** species
provides different colors and
shades in the vegetation.

Larger-leaved plants are placed
toward the background and
"graded" toward the foreground.

A few longer-leaved **Aponogeton**
species are placed among the
cryptocorynes to add a little variety.

Bamboo cane is cut to different
lengths and placed amid areas
of dense planting.

The abundant plant growth in
this display would benefit from a
nutrient-rich substrate additive.

Over time, the plants will spread and
some will do better than others, so the
display will constantly change.

165

Southeast Asian swamp

The habitat of the lowland swamps of Southeast Asia is unique and the fish that live in its waters have developed specific methods for feeding, hunting, and breeding in it. In most swamps, there is an abundance of vegetation both under and above the water. In shallow areas, marginal plants, reeds, and bamboo grow at the edges of the swamps, often in dense patches next to outcrops of dry land. In many places, the swamps are interspersed with patches of dry land where large bushes and trees provide some shade and cover. In the open waters, there is a mix of aquatic vegetation, floating plants, and reed beds, forming a crowded underwater environment. Beneath the surface, the water is often muddy and shaded from sunlight by the abundant vegetation. As a result, the fishes use their senses of taste, smell, touch, and hearing, rather than sight, to find food and avoid predators.

The swamps vary throughout the year in size and depth, in relation to the rainy and dry seasons in the tropical environment. In dry seasons, they become shallow and separate, creating isolated pools and marshes. When the rains arrive, the water level rises and the swamps grow larger, often joining together. Most fish breed when the water levels are high, because new food sources are abundant and there are more potential mates to choose from.

PLANT PARADISE
The soil beneath the swamps is made up from silt and debris and contains a large amount of iron-rich substances, including clay, which also helps to prevent water from seeping away through the ground. The warm,

Southeast Asian swamp habitats

Most swamps occur in lowland areas where water collects in vast flood plains.

Rainfall is high in the Indonesian islands, ensuring that swamps remain throughout the year.

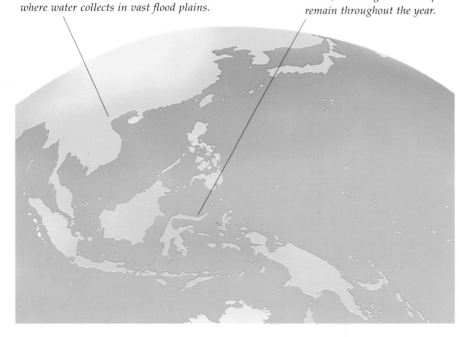

The muddy lowland swamps of Southeast Asia often cover vast areas of land, yet in many places are quite shallow. Beneath the surface, a dense collection of aquatic and marginal plants creates an underwater jungle. Hiding among the vegetation are a number of fish species, all perfectly adapted to the dark, murky, and low-oxygen environment.

are dominant, being able to "divide and conquer" rapidly at the surface without having to root in the substrate or compete for light beneath the water. In this environment, only those plants that can grow fast enough and produce leaves in sunlit areas will survive.

BREATHING DIFFICULTIES

Because the swamps cover a large area, water movement is minimal and is reduced further by the dense vegetation. The result is that little gas exchange occurs at the water surface. During the day, plants photosynthesize rapidly and absorb large amounts of carbon dioxide from the water, substrate, and the atmospheric air, and in return, produce large amounts of oxygen. The oxygen produced by the plants is vital to the ecosystem, as it prevents the water and the substrate from becoming stagnant and toxic, which could kill some aquatic life and encourage algal blooms. At night, however, the plants stop producing oxygen, yet continue to respire and the reverse of photosynthesis occurs; the plants begin to use up oxygen and produce carbon dioxide. Although the plants produce more oxygen than carbon dioxide in a 24-hour period, much of the oxygen is lost through the surface, despite a lack of water movement. In the early hours of the day, before sunrise, the swamps are often incredibly low in oxygen, following the nighttime respiration of plants, fish, bacteria, and other animals.

During the hot season – from about October to February – the water quickly warms up to 28°C (82°F) or higher. This causes further reductions in oxygen, as warmer water holds less dissolved gas. The smaller rasboras and barbs that inhabit the swamps can cope with low oxygen levels because their smaller bodies require less oxygen to function properly. To reduce their oxygen consumption, they slow down and

Stargrass (Heteranthera zosterifolia) *is a South American species, but can be used in this aquarium to represent typical swamp vegetation.*

shallow water, exposed to the tropical sunlight and the iron- and nutrient-rich substrate combine to form an ideal environment for aquatic plants. In the swamps, plants grow quickly and aggressively compete for space. Stem plants regularly grow rapidly and produce leaves only at the surface, where light is available. In many places, the water is filled with leafless stems, and leaves at the surface block out a large proportion of the light.

In open areas, floating plants

WATER QUALITY

The fish of the lowland Southeast Asian swamps inhabit a harsh environment in which many other fish would not survive. In a typical day they endure extremes of oxygen content, murky waters, and often high temperatures. The high organic content and lack of minerals result in water with a low, sometimes almost zero-hardness level. This causes daily fluctuations in pH levels, which are often on average as low as pH 5. However, the fish are not all hardy aquarium species; some are very sensitive to water conditions that do not occur in their natural environment. In the aquarium, it is not uncommon to experience high nitrates and chemical pollutants from tapwater, whereas in the Southeast Asian swamps, biological pollutants, such as ammonia, nitrites and nitrates, and chemical pollutants are quickly absorbed by the vast amount vegetation. The fish, therefore, are not adapted to cope with such pollutants, and many soon suffer when faced with them in the aquarium, becoming prone to bacterial infections or other diseases. The clown loach is sensitive to many aquarium treatments, notably many snail treatments, so take care when using such chemicals. Most treatments will carry a warning if any fish may be harmed. Some of the sensitive anabantoids, such as the dwarf gourami or Siamese fighter, can be prone to skin problems such as ulcers, caused by pollutants in the water. When setting up an aquarium for these fishes, add the most sensitive species last. The filtration should also include a large amount of biological media, so consider an external filter with a larger capacity. Reverse osmosis water may also be beneficial. As well as providing a soft, acidic environment, it is almost pure and contains hardly any contaminants.

hover among hiding spots near the surface, where oxygen levels are highest. However, larger fish would normally quickly perish under such harsh conditions. The larger gouramis, catfish, and loaches have had to develop specialized methods to obtain oxygen from the air, rather than the water. Catfish and loaches are able to take gulps of air from the surface, from which they slowly absorb oxygen into the blood.

This is a minor adaptation, however, compared to the method that gouramis use to obtain oxygen. Gouramis are part of the Anabantoid family of fish, which all possess an additional organ, the labyrinth organ, so called because of its mazelike appearance. These fish also take gulps of air from the surface, but can absorb oxygen much more quickly and efficiently. The labyrinth organ provides a membrane with a massive surface area through which oxygen can travel into the bloodstream.

TOUCH AND TASTE

Catfish and loaches can be found throughout the swamps. The highly fertile substrate is home to many small organisms that feed off the organic debris and provide a welcome food source for the fishes. Bottom-dwellers rarely use sight to locate their food; in the murky, shaded swamps, even excellent eyesight would be of little benefit. Instead, the catfish and loaches

use specially adapted barbels or "feelers" to touch and taste their way around the substrate, finding food as they go. The pectoral fins of gouramis have also adapted into sensitive feelers, which are used by the fish to touch their way around the environment and to recognize other fishes and food. In the aquarium, gouramis can often be observed "testing" objects, such as other fish and food, with these highly sensitive feelers.

Bottom-dwellers, which spend much of their time hidden away from other fishes and predators, also use their sense of smell to locate prey from a distance. In the aquarium, these fish can sometimes be quite shy and timid, often the result of being kept in a bright, open environment. Given plenty of hiding spots and dark areas to retreat to, they become more outgoing.

CREATING A SWAMP AQUARIUM

Fish are a vital part of any display, but in this case, more effort and equipment may be required to support the large number of plants in the aquarium. However, if a thriving population of plants can be established, the conditions created as a result of

Below: The long pectoral fin extensions help the gold gourami (Trichogaster trichopterus) to feel around its environment, and the upturned mouth allows it to pick insects from the surface.

their biological processes, plus the addition of carbon dioxide, will be more than suited to the fish found in the natural environment. Because plants dominate the display, other items of decor are less important, although a few rocks and wood will break up the display. However, bamboo is an important aspect of the design, and helps both to separate and enhance the appearance of the plants. The bamboo also helps to create the feel of the Southeast Asian swamp in the aquarium.

SUBSTRATE
In this aquarium, silver sand is the main substrate, along with a sprinkling of pea gravel and small pebbles for added interest. Silver sand is a reasonably good planting medium, but it can compact and may not distribute nutrients effectively. If the plants are growing well, they should prevent the sand from stagnating by releasing oxygen from the roots.

Bamboo canes add a distinctive character to the overall display and help create the swamplike environment.

A heating cable will also help to prevent stagnation and distribute nutrients (see page 29). An alternative, and preferable, rooting medium can be created by mixing or layering substrates. A typical mix would be a layer of silver sand, preferably around a heating cable, followed by a fine lime-free substrate mixed with, or containing, a layer of nutrient-rich substrate additive.

ROCKS AND WOOD
Although rocks and wood are important ingredients of this display, they should be used in small quantities. A few well-placed rocks with a solid, bold appearance, such as slate, can be used as a backdrop to the foreground plants, separating them from taller, but similarly colored, background species. Driftwood can be used in a similar way, and it is often highly effective to use smaller, bushy plants to hide all but the upper parts of large pieces.

The strong presence of bamboo cane in this aquascape distinguishes it from just a heavily planted display. Cut the cane into varying lengths and place them randomly among the plants. Use some pieces singly and others in groups. Over time, the cane will begin to rot, turning a slightly dark brown color. To prevent this, treat the

Ludwigia repens alters its growth pattern depending on lighting conditions. In bright light, its leaves grow closer together and turn an attractive bronze-red color.

bamboo with a clear polyurethane varnish before use. However, it may be just as easy and inexpensive to replace the cane every few months. Bamboo cane can also be very buoyant and will need to be firmly wedged in the substrate. Alternatively, silicone small pebbles to the base of the bamboo.

THE PLANTS
The most important aspect of this aquarium is the large number of plants used to recreate the swamp environment. A number of bushy plants, some with a messy appearance, represent the random nature of the swamp's vegetative growth. Bushy plants, such as stargrass (*Heteranthera zosterifolia*), are ideal for

The feathery leaves of this Myriophyllum *species add a contrasting texture to the aquarium's background.*

the middle to foreground area and can be trimmed to varying lengths. Taller, unusual plants, such as *Hydrocotyle* spp., can also occupy the midground area. This plant, in particular, has an unusual round leaf shape, supported by a stem that often sprouts in random directions and produces roots from the leaf base.

169

Taller stem plants work well toward the background, including bushy, fine-leaved plants such as *Cabomba* and *Myriophyllum* spp. A few floating plants add to the effect. The water lettuce (*Pistia stratiotes*) used in this display produces fine, feathery roots that are ideal hiding spots for some fish, and may even make potential breeding sites for some anabantoid species.

FISHES FOR A SWAMP AQUARIUM
A number of popular aquarium fish originate from the Southeast Asian swamps, including many gouramis, catfish, loaches, barbs, and rasboras. The gouramis, in particular, are ideally suited to this display and will appreciate the crowded and densely planted aquarium. Unlike other large midwater or surface-dwelling fish, the slow-moving gouramis prefer a crowded environment because it resembles their natural environment. Hardy midwater to surface-dwelling species include the pearl gourami (*Trichogaster leeri*), moonlight gourami (*Trichogaster microlepis*), and snakeskin gourami (*Trichogaster pectoralis*), which all grow to about 10cm (4in), and the smaller pygmy gourami (*Trichopsis pumilus*) and croaking gourami (*Trichopsis vittatus*). Large gouramis include the gold, opaline, and three-spot, which are all varieties of *Trichogaster trichopterus*. These popular gouramis must be kept in groups of four, five, or more, or should all be females, otherwise a dominant male may emerge and become a "bully" fish.

Another popular anabantoid is the beautiful Siamese fighting fish (*Betta splendens*). This amazingly colored fish with long flowing fins is often sought after by new and inexperienced aquarists, although it is unsuitable for many aquariums. Its long fins, slow movement, and bright colors make it an easy target for fin-nipping or aggressive fish. However, the Siamese fighter is a very peaceful fish, except where two males are concerned, and these should never be kept together. If two males find each other they will fight constantly, often until one is dead or dying. However, providing no nippy barbs, such as the tiger barb (*Puntius tetrazona*), are included in the tank, this style of aquarium is the ideal environment for a male Siamese fighter, possibly along with a few females. Unfortunately, they do not sport the same stunning finnage color.

The chocolate gourami (*Sphaerichthys osphromenoides*) and dwarf gourami (*Colisa lalia*) are two more attractive anabantoids that will occupy the lower areas of the aquarium. Both are sensitive to biological pollutants including ammonia, nitrites, and nitrates, so good filtration and maintenance are essential.

BOTTOM-DWELLERS AND SHOALING FISH
Several loaches are ideal for the lower reaches of the aquarium. Two particularly interesting fish with similar colors, but otherwise very different appearances, are the kuhli loach (*Pangio kuhlii*) and the clown loach (*Botia macracanthus*). The small kuhli loach will spend most of its time in hiding; many aquarists add them to the tank, only to find that they disappear for weeks or even months. In a planted aquarium such as this, they may be seen only occasionally when they emerge to feed on a sinking pellet or when excited by the smell of other foods. However, the kuhli loach is an interesting fish and well suited to this display, if only so the fishkeeper can play the odd game of "spot the kuhli loaches."

The open-water areas can be populated by a few shoals of small, peaceful rasboras, including the harlequin (*Rasbora heteromorpha*), slender harlequin (*Rasbora hengeli*), and the pygmy rasbora (*Rasbora maculata*), also called the dwarf or spotted rasbora. All these small fish have attractive coloration and a peaceful nature, although when young, they should not be mixed with the larger gouramis, for whom they will soon become a welcome meal.

Right: The strikingly patterned kuhli loach (Pangio kuhlii) *will disturb the substrate while searching for food. Although it is often hidden from view, its activity helps to reduce algae and remove waste matter.*

*Above: Small
shoaling fish are
ideal for this heavily
planted display. These
harlequin rasboras
(Rasbora
heteromorpha) add
movement, and
complement larger,
slow-moving fish,
such as the gouramis.*

Southeast Asian swamp aquarium

Bushy plants and bamboo combine with partially hidden rocks and wood to create a packed display representative of a Southeast Asian swamp.

Place feathery leaved plants, such as this **Cabomba** *species, in areas of gentle water flow to prevent clogging from debris.*

A few shorter plants with large leaves cover areas of substrate, but leave open swimming space above.

Rocks can be used to divide planting areas and help define individual groups of plants.

"Messy" plants, such as this Hydrocotyle *sp. help to create a less formal and more natural swamplike display.*

This piece of driftwood is placed vertically, as though it were an old tree stump.

Myriophyllum *will turn an attractive reddish color under bright lighting.*

Floating plants provide cover for surface-dwellers and create variations in the aquarium lighting.

Bamboo canes are placed in a random fashion to create a more natural appearance.

Bushy plants, such as this Heteranthera zosterifolia, *can be trimmed to different lengths.*

Silver sand is aesthetically pleasing, although a mixture of substrates may be preferable to provide nutrients for the plants.

Indian river

Geographically, India is an interesting continent, with a wide range of environmental habitats. In northern areas, the mighty Himalayan mountains provide a mass of meltwater that forms the beginning of many streams and rivers. Elsewhere, there are deciduous forests, dry deserts, and evergreen rain forests, as well as a number of brackish environments around the vast coastline. The fast-flowing streams and small rivers in the mountainous areas are home to numerous smaller barbs, danios, and loaches. In forested regions, anabantoid fishes live in the many pools, swamps, and slow-moving streams, as well as in a number of manmade pools. In the open and often dry areas, larger rivers carve through the dusty landscape. They contain considerable amounts of sand, dust, and sediment and often appear brown and muddy, but beneath the surface is a wealth of larger barbs and catfish. Eventually, when the rivers reach the sea, the extended coastline provides a number of brackish habitats for pufferfish, gobies, and perches.

THE UPPER REACHES

Toward the source of the river, the water is fast flowing and periodically tumbles over long and rocky rapids. The size and height of the river depends on the time of year; in rainy seasons and in spring, when meltwater flows into the rivers, the waters are high. During this period, the water is highly turbulent and well oxygenated. The fishes in the upper reaches are normally smaller species of loach, barbs, and danios. Many of the loaches are not common aquarium fish, mainly due to their often subdued, mottled-brown coloration. They are algae-eaters whose specially adapted mouths enable them not only to graze algae, but also to keep a firm grip on the rocks against the powerful flow of water. Smaller barbs occupy calmer, yet still fast-flowing,

Indian river habitats

The Himalayan mountains provide a constant influx of water that soon collects to form large rivers throughout India.

The Indian landscape is covered with many rivers, canals, and marshlands that provide habitats suited to a wide range of fishes.

In India, a number of freshwater habitats combine. A typical river may pass through fast-flowing rapids to open, calmer waters and eventually estuaries and brackish habitats before it reaches the oceans. The fish in these rivers are similar to those found in nearby Indonesian habitats. Gouramis and barbs are the most notable aquarium fish, but many species of loach, catfish, and more unusual brackish fish are also abundant. India offers some interesting habitats to recreate in the aquarium.

Above: Some rivers are affected by major annual rainfall changes. In this section of the Ramganga River, the larger riverbed is visible around the central flow of water.

Below: Danios are common in many Indian rivers and are accustomed to the cooler conditions found at high altitudes or in rivers formed by meltwater.

pockets of water and small pools that often form beneath or around waterfalls. Groups of shoaling barbs search incessantly for food items such as insects and small aquatic animals. Common species, such as the rosy barb (*Puntius conchonius*) and melon barb (*P. fasciatus*), are abundant in these types of habitats.

Danios are found in the same waters as the barbs and loaches. These small fish are highly adapted to make quick darting movements and to swim continually against the flow of water. Their streamlined, torpedo-shaped bodies help to minimize drag, while short, powerful fins enable the fish to move rapidly between different areas, minimizing the energy needed to swim against the current. The danios also have an upturned mouth for picking insects at the surface – their main diet.

THE OPEN RIVER

Once a few mountain streams or small highland rivers combine, they form a larger central river that travels either through rain forest, deciduous forest, or more open desert or savannah landscapes. In many cases, a river will pass through more than one of these environments. Catfish and barbs are found in these rivers, as well as some smaller fish along the riverbanks. Predators are common in the open river and some, including many catfish, can grow to massive proportions. Even species too large for most aquariums, such as the Indian tiger shark (*Pangasius pangasius*), which grows up to 150cm (60in), are dwarfed by the real giants, including the killer catfish (*Wallago attu*) and the giant river catfish (*Bagarius yarelli*), both of which will grow to over 2.5m (8ft). These catfish patrol the open waters and the lower areas near the substrate searching, or more often, waiting, for prey to arrive. As well as the catfish, the open waters are home to larger species of trout and barb, while smaller barbs and rasboras hide in the relative safety of the riverbank vegetation.

POOLS AND SWAMPS.
In the forested regions there are many large swamp areas, pools and small waterways. Some of these may be connected to a nearby river, while others are self-contained. Many of the most colorful Indian species, and consequently, a majority of the fishes suitable, and sold for, aquariums are found in these scattered habitats. The most notable are the gouramis, or anabantoids. They are small (10cm/4in) and many, such as the popular *Colisa* species, sport beautiful coloration. These include the dwarf gourami (*Colisa lalia*), honey gourami (*C. sota*), and banded gourami (*C. labiosa*).

Smaller catfish and loaches are found toward the bottom of the pools and swamps. They include common aquarium species, such as the pyjama catfish (*Mystus vittatus*), Pakistani loach (*Botia lohachata*), striped loach (*B. striata*), and chain loach (*B. sidthimunki*). The loaches are scavengers, searching the muddy substrate for the many small aquatic animals that lurk there and feeding off the fertile, organically rich substrate. Some smaller barbs and

rasboras also live in these waters, although very few are common aquarium fish or of particular interest.

AN INDIAN RIVER AQUARIUM
Any of the distinct habitats of the region could form the basis of an Indian river aquarium. Sizeable aquariums representing the open river could be stocked with larger barbs and catfish. However, this type of display is relatively barren and the fish would be the main objects of interest, since they quickly destroy any delicate planting or carefully positioned decor. Brackish and swamp areas make a good basis for a well-aquascaped aquarium, although they would resemble the mangrove or brackish and Southeast Asian designs. This display represents the calmer riverbank and stream areas, a unique design suited to the popular gouramis, smaller barbs, loaches and rasboras.

SUBSTRATE
A mixture of substrates is used in this aquarium, including a main substrate of lime-free quartz gravel and medium-grade pea gravel, plus a sprinkling of red chippings and black quartz. This mixture, combined with a number of small pebbles, creates a varied and interesting substrate that is also a good planting medium. The substrate also resembles the mixed sand and gravel substrates found in streams and riverbanks near or in many larger Indian rivers.

DRIFTWOOD
Twisted roots and mopani driftwood are both included in this display. Since they are almost identical in color and texture, they can be used together in the same aquarium without creating an

Lime-free gravel is the main substrate and a good planting medium.

Black quartz darkens the overall substrate.

Mixed-grade pea gravel creates a realistic "riverbed."

Red chippings add a little color and texture.

unwanted contrast. The mopani wood is used as a backdrop and a divider between the two groups of tiger lotus plants, which are different varieties. The wood also has a few small cracks and crevices into which a number of small, green-leaved cryptocorynes can be placed. Planting in this way partially hides the driftwood and creates a more natural setting, where plants would naturally root in microhabitats, shielded and sheltered by larger objects. The twisted root fills the upper areas of one end of the aquarium and also forms a planting "scaffold" for Java moss and tiger lotus leaves that grow up around it. This piece of twisted root creates an area of vegetation that extends upward to the surface and is the main focal point of the aquarium.

Choose unusually shaped twisted roots.

THE PLANTS

Many biotope aquariums benefit from having only a few varieties of plant, rather than a jumbled mass of individual species. In this display, there are only three types of plant. Along the substrate floor underneath the twisted root, a dense planting of *Cryptocoryne undulata* creates a bushy area with ideal hiding spots for smaller loaches and catfish. The green area created by the numerous leaves of the cryptocoryne contrasts well with the bright red-orange leaves of the red tiger lotus (*Nymphaea lotus* 'Zenkeri') at the opposite end of the aquarium. There are two color types of the red tiger lotus in this display; the "traditional" bright red-leaved plant is used toward the back, with a more subdued orange-brown variety toward the foreground and among the twisted root. The subdued variety helps to blend in the brighter one with the rest of the aquarium. Without it, the brighter plant may contrast a little too strongly and appear out of place.

The tiger lotus is an interesting plant and easy to keep if it is provided with a good substrate combined with reasonable lighting and nutrients. However, it will need room to grow and can become quite tall. In most cases, the leaves will reach the surface although this can be prevented with regular pruning. In this aquarium, the area containing the majority of the tiger lotus has a large open space at the surface for the plant to grow into. The plants in the area underneath are suited to shady conditions, so they will not be starved of light as the tiger lotus grows.

Finally, Java moss (*Vesicularia dubyana*) is planted among the driftwood pieces and along the twisted root. This hardy plant attaches itself to solid objects rather

Above: *The tiger lotus* (Nymphaea lotus) *is available in various different leaf colors and makes an interesting specimen plant.*

than rooting in the substrate, and does well in most aquariums where liquid fertilizers are used regularly. When first planted in the aquarium, Java moss can appear quite messy, but this often creates a more natural and effective display. However, if you prefer to keep it short and tidy, allow it to grow for a month or two, so that portions can become attached to the wood and then trim it down to just a few centimeters.

Cryptocoryne undulata *has contrasting brown stems and green leaves that look effective when planted in groups.*

177

CHOOSING FISHES

The smaller fishes, such as the danios and gouramis, are ideal for this style of aquarium. You could also add some smaller loaches or even catfish. Since gouramis are slow moving and timid, mix them with only a few of the fast-swimming, active danios. A large shoal of danios (more than eight) may cause undue stress to the calmer gouramis, so a group of four to six is preferable. Although the majority of loaches are peaceful species and can be kept either singly or in groups, some, such as the Pakistani loach *(Botia lohachata)*, may occasionally harass slow-moving fishes, including gouramis.

BARBS AND DANIOS

Although barbs have a reputation for fin-nipping, this is only true of a small number of species, and often only when shoaling barbs are kept in small numbers. However, most barbs that grow to more than 5-6cm (2-2.4in) are active and boisterous, so would not make suitable companions for small, timid gouramis in the aquarium.

Some of the barbs native to Indian regions are brightly colored or patterned, make excellent aquarium fish and can be safely mixed with catfish, loaches, and danios. The rosy barb *(Puntius conchonius)* is an ideal aquarium fish and mature males will exhibit a stunning deep red color, often with black tips to the fins. Another colorful barb, the longfin or arulius barb *(Puntius arulius)*, will grow long, trailing finnage and develop an iridescent mix of colors, although the full color appears only as the fish ages. The melon barb *(Puntius fasciatus)*, filament barb *(Puntius filamentosus)*, and Odessa barb *(Puntius ticto)* are also suitable Indian barbs for this aquarium. They will all grow to about 10-15cm (4-6in) in length.

GOURAMIS

The cover provided by the tiger lotus leaves and the hiding places among the twisted roots and vegetation make this display an ideal environment for the timid and slow-moving yet beautiful gouramis. In fact, there is only one true gourami, the giant gourami *(Osphronemus gorami)*, also a native Indian species. However, as this fish can grow to over 60cm (24in), it is suitable for only the largest aquariums. Of the anabantoids commonly labeled as gouramis, the banded gourami *(Colisa labiosa)*, honey gourami *(C. sota)*, dwarf gourami *(C. lalia)*, and croaking gourami *(Trichopsis vittatus)* are all peaceful species native to Indian waters. The honey, dwarf, and croaking gouramis will grow no bigger than 6-8cm (2.4-3.2in), while the banded gourami will reach up to 10cm (4in).

Many of the nonnative gouramis, including the moonlight gourami *(Trichogaster microlepis)*, pearl gourami *(T. leeri)*, and chocolate gourami *(Sphaerichthys osphromenoides)* would also make ideal fish for this aquarium display.

Above: The peaceful honey gourami (Colisa sota) *will grow to only about 5-6cm (2-2.4in). In this aquarium, the hiding spots provided by dense vegetation will give these timid fishes more confidence. The fish shown here is a color variation often called "sunset."*

The dwarf gourami (Colisa lalia) *is a stunning metallic red and blue color.*

LOACHES AND OTHER SPECIES

The lower reaches of the aquarium can be inhabited by a number of loaches that will appreciate hiding spots under pieces of wood or among dense planting. Common Indian loaches include the Pakistani loach (*Botia lohachata*), striped loach (*B. striata*), chain loach (*B. sidthimunki*), and the Indian kuhli loach, often called the black kuhli loach (*Pangio* sp.). There are many colorful loach species in Indian waters, but these are rarely seen in the aquarium trade. Some are similar in shape, size, and appearance to the flying fox (*Epalzeorhynchos siamensis*) or Siamese flying fox (*Crossocheilus siamensis*) and the kuhli loach (*Pangio kuhlii*), which could also be included.

Of the catfish found in Indian waters, the pyjama catfish (*Mystus vittatus*) is the only commonly available species that will not grow too large (15cm/6in). This attractive and relatively peaceful fish can be kept with most other fishes. A final, and very interesting, fish suited to the aquarium is the black knifefish (*Notopterus notopterus*). It has an unusual "butter knife" shape and interesting behavioral habits that make it an excellent specimen fish. The black knifefish is peaceful and will mix well with gouramis although it can reach up to 25cm (10in) and will eat small fish.

Above: The mazelike patterning of Botia lohachata *helps to camouflage the fish against the riverbed substrate. This active scavenger may hassle other fish.*

Below: The graceful knifefish (Notopterus chitala) *is a slow-moving but fascinating species that makes a good tankmate for larger gouramis.*

Indian river aquarium

The mix of cryptocorynes, Java moss, and the stunning tiger lotus combine to create a display that is complex yet not overcrowded.

Java moss (Vesicularia dubyana) *will spread along the wood and can be trimmed or left to spread naturally.*

Attach plants to the *driftwood using black cotton; it will be "invisible."*

A dense patch of cryptocorynes creates ideal hiding spots for loaches.

These twisted roots are a major feature of the display.

The mixed substrates create a more realistic "riverbed" than using a single substrate.

This open space provides swimming room for more active fishes, such as barbs and danios.

The leaves of the red tiger lotus (Nymphaea lotus 'Zenkeri') make a big impact in the display.

To prevent the tiger lotus from growing too large, remove tall leaves periodically.

A few small pebbles and larger cobbles complete the riverbed substrate.

This raised area allows shorter plants, such as these cryptocorynes, to be placed in the background.

Brackish estuary

A typical estuary can stretch for many miles, varying in salinity along its length. In massive river systems, such as the Amazon River, the estuarine area continues for hundreds of miles upstream and for a great distance into the ocean. The amount of salt in any particular body of water (salinity) depends on a number of factors. The salinity rises as water reaches the ocean, but also varies according to the depth and height of the tides. Because salt water contains dissolved salts, it is heavier than fresh water, which contains few salts. As fresh water from the river reaches the salt water of the oceans, it does not mix immediately, but actually "floats" on top of the heavier salt water. In deep estuaries, the water at the surface may have a very low salt content, while toward the substrate it is almost as salty as the ocean.

Most estuarine areas are flat and therefore affected by the rising and falling tides. As the tide rises, salt water from the oceans travels upstream, often for a some distance. When the tides fall, the salt water recedes and fresh water from the river continues down toward the sea. The tidal fluctuations create large mudflats, home to many fish and animals that live in the daily rise and fall of the tides.

A FINE BALANCE
The majority of fish species are physically adapted to cope with either fresh water or salt water, and although a very slight increase or decrease in salt content would not affect them, they

SPECIFIC GRAVITY

Salt levels can be measured as "specific gravity," which is the ratio of the density of a liquid compared to that of distilled water. The higher the density and level of minerals and trace elements, the higher the specific gravity (S.G.). Pure water has a specific gravity of 1, while seawater is normally about 1.022-1.024.

Brackish habitats

Small islands have a large coastline and small rivers, so brackish habitats are smaller but more numerous. Lowland areas often produce brackish lagoons.

Larger land masses have the same small brackish habitats, as well as estuaries in larger river systems.

Every stream and river must reach a final destination, and for most it is the vast expanse of the ocean. The meeting of these two bodies of water is rarely a sudden event and fresh and salt water will mix for some distance, often fluctuating upstream with the tides. In this area – the estuary – the habitat is constantly changing and houses its own unique group of underwater creatures, including many popular fish species.

Above: The shark catfish (Arius seemanni) *uses its sensitive barbels to search through the muddy substrate for items of food.*

salinity changes using both the freshwater fishes' methods of retaining salts and the marine fishes' methods of excreting them. Although this causes the fishes to expend more energy maintaining their osmotic balance, their reward is the ability to inhabit an area of water that is rich in food sources, but relatively uninhabitable by other fish species.

LIFE IN THE MUD

Most estuarine areas have a high organic load and are a rich source of food for many creatures. All the nutrients, organics, silt, and debris picked up by the river is collected in the estuarine areas and deposited in the deep, muddy substrate. This buildup of nutrient-rich sediment is home to vast numbers of detritus-feeders and filter-feeders. The deep mud harbors a wealth of small worms, amphipods, and invertebrates, as well as larger creatures, such as mussels, crabs, shrimp, and some sponges and anemones.

Toward the sea, where tidal influences raise and lower the water level on a daily basis, many of these substrate-dwelling creatures will spend half their time hidden in the mud, while the water above them disappears. When the mudflats are exposed to the open air, masses of birds descend to search for the small worms, crustaceans,

Above: As silt and sediment are deposited by a river toward the ocean, a large area of land is created where brackish lagoons and pools are found. The silt and sediment provide food for birds and aquatic creatures.

certainly would not appreciate a major change. A significant increase in salt content would cause a freshwater fish to take in far too many salts through its gill membranes, upsetting its osmotic balance (concentration of salts in the body fluids). The kidneys, which normally retain salts, would become saturated with them and the fish would die from kidney failure.

Marine fish would suffer a different fate if placed in fresh water. They would be unable to retain the salts already present in the body and would absorb large amounts of fresh water, possibly dying from a buildup of fluid in the body. In most cases, the stress alone would kill the fish before any physical problems developed.

Interestingly, fish that live in estuarine habitats are adapted to changes in salinity. Some can cope with the daily change from fresh to salt water, while others will "follow" the moving water to stay in areas of similar salinity. The fish have adapted to and invertebrates in the mud. When the tide rises again, these creatures emerge from the mud and begin to feed on microscopic bacteria and organisms, both in the substrate and floating by in the open water. For the scavenging fish that inhabit the brackish estuaries, these substrate-dwelling creatures are an abundant source of food that make the harsh and changing conditions a worthwhile inconvenience.

TWO COMMUNITIES

Because salt water is heavier than fresh water, when the tides are high, the water toward the substrate is salty for a great distance into the river. The deep saltwater area enables many marine substrate-dwelling fish, such as gobies and blennies, to travel upstream and search for items of food in the muddy substrate. As the tides recede, these fish journey back toward the ocean.

Not many plants survive brackish water. Vallisneria spp. are hardy and resembles the reeds found in estuaries.

Surface-dwelling fish from the rivers also follow the tides, seeking out areas of low salinity at the surface. The moving divide between fresh and salt water thus allows species from both the river and the sea to inhabit the same stretches of water. Although the brackish fish found in these areas can tolerate a wide range of changing conditions and salinities, most will try to follow the movement of water and stick to areas of the same salinity. By doing this, they can adapt to salinity levels that do not change to a significant degree, thereby

The sandy texture and color of these Westmorland rocks fit in well with the similar tones of the substrate and mopani wood.

creating less stress on their bodies. Most brackish fish will have a "preferred" range of salinity, although some, such as the popular molly (*Poecilia* spp.) are quite at home in either extreme of salinity.

NOT FOR PLANTS

Despite the nutrient-rich sediment in the estuary, plants do not grow in abundance in the brackish waters. Plants are normally unable to adapt to changing salinities, and freshwater species have virtually no control over the absorbtion of salts and minerals from the surrounding water. Most freshwater plants would therefore not survive in brackish waters for long enough periods to grow and reproduce. A

number of marine algae and some seaweeds can cope with the changing conditions, although the moving substrate makes it hard for this type of vegetation to grow.

In many rivers with muddy substrates, it is the plants that keep the substrate in place, since it is their complex root systems acting as "bolsters" that prevent the substrate from moving. These roots are not present in the estuaries, and the constant water movement caused by tidal and river influences disturbs the fine substrate, creating muddy water and very low visibility.

AN ESTUARINE AQUARIUM

An aquarium design truly representative of a brackish estuary would be relatively unattractive to many aquarists, as it would contain little else but mud and the odd rock. However, for aesthetic purposes, you could draw together the various elements found in brackish areas, along with some hardy plants, to create an interesting display, well suited to brackish estuarine fishes. The large majority of suitable brackish aquarium fish are freshwater species that prefer a slight salt content rather than the marine species that travel upriver. For practical purposes, a brackish estuarine aquarium would have only a low salt content.

SUBSTRATE

A muddy substrate in the aquarium would present many problems, so it is best to choose an alternative material. In this aquarium, silver sand is the main substrate, with a sprinkling of pea gravel to add extra interest. Different effects can be achieved by scattering additional substrates on top or mixing them in with the silver sand. Fine, darker gravels, such as black quartz, create an impression of debris and are closer in color to the natural muddy substrate. A similar, and perhaps more realistic, effect can be created by mixing black sand in with the silver sand, although black sand is sometimes hard to obtain.

Whichever substrate mix you combine with the silver sand, it must be regularly disturbed to prevent compaction. If the fine silver sand is allowed to compact, then anaerobic patches (areas with a very low oxygen content) will be created in the bed. This may cause stagnation and the release of dangerous gases. The sand turns black and algae may grow on the substrate surface. Compaction and algae growth can be easily prevented by gently disturbing and stirring the substrate on a regular basis. Ideally, you should do this at least two or three times a week.

ROCKS AND WOOD
Because the aquarium water is brackish, meaning that it contains a fair amount of salts, the hardness and pH levels will be naturally high. This

This smooth, two-toned wood appears weathered and twisted. Small catfish and gobies will hide beneath it.

means that calcareous rocks, which would normally be unsuitable for a freshwater aquarium, can be used in this display. In fact, calcareous rocks would be a benefit, because they release minerals that will "buffer" the pH level and stabilize water quality. Chalk, limestone, marble, ocean rock, and tufa are all calcareous rocks that can be used to buffer the water.

This aquarium features some pieces of Westmorland rock, because its color is close to that of the sandy substrate. Keeping to the yellow-brown color throughout the aquarium – in the substrate, rocks, and wood – gives the display a unique visual feel. The driftwood is a precleaned and smoothed variety, often called "mopani," and is a lighter color than many other woods, so it matches the substrate and rocks. The rocks and wood in this aquarium are used across the entire length of the tank to create a partial background for the fish and plants. It also imitates the river or estuary bank and provides plenty of hiding spots for the fishes.

THE PLANTS
As we have seen, the brackish water of this aquarium is not ideally suited to aquarium plants and many would not survive under these conditions. However, some species are relatively hardy and can adapt to low-salinity conditions. How well the plants cope may be largely a matter of "trial and error," as some will do better than others. Suitable species include *Microsorium*, *Vallisneria*, *Anubias*, *Egeria*, and some *Sagittaria* and *Hygrophila* species. In this aquarium, *Vallisneria* is used as a background plant, while Java fern (*Microsorium pteropus*) and dwarf anubias (*Anubias barteri* var. *nana*) are planted on the wood

Many rock-dwelling plants, such as this Java fern, are used to harsh environments and should adapt to slightly brackish water.

CREATING A HIGH-SALINITY DISPLAY

This aquarium is largely based on a low-salinity environment and contains fishes that often inhabit river areas and freshwater plant species. A different style of aquarium could also be created based on a high-salinity environment. It could include some of the same fishes, along with a few marine species and marine algae, such as the commonly available Caulerpa *spp. This attractive algae has a highly developed structure and looks more like a typical plant than an algae. A high-salinity aquarium also allows you to add some anemone species and marine gobies and blennies.*

It may be difficult to obtain fishes and invertebrates suited to a brackish aquarium, and a little extra research may be required. Generally speaking, most of the marine fishes and invertebrates commonly found in rockpool environments are suited to slightly lower-salinity environments. In rockpool conditions, salinity often fluctuates, either as a result of evaporation or rainfall, and the fish that inhabit these areas are hardy and adaptable enough to thrive in the aquarium environment.

185

as midground plants. Using the wood as a planting medium will help to reduce the stark appearance of larger pieces of wood and rock.

Bear in mind that many common brackish fish, especially the scats and monos, are highly herbivorous and if included in the display, may quickly destroy certain plant species. Tougher plants, such as the *Anubias* and *Microsorium* species in this aquarium, should be unattractive enough to these herbivorous fish to avoid being eaten.

BRACKISH FISHES

Many of the brackish water fishes suitable for the aquarium are some of the hardiest and most visually interesting aquarium fish available. Aquarists often avoid keeping brackish water fish, assuming that they may be difficult or demanding, but in many cases the opposite is true. Because these fish have to adapt to daily changes in water conditions, not only in terms of temperature and salinity, but also hardness and pH levels, they are actually extremely robust. Added to this is the fact that some common disease organisms find it hard to survive in brackish water. Brackish fish therefore are an ideal challenge for fishkeepers of any experience level and offer an unusual and interesting alternative to standard tropical fish.

Introducing brackish fish to the aquarium should be done with care. Although they can withstand salinity fluctuations, sudden changes will be stressful and damaging to them. The salinity of the water in which the fish are kept before you buy them may be quite different to the level in your brackish aquarium. While many retailers keep the fish in brackish water, it is not uncommon to find them in fresh water. A good method is to set up your aquarium with the same water conditions as the fish are housed in at your retailer. Once the aquarium is fully stocked, gradually alter the salinity to a more suitable level.

SUBSTRATE-DWELLERS

For the lower portions of the aquarium, there are a few catfish and goby species suited to brackish waters. The shark catfish (*Arius seemanni*) is an active species with a striking silver body color and finnage. Since these catfish can grow up to 30cm (12in), provide a large aquarium. Similar-looking *Arius* species can grow even bigger and are also often sold as shark catfish.

A popular goby species for this display, the knight goby (*Stigmatogobius sadanundio*), is a peaceful fish, although some males may become territorial. The knight goby will grow to about 8-10cm (3.2-4in) and its unusual behavior and swimming motions make it a good addition to any aquarium. A smaller, but equally popular, goby species is the bumblebee goby (*Brachygobius doriae*). This tiny fish (up to 5cm/2in) has bright yellow stripes that contrast with an almost black body. Although popular and peaceful, the bumblebee goby should be kept only with other small fish, otherwise it will soon become food for larger species.

SMALL MIDWATER AND SURFACE-SWIMMING FISH

Many livebearers and rainbowfish species are suited to slightly brackish environments. The livebearers are of particular interest and include suitable fish such as the sailfin molly (*Poecilia velifera*) and the halfbeak (*Dermogenys pusillus*). Some ambassids are brackish, although only one species, the Indian glassfish (*Chanda ranga*), is regularly

Left: *The attractive plant-eating scat* (Scatophagus argus) *is a dominant fish that may be aggressive toward its own kind. If kept in groups of at least four or five with larger or medium-sized fishes, their aggression is diminished.*

available. The glassfish, so called because of its virtually "see-through" body, is an interesting aquarium subject, but always keep it in large groups to prevent aggressive individuals from bullying others.

LARGER MIDWATER AND SURFACE-SWIMMING FISH

For the larger aquarium, there are some interesting brackish fish that reach a considerable, although not massive, size. The best-known brackish fish are the monos (*Monodactylis* spp.) and scats (*Scatophagus* spp.). Different color varieties of these fish are available and most species will grow to about 15cm (6in). Although they can become territorial and aggressive, serious problems can be avoided if they are kept in groups of about six fish. Other moderately sized fish include the orange chromide (*Etroplus maculatus*), a relatively peaceful cichlid that is also available in a silver variety, and the highly unusual pufferfish group of fish. The pufferfish, so called because they are able to inflate their bodies to

scare off predators, can become quite tame in the aquarium. Be sure to offer them occasional feeds of items such as cockles, so they can wear down their continually growing sharp teeth by grinding the shells. The sharp teeth are developed exclusively for the purpose of breaking crustacean shells, often found in the muddy estuarine substrate, to obtain food. A good pufferfish for the aquarium is the figure-eight puffer (*Tetraodon biocellus*), so called because of an attractive green figure-eight pattern on its back.

Above: The halfbeak (Dermogenys pusillus) *has an extended lower jaw that makes surface feeding easy. Position plants around the edges of the aquarium so that if it becomes stressed, the fish cannot swim into the glass and damage its jaw.*

Below: The tiny bumblebee goby (Brachygobius doriae) *will spend much of its time resting on the substrate floor, but is nevertheless an ideal addition to a brackish community of smaller fishes.*

Brackish estuary aquarium

The sandy yellow-brown colors and textures provided by the substrate, wood, and rocks give this display a distinctive style.

Large, bold items of wood and rock decor are used to create a central feature along the whole display.

Wood is a useful planting medium for species such as Java fern and anubias.

This thick-leaved Vallisneria sp. can represent the reeds found in estuarine waters.

Westmorland rock has an unusual color and texture that are well suited to this display.

A sprinkling of pea gravel creates a more interesting texture to the substrate.

Groups of vallisneria are prominent in this display.

Driftwood may soften the water, so adding a pH buffer or making regular water changes may be beneficial.

Filters and heaters can be partially hidden by careful positioning of plants and decor.

The smoothed mopani wood has a pale top surface that fits in with the other decor, while the dark underside provides hiding spots for fishes.

A few empty shells in the substrate add a "marine" feel.

Many larger brackish fish will eat most plants but they find Java fern distasteful.

189

Mangrove swamp

The mangrove trees, which grow in a number of brackish water areas throughout the tropics, form a "framework" that creates a unique habitat on which many of its inhabitants depend. In the larger estuarine brackish waters, the flow of the sea and large volume of river water constantly disturb the substrate, creating a large muddy, low-visibility habitat. However, the mangroves are found either further inland or in areas where the water volume of the river is spread over a large area. The waters still rise and fall with the tide, but the overall environment is much calmer and the mangrove tree roots help to keep the sandy substrate in place. In most mangrove swamps, the water is calm and clear, yet the substrate is still highly fertile and full of the same animals found in the estuarine environment.

The mangrove tree, of which there are several species, is a highly adapted plant, well able to cope with the saline water in which many plants would perish. The mangroves have a number of specialized methods to prevent the uptake of salts, or to remove them from their vascular systems. Most mangroves are able to filter out more than 90% of the water's salt content before it enters the roots. The rest is either excreted through special glands in the leaves or concentrated in old leaves or bark, which then fall from the plant.

Despite the relative calm of the mangrove swamps, a daily rise and fall of water with the tides constantly moves the sandbanks in which the trees root. However, a complex and unique root structure enables the mangrove tree to cope with these shifting sands. To keep themselves firmly in place, the mangroves produce a number of long, thick and twisting roots, which are visible above the sands. The deeper roots beneath the sand are exposed to stagnant, low-oxygen conditions and are used only for support. The nutrient-collecting element of the root system appears above the substrate as smaller roots that branch off the main root. This complex root system allows the mangrove tree to stay in place with the

Mangrove habitats

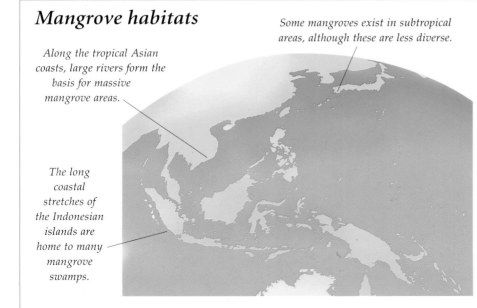

Some mangroves exist in subtropical areas, although these are less diverse.

Along the tropical Asian coasts, large rivers form the basis for massive mangrove areas.

The long coastal stretches of the Indonesian islands are home to many mangrove swamps.

As tropical rivers and streams head toward the sea, many pass through a number of brackish habitats. One of these is the mangrove swamp, a muddy yet clear water area, where a fertile substrate is kept in place by a jungle of mangrove tree roots. The mangroves provide a habitat for many animals and fishes that thrive in this unusual environment.

rise and fall of the tides and with the constantly moving sandbanks.

The mass of roots also provides plenty of hiding spots beneath the surface in which a large majority of the mangrove swamp fishes can be found. Above the water, the mangroves form a habitat suited to many birds, insects, and mammals, and these animals also interact with the underwater world, either by dropping waste, providing food, or acting as predators. Without the mangroves and their complex root systems, the brackish waters would quickly become muddy and unable to support the diverse number of species that make their home here.

CRUNCHERS, SKIPPERS, SPITTERS

Like the brackish estuaries, the mangrove swamp is a highly fertile and productive environment. A mass of organic waste and silt is deposited from the river systems, and combined with fruits, waste leaves, and wood from the mangroves, the environment is a haven for bacteria, fungi, and detritus-feeders. In the sandy substrate, many worms, mollusks, and crustaceans feed on waste matter and tiny detritus-feeding organisms. Most of the fish that live in the mangrove swamps are either scavengers, mollusk-feeders, or insect-feeders. Scavenging fish will search the

Above: When the tides are at their lowest point, the exposed roots of the mangrove trees can be clearly seen. In the mud beneath these roots is a vast collection of living organisms.

Right: At high tides, only the green tops of the mangrove trees are visible and the area truly appears to be a swamp. However, beneath the surface there are many fish feeding on creatures in the mud.

sandy substrate for small detritus-feeders, worms, and amphipods. Some scavengers, such as the mudskipper, actually leave the water and head up to the wet sandy banks to search for small food items. When the tide falls, many small puddles and pools are left on the wet sandy banks. The mudskipper then heads out of the water and into these pools in search of food. Once the tide is out, a number of insects, worms, and amphipods are also found in and around these wet pools and the mudskipper can search for these without much competition from other fish. In many cases, the mudskipper is joined by crabs and birds searching for the same food items.

The mudskipper is able to remain out of water for long periods due to its highly adapted skin, which contains many liquid-filled cells that reduce atmospheric pressure and prevent it from drying out. The inside of the mouth and the gill cavities are also kept moist and have a thin membrane that allows oxygen to be absorbed into the blood.

A few fish, such as the pufferfish group of fishes, will feed on mollusks and crustaceans. These fish have powerful "teeth" – actually an extension of the jawbone – which can easily crunch through the tough shells of snails, mussels, clams, and other crustaceans. Insect-feeders also swim among the mangrove roots. Most of these fish are small, shoaling species, opportunistic feeders that take any unfortunate insects that fall into the water. Seeds and fruits dropped by the mangroves and other plants will also become food for many of the insect-feeders. The four-eyes fish commonly found in mangrove swamps has highly developed sight. As it swims along the surface, its specialized eyes enable it to see both above and below the water surface at the same time, making it easy for the fish to hunt insects while keeping a lookout for predators.

Another highly adapted insect-feeder found in the mangrove swamps is the archerfish. This unusually shaped fish has an incredibly powerful jaw muscle that is used to fire jets of water at high speed toward insects resting on an overhanging branch. Any insect unlucky enough to be hit by one of these jets will fall into the water and be quickly eaten by the archerfish. In its natural environment, the archerfish can fire jets of water up to 150cm (60in) above the water with an incredibly accurate aim.

A MANGROVE SWAMP AQUARIUM

It is possible to obtain small mangrove trees and plant them in the aquarium environment, but growing them is not easy and a suitably sized specimen would need a very deep and complex substrate. For practical purposes, most aquarists prefer to try to recreate the environment of the mangrove roots with alternative decor. A mangrove swamp aquarium can be one of a number of different designs, the easiest of which is simply to recreate the underwater environment beneath the mangrove roots. A more interesting display could include both the underwater element and a sandy bank that extends above the water surface. This style of aquarium allows you to keep the crabs and mudskippers that will regularly venture out of the water.

THE SANDY SUBSTRATE

Silver sand is an ideal substrate for recreating the sandy bottom of the mangrove swamp, but it does have certain problems. A deep sandy substrate will soon compact and stagnate, encouraging algae and producing small amounts of toxic chemicals. This can normally be

Above: A male fiddler crab can be easily identified by the presence of a highly enlarged claw. This fierce-looking appendage is used not for fighting or feeding, but is displayed to attract a suitable mate.

The mudskipper is often associated with mangrove swamps. This attractive and adaptable little fish is quite at home on the mudflats, often out of water.

These smooth, flat slate pieces can be used to hold the steep sandbank together. Crabs and smaller fish will also use them for hiding spots.

prevented by regular stirring and disturbing of the sand, which should be done at least two or three times a week. In this aquarium, the raised area is simply made by piling up sand and "bolstering" it with some rocks. To prevent long-term problems, the sandbank in this aquarium would need to be replaced every few months. A more permanent raised sandbank could be created by using a larger substrate, such as lime-free or coral gravel. Construct the basic shape of the sandbank using rocks, wood, or any large decor and place a fine plastic mesh (a "gravel tidy") on top to hold a thin top layer of substrate. In this

aquarium, the sandbank is quite steep and may be prone to a slow and steady collapse due to the attentions of the aquarium's inhabitants. In larger tanks, a more gently sloping sandbank would be far more manageable.

Above: *Silver sand is almost identical to the sandy or muddy substrate found in mangrove swamps. In the aquarium, it should be regularly stirred and siphoned to keep it clean and looking fresh.*

USING WOOD IN THE DISPLAY
The main aim of the wood in this aquarium is to recreate the roots of the mangrove tree. Although it is almost impossible to obtain wood that is the same shape and thickness as mangrove roots, there are suitable alternatives. Some "traditional" driftwood sold for aquariums, often called twisted root, is very similar to natural mangrove roots. However, in the aquarium, twisted roots may appear too large and can only be used in limited numbers. In this aquarium, dried brushwood is highly effective at recreating a "miniature" mangrove root environment.

Brushwood consists of dead and dried twigs and branches and is often sold by florists rather than aquarium retailers. It is important that the wood is completely dead before it is used in an aquarium. If any green (living) areas are present, fungus or a bacterial bloom may appear in the water once the wood is submerged. Check a branch by testing the flexibility

at the widest part. If it snaps easily it is normally safe, but if it bends it may still contain living tissue. Brushwood normally remains intact for two to three months before it begins to rot underwater; when this happens, you should replace it. Alternatively, coat the wood with clear polyurethane varnish and allow it to dry before using it in the aquarium. With this treatment, the wood should last far longer.

ROCKS, PEBBLES, AND GRAVEL
The small rocks or cobbles in this aquarium are not a vital part of the display, but they do add a little extra visual interest. They can be used to hold the sandbank in place, so they have a practical purpose as well as an aesthetic one. You could place a few small pebbles and a scattering of large gravel pieces across the substrate, but use small pieces sparingly to retain the bold effect of the sandy substrate.

Brushwood must be completely dry and dead before use or it will soon rot. The fine branches recreate mangrove roots in a small space.

THE PLANTS

Aquatic plants are rarely found in the brackish environment of the mangrove swamps, which is too harsh for many to survive in. However, in the aquarium a few plants can add a little greenery, but use them in moderation to keep the mangrove style design. In this aquarium, we have used giant hygrophila *(Hygrophila corymbosa)*. This hardy and adaptable plant should survive low-salinity conditions and its leaf shape is very similar to many mangrove leaves. Species of *Anubias, Microsorium, Vallisneria,* and *Egeria* would also survive low-salinity conditions and could be used in this aquarium, but they would not be representative of the mangrove habitat.

THE FISH

Several brackish fish are suitable for the mangrove aquarium, and many naturally live in mangrove swamps. A number of rainbowfish and livebearer species, plus popular fish such as scats and monos, will all do well in the brackish environment. However, the design of this aquarium is ideal for

some of the more interesting mangrove subjects, such as the mudskippers, four-eyes, and archerfish.

The quirky behavior of the mudskipper *(Periophthalmus barbarus)* makes it a fascinating aquarium fish, and it is worth setting up a mangrove aquarium purely in order to house it. The mudskipper spends a considerable amount of time out of water if it is able

Most aquatic plants will not tolerate salty water, but Hygrophila corymbosa is a hardy species. The leaf shape is similar to that of the mangrove.

to, and will also become very tame. In some cases, mudskippers can become trusting enough to take food from the aquarist's hand while out of water. It is often the unusual behaviors of fish that make them worth keeping, rather than their shape or color, and attempting to encourage natural behavior in the aquarium is a worthy challenge for any aquarist.

Another fish with equally interesting behavior is the archerfish *(Toxotes jaculator)*. If the aquascape has an above-water element, with plenty of brushwood and a tight-fitting lid, you can add insects such as small crickets or flies to the display. The archerfish can then use its natural ability to fire jets of water at the insects, knocking them into the water as food. Observing such behavior in the aquarium is a fascinating and rewarding experience for any interested aquarist.

MIDWATER AND SURFACE FISH

The unusual four-eyes *(Anableps anableps)* is an ideal addition to this style of aquarium, swimming constantly at the surface, with the upper portions of the eyes just poking above the water. The mosquitofish *(Gambusia affinis)* is another mangrove swamp fish that spends much of its time at the water surface. To fill some of the midwater areas of the aquarium, add a few brackish water characins. The most notable of these is the Indian glassfish *(Chanda ranga)*, a small fish

Left: *The four-eyes fish* (Anableps anableps) *has an unusual "hourglass"-shaped eye that enables it to see above and below the surface at the same time. This intriguing species is ideal for the mangrove aquarium environment and easy to care for.*

Right: *Even in the aquarium, the archerfish* (Toxotes jaculator) *will use its natural instincts to locate food. Here it is firing a jet of water at an insect on an overhanging leaf to bring it down to the water surface.*

with a virtually see-through body. Mollies *(Poecilia* spp.) are often found in a wide variety of brackish habitats, including the mangrove swamps. These colorful, peaceful, and hardy fish will mix with almost any other species, so they are ideal for this display.

BOTTOM-DWELLING CRABS

Although there are some catfish suitable for brackish aquariums, they are often hard to obtain or they grow to large sizes. However, the substrate of the aquarium could be populated by the colorful fiddler crab *(Uca pugnax)*. This scavenger will search the substrate for food items and may occasionally climb up the odd branch or venture out of water onto any raised areas. Being a scavenger, it will accept almost any food, although it often prefers meaty foods, such as cockles or bloodworms.

Fiddler crabs are very easy to care for, although occasionally they can be a danger to small fish that venture too close. The male's powerful front claw could easily damage any fish that irritates or threatens the crab. However, the majority of fish suited to this display are surface-dwellers and would not bother, or be bothered by, the crabs. Mudskippers will inhabit the same areas as the crabs, both in and out of the water, but these fish are perfectly used to living with the interesting fiddler crabs. A few species of tropical crab are sometimes available for the aquarium and since most of them are very similar in size and temperament to the fiddler crabs, they would make worthy substitutes.

Mangrove swamp aquarium

This display is relatively easy to construct. In a larger aquarium, you could extend the dry land area and use a greater diversity of plants.

Brushwood represents the dense tangle of roots found in the mangrove swamps and provides an environment well suited to smaller fishes.

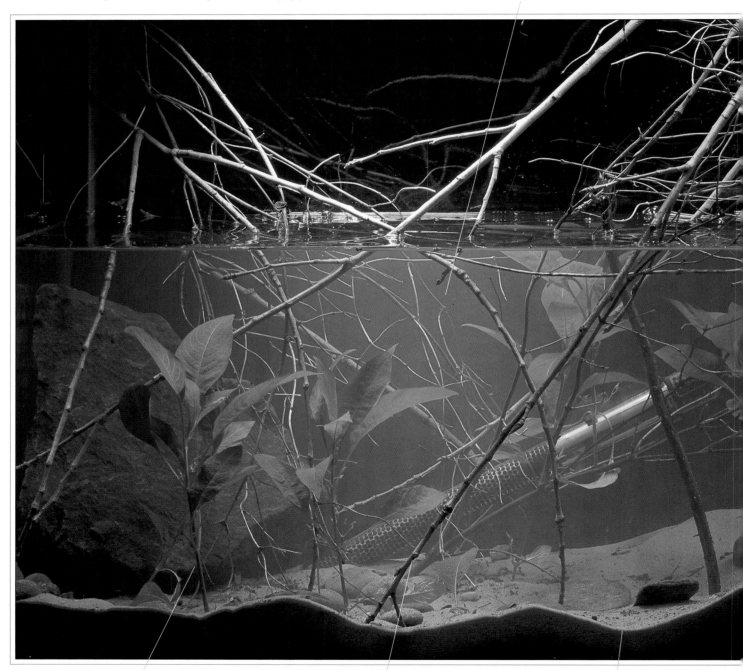

With its thick stems and dark green leaves, Hygrophila corymbosa *makes a good substitute for mangrove plants.*

The light color of the brushwood will darken as it becomes waterlogged and algae begins to grow on it.

Silver sand is almost identical to the natural mangrove substrate.

Some of the brushwood is placed upright in the substrate while other pieces are laid horizontally on the raised sandbank.

Driftwood helps to support the sandbank and provides resting spots for crabs and mudskippers.

This raised area may need to be rebuilt occasionally as it becomes eroded by the movements of fish and crabs.

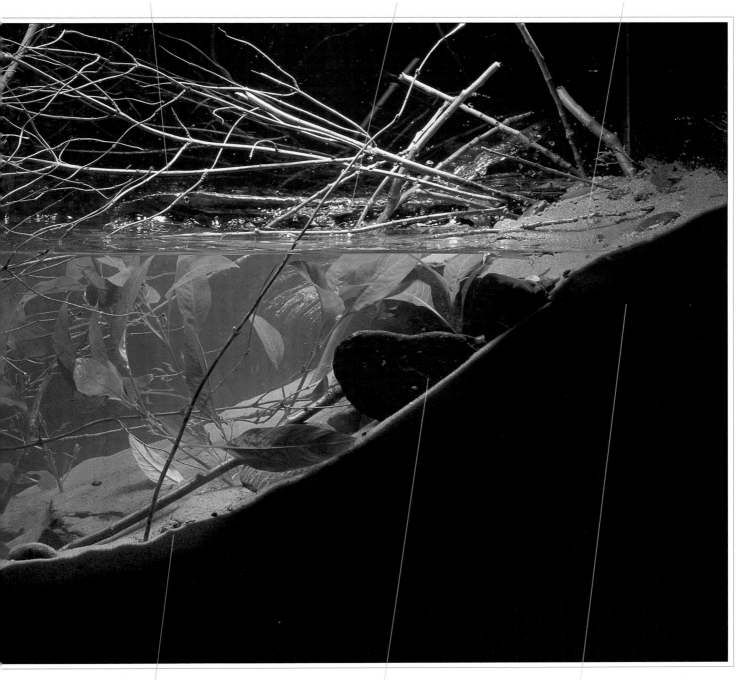

A few pebbles and stones scattered across the substrate helps to create a less barren appearance.

Pebbles and pieces of rounded slate are used here to hold the steep sandbank together.

In larger aquariums, this raised area could be extended and could include terrestrial plants.

General index

Fish index

Plant index

Credits

The publishers would like to thank the following photographers for providing images, credited here by page number and position: (B) Bottom, T(Top), C(Center), BL(Bottom Left), etc.

David Allison: 25, 76, 97(B), 108, 130(T), 155(T), 162(B), 163(T)

Aqua Press: (M-P & C Piednoir): Half-title (fish), Copyright page, 10(TL), 16, 18(T), 19(B), 22-23, 39(BR), 58(T), 69(B), 73(BR), 77(T,B), 81(B), 85, 90(B), 93(T,B), 101(CR), 108(T,C,B), 116, 117(T,C,B), 121(B), 124, 125(C,B), 133(T), 141(T,B), 145(C), 154, 160, 162-163(B), 170-171(T,B), 179(T,B), 187(T), 192(BL,BR)

Ardea London: 57(Jean-Paul Ferrero), 166-167(T, Joanna Van Gruisen), 182-183(T, Eric Lindgren)

John Feltwell/Garden Matters: 64-65(C), 104-105, 112-113(T, Jeremy Hoare), 191(B)

Frank Lane Picture Agency: Contents page (fish), 13(Fritz Polking), 15(B, Silvestris), 68(Foto Natura Stock), 72-73(T, Peggy Heard), 80-81(T, W. Meinderts/Foto Natura), 89(B, W. Meinderts/Foto Natura), 90-91(T, Derek Middleton), 96-97(T, W. Wisniewski), 101(T, W. Meinderts/Foto Natura), 150-151 Terry Whittaker, 155(B, Silvestris Fotoservice), 168(W. Meinderts, Foto Natura), 174-175(T, Robin Chittenden), 175(B, Linda Lewis), 178(C, W. Meinderts/Foto Natura),183 (TR, Linda Lewis), 190-191(T, Terry Whittaker), 195(Alan Parker)

Jan-Eric Larsson-Rubenowitz: Title-page (fish right), 19(T), 54(TL), 60(B), 60-61(T), 61(B), 84(B), 146, 152, 187(B), 194(T)

Natural Visions/Heather Angel: 120-121(T, Richard Coomber), 128-129, 136-137(T, Brian Rogers), 159(Brian Rogers)

Photomax (Max Gibbs): 69(T)

Sue Scott: 40(T), 144-145(T)

William A Tomey: Title-page (fish left), 46, 51, 65(TR), 84(C), 98(T), 133(C,B), 137(B), 140, 178(B), 186

Tropica (Ole Pedersen): 18(B), 40(B), 122(T)

Stuart Watkinson 14 © Interpet Publishing

All other photographs by Geoffrey Rogers © Interpet Publishing.

Computer graphics on page 35 by Phil Holmes © Interpet Publishing. All other computer graphics by Stuart Watkinson © Interpet Publishing. The maps have been produced using Terra Forma files created by Andromeda Interactive Ltd., Abdingdon, Oxfordshire, U.K.

Acknowledgments

The publishers would like to thank Martin Petersen of Tropica Aquarium Plants A/S, Hjortshøj, Denmark and Anglo Aquarium Plant Company, Enfield, U.K. for supplying plants for photography. Thanks are also due to The Water Zoo, Peterborough, U.K. for providing photographic facilities; to Kerry at Heaver Tropics, Ash, Kent, U.K.; to Swallow Aquatics, Southfleet, Kent, U.K.; and to Juwel Aquarium Ltd., U.K.

Publisher's note

The information and recommendations in this book are given without any guarantees on the part of the author and publishers, who disclaim any liability with the use of this material.